D1806388

LORDS of the CHASE

No worthier theme than hunting can a poet's soul inspire,
The stirring music of the chase shall tune my muse's lyre;
Men, hounds and horses I will sing, and ever as you listen
Your pulses shall beat faster yet, your eyes with fire shall glisten.

- Sir Herewald Wake

Reader, tread lightly o'er the sod,
For men of nerve lie here;
Their spirit bowed before their God
But knew no other fear.

Adapted from an epitaph found in the diary of
Will Dale, huntsman to Lord Yarborough and the
Brocklesby Hunt for twelve years (1884-96).

H.R.H. The Prince of Wales inspects the Belvoir.

Lords of the Chase

Tales from The Shires and Beyond

LEVENSTON PSMITH

WORDPECKER

London

LORDS OF THE CHASE

First Published In 1995

Published by WORDPECKER PUBLISHING
P.O. Box 6754, London, N3 3NT England, U.K.

© Copyright LEVENSTON PSMITH and
WORDPECKER PUBLISHING

All rights reserved. No part of this
publication may be reproduced by any means
in any form: electronic, graphic, mechanical,
photo-copying, recording, taping or in any
storage or retrieval system without the prior
permission of the author and publisher in
writing.

ISBN 0 9525001 0 8

While every reasonable care has been taken
to ensure the historical accuracy of actual
events related in this book, allowance must
be made for variations in original sources and
the degree of imaginative projection
employed in some episodes.

Printed and bound in England by
Antony Rowe Ltd., Chippenham, Wilts.

CONTENTS

CHAPTER ONE

TALES FROM THE SHIRES

HIGH GAME: LOW COMPANY

Leicester harboured a secret which few
Of the high-flying gentry e'er knew,
After Boothby and Meynell
Had charge of the kennel,
And the Quorn to such high stature grew . . .

In that country of elegance chaste,
With refinement and nobleman graced;
In that field of rank snobbery,
Exclusive hob-nobbery,
High fashion and corseted taste . . .

For, veiled in the mists of antiquity,
Well sunk in the stews of iniquity
Was a custom barbaric,
Emetic, Tartaric;
A chase of disgraceful obliquity.

Neither riot nor bagman whereat
To tilt in their own habitat,
But a rough cart-horse leading,
Without dignity or breeding,
Drag hunt with a stinking dead cat.[1]

HUGO MEYNELL

A GOLDEN AGE

Before oxer and railroad and wire
Drew rein of the hard-riding Squire,
Fast hounds from the kennel
Of whoo-whooping Meynell
Spurred Nimrod to Nirvana nigher . . .

Over wide, open shrievedom of Leicester,
Unspoiled by unsporting purpresture,
After fleet, racing fox,
Round mazed, white-faced flocks,
Led by bold but judicious young Nestor.

Under Meynell the Quorn soon became
A hunt of great fashion and fame;
Meynellian science
A code for compliance,
The Master a man of acclaim.

His hounds were in-bred for their beauty,
High mettle, devotion to duty;
Open bosoms and strength,
And backs of no length,
Fine noses, straight legs and tongue fluty.

With "the best pack in England" there rode
Three-score nobles, *éminences, à la mode,*
Enthralled by their leader,
Skilled huntsman and breeder,
Dashing sportsman and bright stellar lode.

The best chase Hugo Meynell e'er squired,
A few weeks before he retired,
From the Coplow of Billesdon,
Two hours, fifteen minutes run
To Enderby Hall, was inspired.

Only four of two hundred men finished,
Stout riding field greatly diminished;
By Tilton Wood scattered,
North-Easterly battered,
Or from Soar in spate ignobly fished.

So ended a great golden age
Of hunting by swift-riding sage,
And began a new order
To hunt the marauder,
And the style of a gentleman gauge.

A TREBLE CHANCER

A single horse, skilfully ridden,
With deft hand on rein gently bidden,
Should bear thirteen stone
Of male flesh and bone
Forty miles and not be o'er-stridden.

Will Long of high Badminton fame,
Made a proud and reliable claim
That he rode the same horse
Once a week, a full course,
For a long seventeen years, without maim.

But Sefton's extravagant code,
When as Master of Quorn he swift rode,
Claimed two extra horses,
Whatever the courses,
And forty more fit for the road.

His Quorndon Hall kennel and stable
Were palaces of legend and fable;
Up to one hundred couple
Hounds sinewy and supple,
Hunt servants with aristo-label.

Gilt buttons with crest were the style,
And a ride down a canopied aisle
When weather dictated,
Or Master laureated
A mount for a bucketing mile.

HUZZAS FOR HUSSARS

Though epigram adroitly hegemonic,
The Iron Duke's attributed laconic
On Etonian comport
In both conflict and sport
Was more likely *bon mot* Napoleonic.

But Wellington undoubtedly said
That a cavalry officer bred
To the horn and the chase
Would outwit and outpace
An enemy less gamefully led.

Transposing the scene once again,
Will Hussar, chasing fox, guide the rein
With superior skill
To more competent kill
Through hazards in hunting terrain?

Confronted by pitchfork and kine,
And farm folk intent on condign
Defence of their border,
Colonel Cheney gave the order:
"Buckle up, chaps, we'll charge 'em in line!"

So with heel pressing hard into hide,
Whips cutting and thrusting aside,
They rode down the yokels
With blood-curdling vocals,
And scattered the foe far and wide.

HARD GOING WITH THE QUORN

Two hundred men jostle and gyre
At the covert, in scarlet attire:
Who's away from the gorse?
But quick! Spurs to horse!
The pace is too good to inquire!

Osbaldeston, best known as the Squire,
Is leading the pick of the Shire;
We are out with the Quorn,
Who's blowing the horn?
The pace is too good to inquire!

The hounds, as a body entire,
Race on at a pace to inspire:
Who's taken a toss
From an unwilling hoss?
The pace is too good to inquire!

A cracking of rails like quick fire . . .
Who's down in the ditch and the mire?
Which gentleman's horse
Has contrived a divorce?
The pace is too good to inquire!

Then up the grass ground, ever higher,
Both horses and riders perspire;
Who's that come a cropper
At the high fence? A stopper;
The pace is too good to inquire!

No choice but a gate past the byre . . .
Much care by the huntsman and Squire;
But who's the Newtonian-
Defying demonian?
The pace is too good to inquire!

A newly-plashed hedge reaching higher
Than rider and horse can aspire:
Which steed is the gasper
Undone by this rasper?
The pace is too good to inquire!

Three horses are blown and retire;
Many more find it hard to respire,
But who's brought to book
By the Whissendine brook?
The pace is too good to inquire!

The killing pace sharpens desire:
The death-wish has never been nigher;
But who broke his neck
At the timber-fence check?
The pace is too good to inquire!

Ere the fox is condemned to expire,
There's a question we'll ask of the Squire:
What spirit Draconian
Spurs on the Meltonian?
But the pace is too good to inquire![2]

SONGS OF PRAISE

A famous Quorn hound known as *Vaulter*,
Wore a halo-like spiritual halter;
He was vouched to be good
As a canine saint should,
Having eaten his mistress's Psalter.

And another, with appetite vaster,
Called *Furrier*,[3] than which none ran faster,
Sired forty fine pups
In regular tups
And an ecstasy shared by his Master.

WHIPCORD AND WIRE

Osbaldeston was one of the best,
A huntsman of courage and zest;
A talented all-rounder,
A genuine astounder,
A hero and champion bless'd.

GEORGE
OSBALDESTON

With the Burton or Pytchley or Quorn
He carried a challenging horn:
Supreme in the saddle
And sturdy as staddle,
He triumphed o'er hedge, ditch and thorn.

His close-knit and muscular frame
Sustained him in many a game;
All whipcord and wire,
He seemed never to tire,
A victor of fortune and fame.

From Eton and Brasenose north riding
To family's rural abiding,
He hunted the hare
With a singular flair,
Thence to Lincoln, the Burton bestriding.

With Lord Monson's redoubtable stock
He savaged the scourge of the flock,
Bred and reared a fine pack
For scrimmage and rack,
Hunting Shire of the Fens round the clock.

At Tattersall's his foxhounds were sold
To fetch a huge levy in gold;
Two-seventy-two guineas
A couple for pedigrees
Of Yarborough and Monson blood bold.

With the Hambledon his sojourn was brief,
Not caring for sear, yellow leaf,
Or woodcraft and snooking
And dank, bosky spooking
'Mid 'Hamptonshire's festering fief.

In the Shires he advanced with great brilliance,
Hard and straight like a rail-riding diligence;
Rampaging for rout
Of carnivore stout
With cohort of concinnous consilience.

But our hero of sinew and zeal
Had a curious Achilles' heel;
On the Turf and o'er sticks,
He got up to tricks
And stratagems less than genteel.

As a Turfite his honourable form
Like his horses' could swerve from the norm,
Affording largesse,
But nobbling noblesse,
Obliging but not to the swarm.

STYLISH ATHLETICISM

The hard-riding style of the Quorn
Invited a measure of scorn
From the neighbouring gentry
Of a more sedate entry
And seemlier approach to the thorn.

John Warde of the Pytchley, inclined
To a leisurely pace, once opined
That heavyweights broke t' backs
Of their much-abused hacks,
And lightweights, horses' hearts, in hard grind.

JOHN WARDE

Colonel Wyndham, who weighed nineteen stone,
Was a Quornite less cavalier in tone:
Kind to horses and hounds
In those vigorous grounds,
And to stylish athleticism prone.

He would leap from his horse at high raddle,
Vault the fence alongside empty saddle,
Remount at far side
Without checking steed's stride,
Or allowing the beast to skedaddle.[4]

CROWNING GLORY

In the reign of King William the Fourth,
Young Billy Coke galloped the swarth,
His spirited entry
Disturbing The Gentry
Of Loughborough and many points North.

Like a doyen of hunt heretics
Or an ignorant lad from the sticks,
Billy Coke of the Quorn
Laughed etiquette to scorn
With a note on his back, " 'Ware, he kicks!"

At a good thirty knots on *Advance*,
He would lead horse and hound a fine dance;
Astride in his braces,
Kicking over the traces
And leaving the visitors askance.

Sartorial flair of the brat
Was enhanced by a carefree cravat,
But his principal claim
To hunting field fame
Was the "wide-awake" billycock hat.

HUNTING ON £300 A YEAR

When the selling of horses subvenes,
A gentleman of moderate means
May follow the hunt
And socially bunt
Where the best of society convenes.

But a man with restricted resources,
Confined to indifferent horses,
Must incline to misogamy,
Candle-ended economy,
And the meanest of menial recourses.

Mr. Carrington's three-hundred a year[5]
Allowed for no very great cheer;
Four hunters, one hack,
In a miserable shack,
And one man to polish the gear.

While others were feasting at table,
Mr. Carrington was down at his stable,
Self-employed as a groom
In the Stygian gloom,
Mucking out as best he was able.

While Meltonians expressed admiration
For Carrington's extreme dedication,
And did not indict him,
They failed to invite him
To attend on a social occasion.

Lord Waterford deemed him so poor
He told him to use the back door,
Which was somewhat bizarre
For a proud ex-Hussar
Who was, by no means, a boor.

Lord Gardner was almost benign,
Inviting the man to take wine,
But refrained, like the rest
Of Meltonian best
From asking the fellow to dine.

Frugality was thus an impediment
To a man from an excellent regiment;
For diligent labours
Ostracised by his neighbours
Whose actions revealed a false sentiment.

OUT-DOOR RELIEF

A pauper on out-door relief,
Not yet in the sear, yellow leaf,
Turning out at hunt meets
And gents' country seats,
Rode to hounds and to mild unbelief.

The Master raised no real objection,
And the huntsman showed no disaffection
When the man shared the chase,
Without causing disgrace,
In a state of dress less than perfection.

But the Guardians, in some indecision,
Were wary of courting derision;
Their patience broke down
For their man about town,
And they opted for rural revision.

They decreed that a man might not hunt
While the ratepayers were bearing the brunt
Of keeping the fellow
In bread, if not furbelow:
A wanton and arrogant stunt.

So the pauper gave up his old bay,
But never his red-letter day:
He refused to stay put,
Instead hunting on foot;
Boot-leather his only outlay.

WORKS OF THE NIGHT

Hunting parsons in Melton terrain
Conformed to a liberal strain,
Stout-hearted, reliable,
Conscientiously pliable,
Vulpinely neither Abel nor Cain.

Mr. Seabrooke, as a good parson should,
Had faithfully promised he would
Restrict his field sport
To two days athwart,
But found four half days quite as good.

Mr. Myerhouse, on a sixteen-hand bay,
Contrived to see most of the day,
No nuptial knot-tying
Nor parishioner dying,
His spiritual repast to gainsay.

But a spoil-sport incumbent, Mr. Karney,[6]
A dissenter from clerical blarney,
Went out of his way,
The next Sabbath Day,
To castigate a nocturnal barney.

Reproving dark works of the night,
He raised ripples of ribald delight,
Condemning a midnight race
As unmanly: a steeple chase
Black as pitch save for pale lantern light.

THE BEAU IDEAL

Whyte-Melville, in command appendicular
At the Crimea, with Turkish irregular,
Abhorred mud and filth
And chaos and spilth,
And soldiers and horses pedicular.

He longed for the pastoral scene,
For English shire pristine and green;
The neat and trim horseman,
The beau-ideal courseman,
The gentleman both courteous and clean.

True sportsman, upright and fastidious,
He chided the drunkard perfidious,
And the card-sharping gambler
And loose-riding rambler,
And conduct unworthy, insidious.

Though never a source of dissension
In the field, his deep-seated attention
To horses and riders,
Galumphers and gliders,
Gave hunting a moral dimension.

As poet-equestrian philomathic,
He strove for affinity empathic
'Twixt a man and his steed,
Safer riding to breed
By abjuring a style antipathic.

He was passionately fond of the chase   **WHYTE-MELVILLE**
And fast where a country gave space,
But took his own line
In a bid to refine
The technique and cultivate grace.

He avoided a bucketing clamour,
Preferring discretion to valour,
Neither spurring nor lashing,
Nothing showy or dashing;
With the Pytchley, a gentleman's demeanour.

The major had very few falls,
Square-toed when he tilted at walls;
His fine riding stance
Deflecting the lance
Of mischance in unsquadronly squalls.

He had an appropriate prescription
For a country of any description;
Over plough, keep to rut,
Muddy furrow or cut,
Avoiding a sad superscription.

With the Vale of White Horse one fine day,
Stylish safety and skill to display,
Gently jogging o'er plough,
He shot stern over prow,
Breaking neck on the Malmesbury clay.

THE YELLOW EARL

Fifth Earl of the second creation,
But first in esteem of the nation,
Lord Lonsdale played hard
For sporting regard,
Earning fame and profound admiration.

He strove for a noble perfection,
Pre-eminence in every direction,
With no expense spared
To attain what he dared;
A sportsman of wide intellection.

LORD LONSDALE

KIRBY GATE, 1893.

1. Frank Gillard.   2. Tom Firr.   3. The Hon. Mrs. L. Lowther.   4. The Hon. L.
Lowther.   5. Capt. T. Boyce.   6. Mr. A. V. Pryor.   7. Lord Lonsdale, M.F.H.
8 and 9. Mr. and Mrs. James Hornsby.

Educated in hunt stableyard
By servants and pugilists scarred,[7]
Private tutors soon beaten,
He'd one year at Eton
But for study a curt disregard.

He lived by an instinct unerring,
A vision far-sighted, unblurring,
Expansive, flamboyant,
Resilient and buoyant,
By valour for fame ever spurring.

To his trustees' perennial sorrow,
He gave little thought for the morrow;
His wife in decline,[8]
He was last of the line,
Determined to spend to the marrow.

When Lonsdale took charge of the Quorn,[9]
Austerity was quickly forsworn;
Extravagant flamboyance
And colourful joyance
Were the style on that bountiful morn.

Kirby Gate was a brilliant affair
Such as none but his Lordship could dare,
With ruby-red riches
And white leather breeches
For servant astride chestnut mare . . .

Thorough-bred and long-tailed and hog-maned,
Exquisitely accoutred, *ordained*,
And carriages, bright yellow,
Dashing up to a bellow
Of cheers from a crowd unrestrained.

As Master of Cottesmore and Quorn,
He rode as a hunting-man born,
Jumping blackthorn and rail,
High-mettled and hale,
To sweet music of foxhound and horn.

Lord Lonsdale had eloquent skills,
Shortest line between coverts and kills,
A superior seat,
Manège quick and neat
And a talent for foxhunting thrills.

A COTTESMORE HAT.

He warned against changing a line
Fox to fox: a policy supine;
They should hunt to the death
Their first fox, to last breath,
No point-to-point gallop benign.

He was also inclined to berate
Jumping fences when using the gate
Would get the pack through
As a whole, to renew
Their pursuit of the fox to his fate.

They should study the flight of the bird,
The movements of ruminant herd;
The eye and the brain
Should scan the terrain
For evidence of creatures bestirred . . .

Before jumping, convey the intention
To the horse by precise intervention;
Fit the speed to the deed,
Firmly pacing the steed,
Giving last two strides careful attention.

In the field he could be autocratic,
Imperious, dictatorial, dogmatic,
Interrupting a run
And the galloping fun
To berate a delinquent fanatic.

He was jealous of winning competitor,
Intolerant of carping admonitor,
But friend to the farmer,
A considerate disarmer,
And generous to suitor or servitor.

He'd a team of well-matched chestnut horses
For The Row[10] and the royal race courses;
Hunting stables and box
For the Barleythorpe fox,
And elegant hounds for the gorses . . .

He floored the world heavyweight champion,
John Sullivan, no handsome ring rampion
But match-makers' joy,
Ex-Boston strong boy,
Too good to fight England's best tampion.

At a cracking, six-mile-an-hour pace,
In a hundred-mile road-walking race,[11]
He beat a professional,
In long-drawn processional,
For a trifling bet: always the ace.

But Lordy's life-long adulation
By a mesmerised and credulous nation
Overlooked seismic faults
In his character vaults,
And deserved a degree of damnation.

Ignoring *angelica vox*,
He chased women as well as the fox;
The pale Jersey Lily[12]
And a high-steppin' filly[13]
From the boards to maternity smocks.

Advised by the Queen to depart
Till impetuous affairs of the heart
And the scandal died down,
He bowed to the Crown
And to Canada aimed his dispart.[14]

From Saskatchewan via Lake Athabasca
He embarked on a Herculean task a
Lesser man would shun,
With dog, guide and gun,
Trekking three thousand miles to Alaska.

A spontaneous public subscription,
A six-figure sporting prescription
For the indigent; a bursary
To mark wedding anniversary,
Disappeared by neglect or surreption.[15]

In post-prandial egoist glow
Anent triumphal feats long ago,
Extolling physique,
Perspicacity unique
He would draw a very long bow.

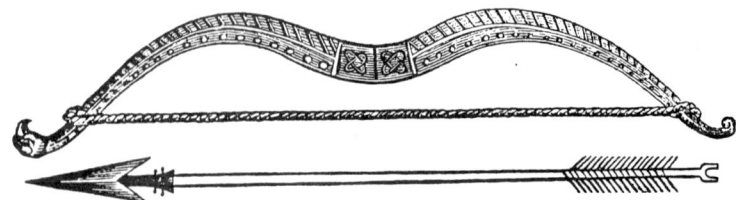

NOTES ON CHAPTER ONE

Throsby in his *History of Leicestershire* relates how, in the 17C, on Easter Monday, the Mayor of Leicester in full civic regalia repaired to a sportsfield nearby and, as part of the holiday programme, started the drag hunt with an aniseeded cat tied to a farm horse's tail. The trail finished at the mayor's parlour where he dispensed hospitality to horsemen and foot-followers alike.

Out with the Belvoir on March 5, 1873, the Prince of Wales pulled up and rode back to apologise to a fallen horseman over whom he had been obliged to leap. Cuthbert Bradley observed that selfish indifference to the fallen was too often characteristic of a hard-riding Leicestershire field. Whyte-Melville described them as fierce as hawks and jealous as women.

Furrier arrived in a draft from the Belvoir and was later seen to be crooked, from an end-on view. But he ran at the head of the pack and once jumped a very high gate. Put to stud, he sired twenty couples of bitches before the end of Mr. Osbaldeston's second mastership. The Squire's packs had admirable conformity but two obvious faults: they ran mute and were indifferent to a middling scent. Nevertheless they showed excellent sport and the Squire, who spent much time in the kennels, was right to be proud of them.

Major Whyte-Melville witnessed this feat and maintained that a finer rider than Col. Wyndham never graced a saddle. In a burst across Leicestershire grass he could go for twenty minutes with the best of the light-weights, despite his giant's stature. George the Fourth described him, when he commanded the Scots Greys at Waterloo, as the handsomest man in the army.

Mr. Carrington was previously a subaltern in the 15th Hussars. He hunted from Melton in the 1820s and rode low-priced, light-weight horses which fetched little at sale. T.F. Dale, the hunt historian, deplored the class of men who sneered at the likes of Carrington. They were people whom wealth had raised socially without elevating either their minds or their manners. Such were few in the hunting field where men were valued for what they were rather than for what they possessed.

6.   Parson Karney's text was from Ephesians V, verse 11. F
     sleep was disturbed by the sound of iron-shod hooves clatteri
     over cobblestones on March 10, 1890 when eleven leadi
     riders wearing ladies' nightdresses over riding kit took part ir
     midnight race. They rode a course of four or five fields a
     double that number of fences about a mile from Melton, after
     dinner at the Bell Hotel to celebrate Lady Gussie Fane
     birthday. The moon was obscured by heavy cloud and t
     course poorly lighted by borrowed railway lamps hung
     poles. Mr. Algernon Burnaby won and was later presented w
     a handsome cup at a supper party given by Count Zborowski.

7.   Hugh Lonsdale was educated in pugilism by Jem Mace, the l
     bare-fist champion of England, and by Trooper Ha
     regimental champion of the Life Guards and his fathe
     batman.

8.   He married Lady Grace Gordon in 1878. She had a fall wh
     hunting and was unable to have children.

9.   Master of the Quorn 1893-98, and of the Cottesmore, 1915-2

10. Rotten Row, Hyde Park, London, where fashionable socie
     rode and drove to see and be seen. Lonsdale paid o
     thousand pounds for the team of chestnuts, an enormous su
     for the times.

11. He took three rests of an hour each and changed his shoes a
     socks every five miles.

12. Lillie Langtree (b.1852), daughter of the Dean of Jersey anc
     famous English beauty, reputedly mistress of the Prince
     Wales.

13. Violet Cameron, another stage beauty, with whom he lived
     Hampstead, North London, as Mr. and Mrs. Thompson.

14. He sailed in February, 1888.

15. The appeal was sponsored by the *Sporting Chronicle* to ma
     Lonsdale's wedding anniversary on June 27, 1928. He was
     administer the fund as a sportsmen's charity for the indige
     The appeal raised £300,000 which was ten times the to
     subscribed after the pit disaster at Lonsdale's Whitehaven c
     mine in 1922. By 1935 the money had disappeared.

CHAPTER TWO

MORE TALES

A CHARACTER WITH BOTTOM

Foster Melliar, of North Aston Hall,
Was a big, heavy man, riding tall
Over cold, Cotswold plough
Or through water-logged slough
With the Heythrop, in bleak winter thrall.

Over stone wall or Deddington Brook,
He soared like a scarlet-robed rook,
A character with bottom,
Supportive sub-stratum,
And as Treasurer, ne'er brought to book.

The Deddington, a formidable beck,[1]
Held many a good rider in check,
But Melliar, who kept it,
Most confidently leapt it,
While a lesser man feared for his neck.

Years later admirers discovered
That the bed of the stream had been covered
And built up with stone
To a rock-solid throne,
Whereupon general confidence recovered.

A STORM IN A BUCKET

John Cradock,[2] a man of great charm,
Used the sweetest of words to disarm
The hard-riding stranger
Courting mayhem and danger
With the Quorn, in mode to alarm.

But one day in his role as field master,
Chasing Reynard from Six Hills, disaster
Seemed certain from one
Such a bachelor's son
On a headstrong, grey horse, ever faster . . .

Horse's hooves hard on heels of the pack
Threatening imminent ruin and wrack:
Mr. Cradock reared up,
Rated insolent pup
In a coarsely vituperative thwack.

"I couldn't hold my idiot horse!"
Cried the *tiger,* in token remorse;
"Then you'd best stay at home,"
Said our sainted Jerome,
In further vulgate intercourse.

"Then tell me which days you are out,"
Rejoined the recalcitrant scout,
Scarce screening his scorn
For the man with the horn,
Whose rule he'd determined to flout.

Mr. Cradock soon rued admonition,
Deplored his own earthy ebullition,
And before the sun set,
Expressed his regret
With courteous and measured contrition.

LE PREMIER CHASSEUR D'ANGLETERRE

Mr. Thomas Assheton Smith,
Though a man of ubiquitous kith,
Was unique as a hunting man,
A *hang-out-the-bunting* man,
A maker of marvel and myth.

Acclaimed by the Emperor Napoleon
As the best from perfidious Albion,
The *premier chasseur*
And *littérateur*
Rode faster than whirlwind Aeolian.

Fine swimmer, good oar, scientist,
Tom Smith was a skilled pugilist:
Disrespect for the hunt
Or other affront
Could lead to a bout with the fist.

TOM ASSHETON SMITH

Etonian, coal-heaver, politician:
All suffered the discourse patrician,
Appealing to reason
In the foxhunting season
Evincing a forceful logician.

Stout batsman and capital shot,
Designer of steamboat and yacht;
A *beau sabreur manqué*,
Connoisseur of fine Twankey:
For a foxhunt he'd give up the lot!

Aged thirty, he picked up the horn
From Lord Foley, to Master the Quorn;
For more than a decade
He carried the accolade,
Pre-eminent, all others forsworn.

As well as a bulldog tenacity,
A firm and unyielding pertinacity,
Tom Smith earned his fame,
And world-wide acclaim
By conspicuous zeal and audacity.

Hard riders, his pace would enthrall,
More timorous members, appall;
His numerous spills
Begetting no ills:
His secret, he knew how to fall!

When pitched into blackthorn or gorse,
He always fell clear of the horse,
Hanging on to the rein,
Despite danger or pain,
And swiftly regaining his course.

First gentleman-huntsman to hounds
In the world-famous Leicestershire grounds,
He was reckless and daring,
For prudence uncaring,
His fervency oft out of bounds.

He could transfer to hunter from hack
Scarce rising from animal's back,
Equestrian ability
And muscular agility
Surpassing the speed of the pack.

Tom Smith's most extraordinary feat
Occurred at a Lincolnshire leat:
Two parallel bridges,
Each fenced by low ridges,
Leaping one to the other *en suite*.

He inherited the Tedworth estate:
Fifty-thousand-a-year from Welsh slate;
And contrived a new pack,
But first had to hack
Through acres of forest ingrate.

Vast woodlands were razed to the ground
To make way for horses and hound,
For coverts and hides
And broad, grassy rides:
The will and the effort astound!

The hunting emprise was immense,
Designed without thought to expense;
Kennels fit for prize beast,
At slumber or feast,
And paddocks of great excellence.

The stables were truly magnificent,
Some fifty fine horses their complement;
Names 'scribed over box,
Clean straw for the hocks,
And the freshest of water and aliment.

A Master less liked than admired:
His skill, not his manner, inspired;
Assheton Smith would enrapture
But never could capture
The hearts of the people he squired.

But an urgent request from the Quorn
For a day in the Leicestershire bourne
Drew two thousand men
From city and fen
To honour the old Master's horn.

Of eminent standing and station,
Of sportsmen, the cream of the nation;
Superbly accoutred,
All rivalry neutered,
United in grand salutation.

Right up to his eightieth year,
Assheton Smith rode to hounds without peer,
Upright in the saddle,
A sportsman *immortel*,
A man's man for the world to revere.

A BRIEF ENCOUNTER

Where in season sweet violets grew,
And sweet pea in riotous hue
With peaudouce entwined,
And all Nature combined
Its bounties abundant to strew . . .

A lady abroad in the grounds
Of her mansion, traversing the bounds,
Made to nature obeisance
In rude *cabinet d'aisances*,
To far-distant cry of the hounds[3] . . .

When a stranger abruptly appeared
In that rustic two-seater and reared
Himself on to seat
Of the cabinned retreat,
By the Badminton hounds sonneteered.

The lady, with grace of a queen,
Averted her eyes from the scene,
Ignored the intruder
As being no ruder
Than barrister by justice unseen.

But the pack, drawing dangerously nigh,
And Will Long in encouraging cry,
The fox hurtled out,
From his cosy redoubt,
No time e'en to proffer *Goodbye.*

WILLIAM LONG.

The lady, her reverie done,
Had emerged from caboose when her son
Rode up to inquire
For vulpecular sire:
Did she know whither Reynard had run?

But his mother, a lady of breeding,
Disavowed House of Commons proceeding:
Curt shake of the head
And the scarlet-coat fled
Whither foxhounds on high scent were leading.

When the pack their sad quarry had savoured,
Salivated and slobbered and slavered,
And the huntsman replete
With a victory meet,
The Master declared him "well flavoured."

THE SQUIRE OF BENTLEY

By a quirk of fate, coincidently
Both Master and Mistress of Bentley,
And known as "The Squire",
Though never a sire,
Mrs. Cheape ruled her realm very gently . . .

By gracious demeanour and rig;
No clumsy, hermaphrodite brig
But a great-hearted sport
Of the temperate sort,
Commanding, in saddle or gig.

THE SQUIRE OF BENTLEY

Mrs. Cheape dearly loved the alliance,
The poetry, the music and science,
Good fellowship and fun
Of a spanking good run,
And Reynard's determined defiance.

So keen were the Squire and her Colonel
On hunting the predator infernal,
Their honeymoon was spent
Amid landscape deep-bent,[4]
In strenuous endeavours fraternal.

The Squire taught her children to ride;
With discipline and confidence to guide
Their rough mountain steeds
By well-founded creeds
To equestrian excellence and pride.

She likened the stiffest of fences
To life's hurdles: a spur to the senses
And a challenge to meet
With a confident seat
And the courage which training dispenses.

They rode to hounds not for a fall
Nor a bucketing, boisterous brawl,
But to be at the finish,
No man to diminish;
No mount too hard-blown to stand tall.

All six of her brood played the game,
Some earning distinction and fame,
But three were sad-drowned
When Ares deep-frowned,
Fierce fathoms beneath angry *faem*.

THE PYTCHLEY RIDE NORTH

A notable ride[5] with John Warde
Found Pytchley and Quorn in accord:
A twenty-seven mile run
Before trophy was won
And constancy earned its reward.

After finding at Marston Wood covert,
'Midst wood pigeon, goldfinch and plover,
To Theddingworth they ran,
Laughton Hills quick to span,
To Gumley, in earnest endeavour.

Past Saddington, the quarry in view,
Up hill into Kibworth, the few
Who were now within hail
Clearing bullfinch and rail,
Straining stirrup strap, muscle and thew.

To Wistow, then running due North,
Through Stoughton to Stretton's green swarth,
Then Norton by Galby,
And Frisby to Botney,
The hounds' joyful note holding forth.

Through meadow, stream, valley and marish,
And into their twenty-sixth parish,
The hounds made their kill
At Tilton on Hill
With only four men at the finish.

Lately Master of Quorn, Mr. Meynell,
A veteran of stable and kennel,
Declared it great sport
Of manly comport
Over Leicestershire grass ground and fennel.

A COLOURFUL MEET

Hark for'ard! And never cast back,
E'er for'ard with sight of the pack:
Thus it was with the Belvoir,
Frank Gillard, chief reiver,
For'ard-looking and rampant for wrack.

But his duties involved *sorry meet*,
Retrospection for life's run complete;
A friend gone to earth
In his last narrow berth
After galloping point all too fleet.

NICOLAS CHARLTON

But where Cromwell's horse sullied the nave,
And Ireton[6] honed regicide glaive,
A hunter found rest
From vulpecular quest,
Bright-mourned by the meek and the brave.

At Attenb'ro' colourful exequies
Illumined uprightly propensities
Of a life full of joy,
Nor e'en death to alloy
By conventional funereal nepenthes.

On a waggon drawn by a white horse,
Decked with flowers and gold-blooming gorse,
A scarlet-draped box
Proclaimed scourge of the fox,
And banished all thought of remorse . . .

For Nicolas Charlton[7], deceased,
Who spent his life taming the beast,
In clamour and stealth
And in sickness and health:
A venerer and horseman-artiste.

Fifteen men of the horn interlink
Belvoir, Badsworth and Quorn to bethink
Glad thoughts of their friend,
Life's chase at an end,
And all except one in the pink[8].

AN INTEMPERATE ENCOUNTER

Lord Waterpark[9] earned a rude rate
When trying to open a gate,
With his whip wrong way round,
At Goosehill, to confound
Harry Baylis, arriving in spate.

Shouting angrily, "Out of my way!"
Farmer Hal cleared the gate on his bay,
Deploring ineptitude
In reprimand coarse and lewd;
To the nobleman, *lèse-majesté*.

His Lordship inquired of the Master
The name of the grammaticaster,
But suave Mr. Ames
Would mention no names
Save to say, "A good sport but a blaster . . ."

Mr. Frederick Ames, ex-Rifle Brigade, of Hawford Lodge, Worcs., a popular Master

On account of his bluff sapience
Over, under or through a stiff fence,
Especially when primed,
With spirit sublimed
For high-flying, hard-running suspense.

Waterpark then told Baylis, with hauteur,
Who he was but, allowing no quarter,
Baylis insolently dared
That for all that he cared
He might be Lord Brandy and Water.

LORD WATERPARK

A WINNING HAND

For centuries the Brocklesby hounds
Have hunted 'mid well-defined bounds
In the Lincolnshire fens,
Rightful heirs, denizens
Of historic and long-halloo'd grounds.

The Master was always a Pelham,[10]
Droit de seigneur sufficient to quell 'em,
From seventeen-fourteen,
Under Protestant Queen,
Later Yarboroughs, illumined on vellum.

EARL OF YARBOROUGH

Every card of a count over nine,
No knaves but bright aces to shine
At Court or in battle,
Bright sabre to rattle,
In earlship an unwavering line.

The huntsmen were likewise dynastic,
Long-lived, highly skilled, esemplastic,
Five Smiths in a row,
The same horn to blow,
Find and kill countless foxes gymnastic.

And the hunt, native-born to a man,
Tenant farmers with wit and *élan*,
Horse-breeders and breakers
Riding hard o'er vast acres
As forebears for centuries foreran.

Dean Buckland,[11] with clerical phlegm,
Inquired whence the tenants should stem:
The first Earl replied
With forgivable pride,
"Get 'em? I don't *get* 'em! I *breed* 'em!"

A MIDLANDS WATERLOO

Though proud of his rank and his Corps,
A colonel who ne'er went to war,
Jack Thomson of Fife
Spent the whole of his life
Courting death leading foxhunts galore.

Eighty years of minute reminiscence
Recounted equestrian omnipotence;
From the Forth to the Tay,
From Land's End to the Spey,
He challenged vulpecular sapience.

Whether Atherstone, Pytchley or Fife,
He rode boldly, as if for his life;
A demon red-coated,
A Master devoted:
No pining for home, hearth or wife.

Ex-Lancer, Jack Thomson might rue
Not being at the Crimean to-do,
But twelve short years later
He gained glory greater
By mastering his own Waterloo.[12]

At the head of the Pytchley he rode,
Down the red-crusted Arthingworth road:
At a quarter to two
Came the first *view halloo*,
And a marathon chase none forebode.

They found in the Waterloo gorse,
'Mid the bounteous Northamptonshire bourse
Of courage and cunning
Of hiding and running,
Straining sinew of man, hound and horse.

JACK THOMSON

Through thicket and copse the hounds ran,
'Cross railway and road in the van,
Towards Shipley Spinney,
Two-score bobbing jinni,
Lean and fit, a brave caravan.

Up the hill towards Clipstone they sped,
Through bullfinch and stile which soon led
To ecstasy brief,
Hard tumbles and grief
'Mongst the riders, now widely outspread.

The hounds careered on without pause,
To the chagrin but silent applause
Of the straggling entourage,
Bogged down in the borage,
Retarded by yokels and yaws.

Eighteen miles in two hours without check,
The hounds running strong, neck and neck;
Only three fields of plough,
Neither despond nor slough:
The quarry must rally and reck.

Three times the Master changed horses,
When the going sapped equine resources,
But his own strength ne'er failed,
Though others soon quailed
In a rabble and rout of near corses.

The Master by now was alone,
Keeping hounds to one line on his own;
For three hours and a half,
A fine *halloograph*
For the rest of the hunt to atone.

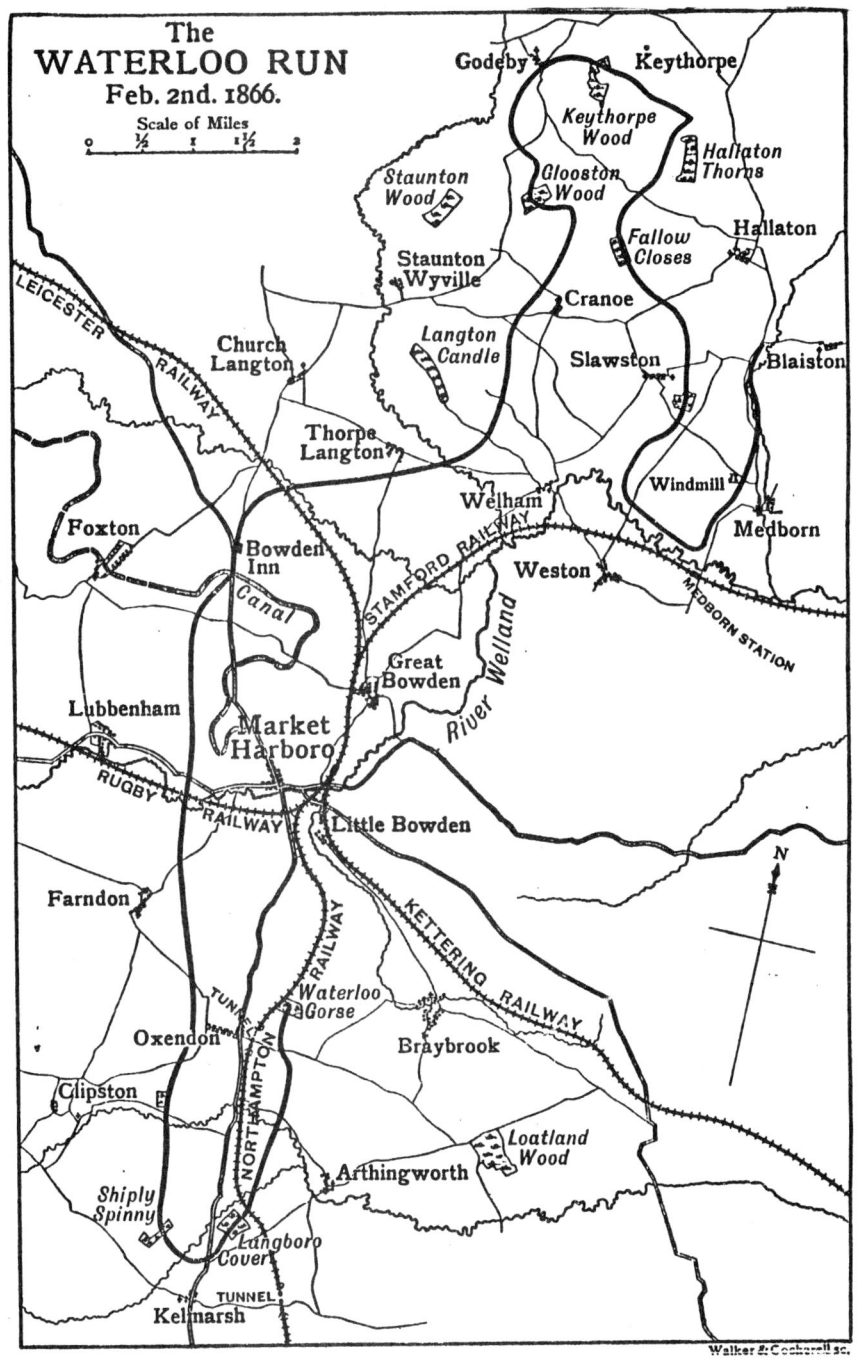

The
WATERLOO RUN
Feb. 2nd. 1866.

Scale of Miles
0   ½   1   1½   2

Godeby   Keythorpe
Keythorpe Wood
Staunton Wood   Glooston Wood   Hallaton Thorns
Staunton Wyville   Fallow Closes   Hallaton
Cranoe
Church Langton   Langton Candle   Slawston   Blaiston
Thorpe Langton
Welham   Windmill
LEICESTER RAILWAY   Medborn
Foxton   Bowden Inn   STAMFORD RAILWAY   Weston   MEDBORN STATION
Canal
Great Bowden   River Welland
Lubbenham   Market Harboro
RUGBY RAILWAY   Little Bowden
N
Farndon
KETTERING RAILWAY
Waterloo Gorse
Oxendon   Braybrook
TUNNEL
Clipston   Loatland Wood
NORTHAMPTON RAILWAY
Arthingworth
Shiply Spinny
Langboro Cover
TUNNEL
Kelmarsh

Walker & Cockerell sc.

With the scent and the light quickly failing,
He stopped them at Medbourne Halt paling,
'Mid goutweed and fennels,
Nineteen miles from the kennels
At Brixworth, a long road a-trailing.

By ten he had whipped the pack home,
By eleven dined by candlelight gloam:
Then off to hunt ball,
The guests to enthrall
With his exploit, to gay metronome.

A MUCH ADMIRED MEMBER

The shortcomings of William John Chute
Were numerous but never acute;
Though not caring for wine,
He headed The Vine,
Riding poorly though fast in pursuit.

From Harrow he went to Clare Hall,
Where scholastic attainment was small,
But finished in France,
Which served to enhance
His burlesque of the histrionic Gaul.

Some thirty years a Member for Hants.,
He displayed neither rages nor rants,
Regarded fine oratory
As akin to idolatry,
Spoke and rode by the seat of his pants.

Though to foxhunting clearly devoted,
And a Master on whom the Hunt doted,
He showed little skill
In the find or the kill,
His huntsmanship scarce anecdoted.

But the Vine Hunt, one frosty December,
Had a day such as all would remember,
When his horse went awry,
Kicked him hard in the thigh:
He and they feared for loss of The Member.

He sat up with fast-beating heart,
Examined the sadly-used part,
Then with feeling restored
And posterity assured,
He resumed the vulpecular art.

A DANGEROUS RADICAL

Sir John Chope, in belligerent mood,
Wrote a letter, suggestive and rude,
To Will Chute of the Vine,
As if to define
A character anti-socially imbued.

He remarked that the nomenclature
Of five hounds to fox entered that year
Had much the same meaning,
Appropriate, demeaning,
Implying a personal slur . . .

On his role as a Tory M.P.,
And on colleagues in garb funerary,
For, the best of the Vine
Were equestrians divine,
Unbeneficed, well-heeled, duty-free.

So *Pensioner*, *Pilferer* and *Parson*,
He equated with Master and Squarson,
And *Plunderer* and *Placeman*
With Huntsmen and statesman,
Devoted to reiving and arson.

Mr. Chute vitiated the viticide
With *Radical, Rebel* and *Regicide,*
Synonym apposite,
A sharp, cutting wit,
With *Rascal* and *Ruffian* allied.

SUMMONED BY BELLS

When honoured by Master with meet,
Churchwardens of Thurnby would greet
The Quorn with church bells,[13]
Ringing welcoming swells
In tribute to sportsmen elite.

But the vicar perversely objected
To paeans of praise misdirected,
And nailed down the door
Of the belfry and swore
He would prosecute men disaffected.

Mr. Waite, sporting farmer, took action
To counter the clerical infraction;
Ignored priestly twinges,
Ordered door off its hinges
To ringers' and hunt's satisfaction.

For two hours the ringers rang rings,
Chimes, changes, Bobs, singles, dongs, dings
And treble Bob hunts,
Joyful dodges and stunts,
Celebrating with springs, clings and flings.

The clerk, in a towering rage,
Took the farmer to court for rampage
And indecent comport,
But the secular court
Dismissed sacerdotal outrage.

NOBLESSE OBLIGE

A pageant of venatic glory
On English lawns verdant and hoary,
The Badminton meet[14]
Was a hunting-man's treat:
A sporting veneration ostensory.

Both royalty and higher nobility,
Knights and squires of conformability,
The ruff and the muff
And the Blue and the Buff
All mixing with great affability.

Then the ladies drive off in their carriages,
Admiring the finest entourages,
And the hunt takes the field
In that bountiful weald
Of venery and graceful seigneurages.

THE 7th DUKE
OF BEAUFORT

Two thousand horse follow the Master
To fame and noblesse or disaster,
The green and the blue
And the ruddier hue
Spurring on at a pace ever faster.

The ninth Duke was considered supreme:
Of amateur huntsmen the cream,
Outranking professionals,
In the van of processionals
And held in the highest esteem.

At polo and coach-driving too,
He excelled as befits a true-blue,
But to turf and the rod
He gave barely a nod,
Preferring the huntsman's *halloo*.

THE 9th DUKE

NOTES ON CHAPTER TWO

W.F. Foster Melliar, who was treasurer of the Heythrop for nearly forty years, built up the bed of the stream at his favourite crossing point to within three feet of the surface.

The Cradock family was settled in Leicestershire for many years. A Mr. John Cradock was a prominent member of the Quorn in the time of Meynell. He died in 1833 and was probably the oldest hunter in the county. His son, John, born about 1792 and a solicitor, was no less enthusiastic. He was field-master in the absence of Mr. Errington (1835-38) and was noted for his easy and persuasive manner in dealing with inconsiderate riders. He died in 1838 and his brother, Thomas, carried on the family tradition. He held office as secretary for twenty-three years.

The hunt found at Tarwood, renowned for sturdy foxes, and the incident occurred near Hailey, two miles north of Witney, Oxfordshire, in February, 1808, when Will Long was second whipper-in.

In the Highlands with three couples of foxhounds and Jack Shepherd, Fife kennels huntsman all his life except for 1906 which he spent at Bentley.

On February 3, 1802.

Henry Ireton, Cromwell's son-in-law and righthand man was born in a farmhouse adjacent the church. He signed the death warrant of Charles 1.

Nicolas John Charlton of Chilwell Hall, Notts., died in June, 1892 and was buried in the churchyard at Attenborough. There is a commemorative slate on the floor of St. Mary's Church.

Another colourful funeral with all the trappings of the hunting field on display took place ten years later when Bobbie Dawson, for sixty years whip for the Bilsdale, was buried on June 18, 1902, at Chop Yat (Gate). He died in his ninetieth year, "shrunken, withered and ancient" but until then "still the tireless sportsman", lastly under the Mastership of Mr. H.W. Selby Lowndes. Dawson asked to be buried upright "seea that

Ah can hear t'hoonds when they come doon t'deeal". His wi
was humoured while he lived but ignored after his dea
However, he was put to earth in the colourful style of Tc
Moody, the famous Shropshire whip, in 1796, with his horse, co
cap, boots, spurs, hounds and scarlet-coated riders in attendan

A gravestone carved in his memory
bore the emblems of the chase: a
fox mask, brush, hunting horn
and whip on a white cross. But
religious prudence prevailed and
the stone was never set at the head
of the grave.

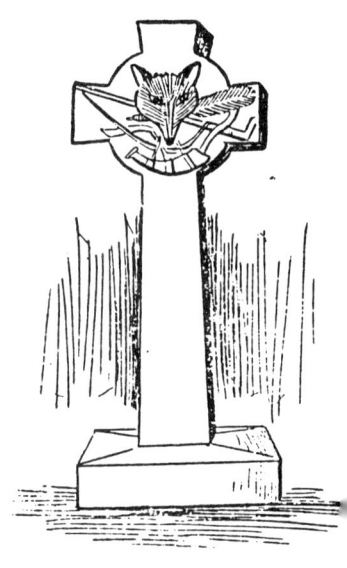

9. Lord Waterpark was a guest at
   Hindlip Hall where a liberal
   luncheon preceded a near two-
   hour run with the Worcester in
   February, 1886.   Harry Baylis
   lived at Netherwood. Mr. Ames
   was Master 1873-76 and 1879-96.

10. The first Master was Mr. Charles
    Pelham (1714-63).

11. Dr.Buckland, Dean of Westminster,
    father of the naturalist.

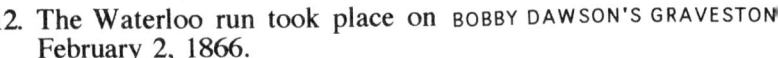

12. The Waterloo run took place on   BOBBY DAWSON'S GRAVESTON
    February 2, 1866.

13. Since 1857, the year after the Earl of Stamford succeeded S
    Richard Sutton as Master of the Quorn, the custom of be
    ringing to welcome hounds and their Master to a village me
    had been followed enthusiastically at Thurnby ($3^1/_2$
    E.Leicester). The Quorn was due on February 27, 1862, but t
    vicar, the Rev. J.C.K. Redhead, forbade ringing the bells a
    threatened proceedings against anyone disobeying his edi
    The Sunday before the meet he locked the door to the belf
    and nailed down the latch. But, at 7 a.m. next day Mr. Waite
    farmer and churchwarden, got the village constable to lift t
    door off its hinges with a crowbar. The ringers went in and ra
    the bells for more than two hours in firm defiance of the vi

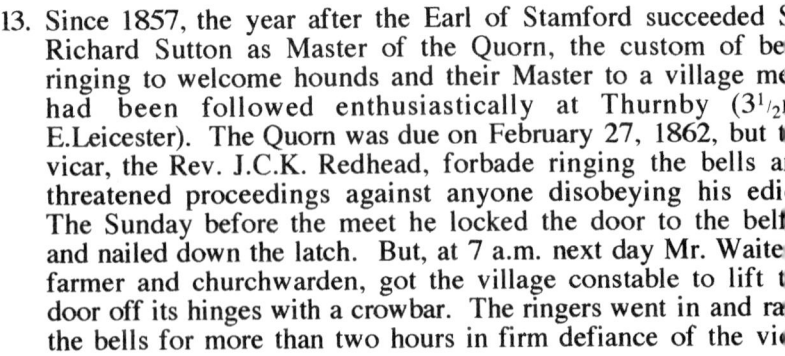

who then summoned Mr. Waite to appear at the county public office in Leicester for "violent and indecent behaviour." (Presumably he was the people's warden.) The bench dismissed the case, holding that they had no jurisdiction. In relating the story, W.C.A. Blew, the hunt historian, opined that an ecclesiastical lawyer might have been puzzled by the decision. He was apparently unaware that the case was later taken to the Court of Arches, the chief consistory court of the Archbishop of Canterbury, and on June 18, 1862, the churchwarden and ringers were admonished and "condemned in costs" of £48 15s 10d. In default of payment the ringers were jailed for five weeks but released when the patron of the living intervened and paid costs of £41.14s 6d. The summons before the magistrates was couched in ecclesiastical terms. Had the warden been charged with malicious damage there might have been a case but that would have hung on the hinges, so to speak. He had a right to be in the church and it was the constable who lifted the door off its hinges. The ringers might have been charged with riot but it would have been a thin case: it was the warden who invited them in. Canon law provides that the custody of the church and its bells is vested in the incumbent and churchwardens and the consent of the minister conjointly with that of either warden is necessary for ringing the bells.

A long succession of Dukes of Beaufort hunted the pack at Badminton, originally for stag. The hounds converted to fox about 1760 under Henry, the fifth duke. He also hunted from Heythrop House in Oxfordshire. He died in 1803. Henry Charles, the sixth duke, took over and the pack became celebrated. He gave up in 1835. The eighth duke, Charles Fitzroy Somerset, carried the horn himself for a few years. Under the sixth and seventh dukes, meets on the lawn at Badminton were great social events, often attended by royalty.

THE EIGHTH DUKE OF BEAUFORT

CHAPTER THREE

THE CHASE

OF THE

WILD DEER

WHIDBORNE   STUDD

DRAMATIS PERSONAE

Mr. John S. Whidborne, solicitor and banker of Teignmouth; Master of the South Devon, 1851-1856, and 1882-1885 (Newton side); previously kept harriers at Teignmouth with kennels at Buddleford Farm.

Mr. Edward Fairfax Studd, MA, BCL, barrister-at-law, of Oxton House, Kenton; Master of the Haldon side, 1882-1884, and of the Exeter division, 1886-1891; kept kennels under the Hang of Oxton.

Sir John Duntze of Exeleigh, Starcross.

The First Baron Haldon; formerly Sir Lawrence Palk, d. 1883.

Dan North, huntsman, formerly of North Devon where he was accustomed to hunting red deer; later huntsman to the Haldon Hunt.

The incident occurred on November 2, 1882.

THE CHASE OF THE WILD, FOREST DEER

In the Year of Our Lord, 'Eighty-two,
There occurred an extraordinary to-do
In the purview of Heaven,
The annals of Devon
And the history of foxhunting, too.

On the very first day of the season,
The South Devon sustained a grave lesion:
A breach at the top,
On High Haldon cop,
A hazard to sporting cohesion.

The chase of the wild, forest deer
Was debated for many a year
By saddle-room lawyers,
Sagacious old sawyers
And huntsmen from far and near.

In pursuit of the quarry vulpecular,
The South Devon was swift and spectacular;
Its *view halloo* roisterous,
Its hound-language boisterous
And couched in a colourful vernacular.

But beneath the apparent impiety
Lay a proper regard for propriety:
A respect for the norm
Of foxhunting form
And a wish to avoid notoriety.

The bone of contention was plain:
Should a Master of foxhounds refrain
From running a deer,
Should that creature appear,
In the absence of beast more germane?

The subject of theories and theses . . .
Should a foxhunt pursue alien species?
Was a Master a boor
To follow the spoor
Of game of superior faeces?

Antlers of an
Exmoor Stag,
23" tip to tip,
Killed in 1881

The argument raged unabated,
Disputants remaining unsated;
Whether ethics or law,
It stuck in the craw:
No judgement was finally stated.

The pack met at Haldon Race Stand
Whence the hounds in their searching out-fanned,
Noses close to the ground,
But no scent could be found
Till they came to the Kenton upland . . .

And there saw a sight to astound,
The sturdiest senses confound:
A magnificent stag
With fine points and knag:
At last! The foxhounds had found!

More than six feet from nostril to tail,
Fully-rigged like a galleon in sail;
A king among beasts
Fit for Valhallan feasts
After sporting up hill and down dale.

A stranger from distant Exmoor
As rare as raw stake or wild boar:
The savage, red deer,
A bold buccaneer,
Never heard of on Haldon before . . .

For a moment he pauses in splendour,
Majestic, supreme of his gender:
A noble audacity,
A graceful sagacity,
A high-born and worthy contender.

He tries to return to the covert
But the amateur tufters recover
Their unlooked-for prize:
No leafy disguise
Shall counter their questing endeavour.

The mastership then being shared,
A decision was somewhat impaired;
Mr. Whidborne said, "No!"
Mr. Studd, "Let 'em go!"
And so the hunt was ensnared.

Mr. Whidborne, old-school, orthodox,
Was all for sticking to fox;
Mr. Studd, young and brash,
Full of vigour and dash,
Gone away with flying red frocks.

Baptised in equestrian salvation,
Dan North needed no confirmation;
Headstrong for the chase,
Come fame or disgrace,
Celestial bliss or damnation.

Young North had a musical voice
And a scream to make foxhounds rejoice;
A good note on the horn,
The hunt to forewarn,
Hound language expressive and choice.

Like the charge of the Light Brigade,
A growing momentum, unstayed:
An impetuous rush
Through bracken and brush,
A hurtling, pell-mell cavalcade . . .

Disdainful but dry in the mouth,
The hart set his head for the South;
Through Mamhead he ran,
Superb in the van,
Oblivious of frost, flood or drouth.

At Luscombe he turned in his track,
Close followed by hard-running pack;
Cross Mamhead once more,
Through Rushycombe gore
To the race-course, hounds close on his back.

The Hunt saw the visitor flee
From Kiddens to Doddiscombsleigh,
To Dunchideock Brake,
Hounds swift in his wake,
On to Perridge, o'er bracken and lea.

Then on to the Exeter road
The valiant ungulate strode,
Below Longdown to cross,
Over hummock and fosse,
Ere imminent peril forebode.

In an orchard a mile from the City,
Exhausted but proud in obtundity,
The stag stands at bay,
Indifferent to fray,
A picture of sporting nobility . . .

The horn like a trumpet resounds
As Mr. Studd whips off the hounds:
A gesture oblatory,
Exultant! Acclamatory!
His ecstasy knowing no bounds.

No blood-lusting hunt predatory,
No grunting, pot-hunting safari . . .
The quarry gave grace . . .
'Twas the point of the chase
But the chase was far more than the quarry.

So furious and strenuous the pace,
Three horses expired in that race:
A near six-hour run
Ere victory was won,
And a fifteen-mile jog back to base.

A great run, the critics conceding,
But a highly improper proceeding . . .
Indignance and wrath
At a lapse from the path
Of rectitude, probity and breeding.

Mr. Whidborne, a Teignmouth solicitor,
Felt his place as the senior coheritor;
He could not be seen
To condone the obscene:
No verdict from him of *absolvitor*.

SIR J. DUNTZE, BART.

The foxhounds were owned by John Duntze,
A veteran of numerous hunts,
Whose seventeen and a half couple,
Still vigorous and supple,
Were not to be used for such stunts.

Though sporting the old Beaufort button,
And preferring red deer meat to mutton,
Sir John loved the Devon,
His foxhunting Heaven,
And censured the indiscriminate glutton.

At the end of the previous season,
He gave up the South Devon for good reason,
But promised the pack
As a gift, taken back
In the face of such unsporting treason.

Mr. Whidborne refused to continue
With a master revealed as a *parvenu*;
'Twas hard to assuage
The heat of his rage
At a master addicted to *detinue*.

But the animal wasn't detained,
So could Mr. Studd be arraigned
For culpable detinue
When the whole of his retinue
Knew the charge could not be sustained?

Mr. Whidborne's animadversion
Turned to *trover* or maybe *conversion*;
There must be a case
'Gainst an action so base
As to constitute a sporting perversion.

But the *finding*, in law, was a fiction,
No question of grave dereliction:
No criminal act
But an immaterial fact,
Not valid in our jurisdiction.

Through the dense legal fog was now creeping
A notion both sobering and sweeping:
Studd didn't kill the stag,
So there lay the snag:
Mere *finding* was not really *keeping*.

Was there taking and leading away?
Even that was inaccurate to say;
Pursuit with intent,
But of no clear extent,
Or just an impetuous foray?

If it wasn't deliberate duplicity,
Merely careless, cavalier catholicity,
Was it right to inflict,
As for *flagrant delict*,
No other attaint than publicity?

The Joint Master's conduct condemned:
It seemed he had hardly a friend;
Mr. Studd must reflect,
In mode circumspect,
How best his good name to defend.

The rising young lawyer foresaw
The folly of pleading at law:
He must keep his own peace
Till the tumult should cease,
Conserving the strength of his jaw.

He inwardly felt no contrition
And outwardly made no admission:
'Twas no common riot
He'd ventured to cry at
But quarry without precondition.

'Twas a matter of custom and usage,
Not hunting-law breach or abusage:
For a rule must be general,
Not rare or ephemeral,
Not unique and incapable of presage.

The Secretary finally called on
Advice from the noble Lord Haldon,
Whose primary aim,
To avoid casting blame,
Prevented a hunt Armageddon. SIR LAWRENCE PALK, 4th B
LATER LORD HALDON

He opined that the Hunt should decide
On a Haldon and Newton divide,
With two separate packs,
On different tracks,
On alternate days, either side.

Thus Whidborne and Studd both remained,
Their pride and their honour unstained;
And the foxhunting cohort
Got four days of sport;
Their choice was in no way constrained.

Was the hot-blooded chase after venery,
Amid the Arcadian greenery,
An aberration venial,
A roguery genial,
Or a blot on the foxhunting scenery?

The case must be left to posterity
To fathom the intricate verity;
To Artemis and Zeus
And the courts of Olympus
To adjudicate with fitting dexterity.

There's a postscript to add to our story
Ere Whidborne and Studd go to glory:
The very next year
Harriers roused a red deer
In the North of the Hunt territory.

Apprehended and fed for a week,
Its condition was brought to a peak;
Then, enlarged in a field
Near Longdown, to yield
Élan to a vast hunting clique.

The South Devon
"receipt button"
introduced in 1888
exempted members
from "capping" in
the hunting field.
The subscription
was then £3.3s.

Set at first on a tortuous route,
The stag ne'er eluded pursuit;
Via Ugbrooke he ran,
Then as if to a plan,
To Kingsteignton, in line resolute.

Perchance by a destiny starred,
Mr. Studd and Dan North *avant-garde*,
By an ironic fate
He goes through the gate
Of none other than Whidborne's backyard.

NOTE TO CHAPTER THREE

Staghunting gradually gave way to foxhunting around the
middle of the eighteenth century but in the time before local
packs owned by farmers and smaller landowners gradually
merged into more formal hunts with well-defined countries,
running riot was not unusual nor considered unseemly. In the
neighbouring county of Dorset, Henry Symonds in his
delightful *Runs and Sporting Notes from Dorsetshire*, 1899,
records a run on November 8, 1830, with Mr. James Harding's
Mountain Harriers from Higher Waterson, near Puddletown,
Dorchester. They met at Puddlehinton, found a hare and after a
half-hour run, killed. In drawing for a second hare in a patch of
turnips "the best energies of this gallant little pack was called
into action and the spirits of the field raised to a delightful pitch
by raising a noble fallow-deer, a most unusual quarry in that
country." He describes a great run with deer and pack
swimming the river Frome to claim victory at Broadmayne after
a ten-mile chase lasting an hour and eleven minutes.

CHAPTER FOUR

THE BEST OF THE WEST

SIR WALTER PALK CAREW

ST HUBERT'S HALL OF FAME

In an old granite quarry at Hayne,[1]
In the C. Arthur Harris domain
Stood a temple of stone,
Rough-hewn, to enthrone
The lords of vulpecular bane.

Bosky-shadowed, round-hollowed and paved,
In-circled, enhallowed, love-laved:
A Valhallan hall
Of rude, rustic stall
Each with hero's appellation engraved.

Thus *Templa quam dilecta* appeared
With the name of knight-Templer revered,
And *By valour not craft*
Was the motto engraft
With the name, *Walter Carew*, deep-sheared.

Might St. Hubert,[2] the patron, presiding
O'er that vermin-fixed, lion-hearted priding,
Be somewhat bemused
At an image confused
Of crucifix 'tween slant ears abiding?

ST HUBERTS HALL

JACK RUSSELL'S HOUNDS AT TORDOWN AMONG THREE TRANSMOGRIFIED,
EQUINE FRIENDS: *BILLY, COTTAGE AND MONKEY,*

THE LEGENDARY TEMPLER OF STOVER

GEORGE TEMPLER

A huntsman who'd been at the booze
Awoke from an afternoon snooze
To a terrible fright,
An incredible sight:
A monkey *en tenue rouge*.

The nimble and liveried *chasseur*,
A huntsman *manqué*, amateur,
Was a pet of George Templer,
The sportsman exemplar,
A horse-flesh and hound connoisseur.

A man of great intellect and wit,
Charming manners, erudition and grit,
George Templer of Stover
Was brought up in clover,
His patrimony there to acquit.

Doyen of the first regular pack
From Prawle Point to Kirton to hack,
From East of the Moor
To Teignmouth's fair shore,
He led the South Devon there and back.

His hounds had a great reputation
For performance and fine conformation:
So much that the Belvoir
Was a noted receiver
Of a draft from the Stover foundation.

At nineteen-inch high, fully-grown,
A marvel of sinew and bone,
The dwarf-hound of Stover,
An intrepid rover,
Was known as a *Let-'em-alone*.

Whether wild fox from moorland or hill,
Or bagfox of cunning and skill,
The hound would not strike,
In ditch or on dyke,
Unless he was ordered to kill.

The Stover pack had a great boon
In a bagfox they called *Bold Dragoon*:
Out thirty-six times
In hunt pantomimes:
Tail up like a pike or spontoon.

The hounds were quick-witted, swift-heeding,
Reflecting the Master's own breeding:
Merest gesture of hand,
Understated command
Or inflection of voice, quickly reading.

By way of a neat paradox
And giving his friends a few shocks,
The Master at Stover
The traces kicked over
By hunting the hare with the fox.

A lawyer's alleged peculation,
And Templer's unwise speculation,
Unbounded hospitality
And benign liberality
Led sadly to hypothecation.

A fall brought an end to a race
Distinguished by wit, style and pace;
For Templer of Stover
Life's steeple-chase was over,
In the family vault at Teigngrace.

SKYLARKING AND SHOW-JUMPING

Mr. C. Arthur Harris of Hayne,
Jack Russell's co-adjutor and swain,
Was no mean equestrian,
No plodding pedestrian,
But a master of horse, spur and rein.

At Tinhay Bridge, under repair,
On *Skylark*, a Foxbury mare,
He cleared five open spans
Before mazed artisans,
A challenge no other would dare.

His friend and co-equal exemplar
Of equestrian stunts, young George Templer,
Once made hackles rise
By a deft exercise,
Leaping toll gate in manner spectacular.

At Shaldon Bridge over the Teign,
The longest in England e'er seen,
In cold blood he rode,
In derring-do mode,
Clearing gate in vertiginous careen.

The by-laws banned football and fives,
And higgling and hawking fish-wives,
Bear-baiting and tennis,
Privateers from Pendennis,
But not hurdling or shackling of gyves.

To discourage such bold expertise,
And avoid further loss of their fees,
The lords of the toll
Reinforced their control
By erecting a *cheval-de-frise*.

Henry Taylor of Ogwell was one
Of that trio for frolic and fun
To make music from Stover,
Scoring skilfully over
Templer's staves for a *strascinando* run.

Though never a Master *per se*,
A man of great mark in his day;
Whipper-in with Jack Russell
In the bustle and justle;
Recipient of Nimrod's bouquet.

THE REV. H. TAYLOR

On occasion they'd counsel the hounds
To cast themselves well out of bounds:
A "brilliant irregularity,"
A bold vernacularity
Except where convention abounds.

Taylor once won a bet at a meet[3]
To jump park gate, half-crowns 'neath feet
On stirrups light-resting,
Thus cunningly testing
Superb riding skill and fine seat.

DOGGED MALFEASANCE

A story in very poor taste,
Which some post-prandial tables disgraced,
Posed a rare permutation
Of the triangulation
'Twixt huntsman and hounds and the chased.

Were it not for bucolic antecedents,
The tale would deserve little credence,
But it ought to be told
As a warning of bold
And disgustingly dogged malfeasance.

A huntsman abroad in his grounds,
Inebriately doing his rounds,
Suffered vicious attack
By his ravening pack
And was swiftly devoured by the hounds.

The narrator would go on to varnish
And the picture excrescently tarnish
With gory details
Of curious entrails
And what the vile beasts used for garnish.

DOWN AMONG THE DEAD MEN

But Davies, Jack Russell's biographer,
Not known as a rustic gastrosopher,
Records as a fact
Such a bestial act
In his role as a vulpine demographer.

Describing a fox-earth at Hayne,
A Y-shaped and narrow-walled drain,
He records that Dick Down
Earned ghostly renown
As a huntsman thus cruelly slain.[4]

And a Cornish correspondent avers
That the worst of the man-eating curs
To Tetcott were drafted,
Discreetly abafted,
To run with John Arscott's *chasseurs*.

One of these was a black and tan hound,
Immense, and invariably found
By the hunt-runner's side,
In the straw of his hide,
In the kennels, in slumber profound.

BLACK JOHN OF TETCOTT

At Tetcott, John Arscott's familiar,
Court jester for moods atrabiliar,
Story-teller, sparrow-mumbler,
Vermin-swallower, comic tumbler,
King pin of carousels conciliar . . .

JOHN ARSCOTT

Was a dwarf four feet high called *Black John*,
A misshapen, uncouth phenomenon,
Atavistic of mien,
Unkempt, none too clean,
Of ugliness a sad paragon.

When Arscott, the hunter, rode out
From his Tamar- and Claw-side redoubt,
Black John at his side,
On foot, place of pride,
Was a faithful and hard-running scout.

So sinewy and swift was his form,
So agile and keen to perform,
He was up with the hounds
In the wildest of grounds,
And in at the death with the swarm.

With the brush of the fox as the crest
Of his hat, then the twain would be blest
The next Sunday at church,
By the priest from his perch;
Both victor and victim confessed.

Once awakening, in pew high and narrow,
To hear parson lamenting in sorrow,

BLACK JOHN

"Peace on earth's *hard to find*,"
He robustly opined,
"Us be sartain to find 'un tomorrow!"

A BOISTEROUS BRUIT

Bold Dragoon, just enlarged at Teigngrace,
Then the flooded Teign halting the chase;
The ford drowned in trough
And Jew's Bridge a mile off,
Escape seemed assured for the ace.

So the hunt galloped off to the bridge
Save Taylor who, spotting a ridge
Of rails near the bank,
Maybe short in the shank,
Plunged forward, the spate to abridge.

But, alas! He was deep in the mire,
Horse and rider both set to expire
'Neath the powering water,
Ignominious slaughter!
Sad end for the best in the Shire.

But Taylor, a wet-bob at Eton,
Skilled swimmer, ne'er knowingly beaten,
Rose up in the bore,
Striking out for far shore,
Though his steed nowhere waitin' to greet 'un.

Then, hooves-first, the hunter appeared,
Body grounded but forelegs engeared,
Jerking head under water,
The reins ever tauter,
'Till swiftly by owner clean-sheared.

Taylor mounted, raced on in pursuit,
Along riverside's tortuous route,
Bagging quarry alive:
Three born to survive
The flooded Teign's boisterous bruit.

THE PASSING OF POOR FANNY TUCKER

The passing of poor Fanny Tucker
Caused many a stern face to pucker
At her ironic fate
From the action ingrate
Of a beast she would tenderly succour.

No creature would e'er vainly ask
For kindness from Fanny, whose task
Was to take corn each day
To her feathered friends gay
At the aviary, in flat-bottomed flask.

Old Dick[5] was a stag in the park
At Powderham, a proud patriarch
Who ruled his domain
With the bossy disdain
Of a proud and demanding hierarch.

He would waylay the maid in her track
For his danegeld: a mouth-watering snack
Of the succulent grain,
Never asking in vain,
Till one day, alas and alack . . .

The ill-fated woman was early
For her tryst with the ungulate knurly;
The punctilious deer
Thus failed to appear,
And Fanny passed on prematurely.

For, on her return, empty-handed,
And lacking the tribute demanded,
Old Dick ran her through,
Tossed her high, cruelly slew
And fatally reprimanded.

The moral is perfectly clear:
No man should keep singular deer
Alone in a park
For fear it embark
On rampage and mayhem severe.

Even reared from a calf and dehorned,
A lone red deer, bald, unadorned,
Will attack without reason
Especially in season,
His victims mere objects, unmourned.

BOGGED DOWN ON BOXING DAY

There are two kinds of bog on the Moor,
The mire in the wet, valley floor,
And the Dartmoor bog proper,
The real hunting stopper,
The dry, powdery peat on the tor.

On a frost-crusted Boxing-Day jog,
The Mid-Devon got stuck in a bog,
With the peat ten feet deep
And the Hunt in a heap,
And one horse sitting up like a dog . . .

And the lead mare in up to her belly,
Mr. Prickman's firm stance turned to jelly;
Hayter Hames in distress
At the sad, sorry mess
And the afternoon's sport wrecked most felly.

Then 'twas off with the coat and the saddle,
A dig round each leg with a paddle,
And a bit of a struggle
And wriggle and juggle
And out on a silver-pink raddle.

HEIRS AND LACES

Sir John Heathcoat-Amory, Bart.,
Much-skilled in the chase of the hart
And science avifauna,
And flora and fauna,
Cared little for mercery mart.

In a life-time devoted to sport,
To hooking and sounding the mort
For hare, fox and stag,
Over moorland and crag,
Sir John rode majestic athwart.

From bluff Buckland Beacon he viewed
The haunt of the deer, vast and rude;
At Stoodleigh he rode,
To knight-errant code,
To cull an excess of the brood.

In the Moriston, Ness and Fintray
And the Spean and the Spey and the Tay,
And the Culm, near to home,
And the Exe, he would roam,
With Jock Scott,* Fiery Brown, Lemon Grey.

'Midst acres of trumpeting bignonia,
With oak, cedar, pine and begonia,
Rhododendron endowed,
He was uprightly proud
Of his beautifully-shaped Wellingtonia.

Six children a-romp in the nursery,
Each assured of due share in the bursary;
A gentleman's life,
Free of striving and strife
Save for fish, fowl and deer-flesh elusory.

---

* Jock Scott (1817-93) created the pattern during a trip to Norway with his master,
  the Earl of Haddington

His fortune was based on a bobbin,
A darting and weaving-round-robin
Taking traverse or weft
Round the warp threads, neat-cleft,
In eight motions of jobbin' and throbbin'.

His grandsire's ingenious invention
Superseded the Brussels convention
Of bobbin on pillow
And pattern on billow,
But led to the Luddite contravention.

His father, a lawyer and banker
From London, was minded to hanker
For pastures more grand,
Rich heiress's hand,
And at t' mill wharf had swiftly dropped anchor.

Anne Heathcoat within his embrace,
Sam Amory secured a new base
O'er the Exe-powering waters,
An heir and fair daughters,
A dynasty founded on lace.

A GENERAL ON EXMOOR

AN EXMOOR STAG

Bluff, burly and bold Mr. Bisset
Had a love of deer-hunting implicit
In twenty-six years'
Mastership 'mid the meres
Of Exmoor stag country exquisite.

He killed more than six-hundred deer,
An average of twenty-three a year,
In eleven-hundred days,
To the rapture and praise
Of the hunt and his visiting peer.

Once a sub. in the King's Dragoon Guards,
But known by his fellow die-hards
As *The General*, forsooth,
For his style, terse and couth,
And appraisal of moorland hazards . . .

He ruled with a gentle severity,
A clement and kindly asperity;
He spoke very little,
In syllables brittle,
Eschewing a garrulous temerity.

To landowner, pauper or peasant,
He was courteous, considerate and pleasant;
To yeoman or farmer,
A magisterial charmer,
A gentleman by general assent.

Never once in his stag-hunting journal,
Recorded in ritual diurnal,
Did the first person rear,
Egotistic chanticleer:
Achievement was communal, fraternal.

In stature just short of a giant,
Large-limbed but physically pliant,
He weighed twenty stone,
All muscle and bone,
A man's man, assured, self-reliant.

At a glance Mr. Bisset could tell
The sex of a deer, and foretell
Its probably route
To counter pursuit,
And the distance and timing as well.

MR BISSET

Without sighting of quarry or hound
For miles in that vast hunting ground,
He would plot his own course,
Backed by native resource,
And by accurate prediction astound.

Persevering o'er cart-rut and quag,
Mr Bisset despatched his first stag
In the Haddeo, by candlelight,
Nigh on eight o'clock o'night,
Determined on "one in the bag."

Despite an unpromising start
Mr. Bisset, ne'er one to lose heart,
Soon vanquished deer-stealing,
Sheep-killing, ill-feeling
Raw hounds and the like, art and part.

The ancient and time-honoured laws
Of the forest, the wisdom and saws
And fieldcraft observed,
The deer were preserved
And order restored, without pause.

There ensued very many fine chases,
Spent horses and hounds, ruddy faces:
Twenty miles without check,
Over hillock and beck,
And blood at the last in far places.

Having built up a fine herd of deer,
To the general well-being and cheer,
He must next do his duty
And limit the booty,
And cull and control, year by year.

But the deer and the visitors grew;
Opening days saw a vast retinue
At Cloutsham, a mob
Contriving to rob
The General of field-marshall's due.

So he started a Horner campaign,
In the heart of the red deer domain,
With the pack lodged near Porlock,
He hunted hind round the clock
With relays of hounds, might and main.

Two or three were despatched in one day,
In morn, noon and night roundelay;
Then the hunt, moving West,
Chased the fleet and the best
From the coverts and banks of the Bray.

'Seventy-eight saw an end to the gladness,
A start of dejection and sadness;
A looming disaster
For the hard-working Master
When a hound evidenced canine madness.

In three months six couple were shot
In a bid to eradicate the blot
From that fair hunting clime,
Sweet pasture sublime:
In eleven months he'd slaughtered the lot.

Perfection and fame dearly bought,
Then a desperate fight bravely fought:
A hard act to follow,
A sharp pill to swallow,
Two decades of work set at nought.

A new pack was formed around *Wellington*,
A well-seasoned hound, nigh a paragon;
As tough as old boots
And good with recruits:
An example to tyro and Bedlington.

Then a new case of rabies appeared:
More hounds were destroyed; it was feared
That deer herds would multiply
And finally stultify
The work of a Master revered.

Forebodings were justified fully,
Huge herds roamed o'er hillside and gully;
The deer, out of hand,
Were free to expand,
A fine job of culling to sully.

Mr. Bisset abruptly resigned
And, although not to politics inclined,
Became an M.P.,
A sad refugee
From the duties of hunting the hind.

He said he would far rather be
In a thick moorland fog by the sea,
Than confusing the nation
With perverse obfuscation
And nebulous riddlemeree.

In property and staghunting lore
He bequeathed a great deal to the Moor;
A hard-questing sleuth,
A *General* in truth,
A legend in seasons of yore.

LORD EBRINGTON,
MASTER, D. & S.S.,
1881 - 1887

THE OLD SQUIRE OF DORSET

Down from Eton and Christ Church he came,
Estate and vast fortune to claim;
College stripling, two-and-twenty,
MFH till two-and-seventy,
Pursuit of the fox his sole aim.

James Farquharson of Langton, the squire,
Hunted country as big as the shire:
Blackmoor Vale, Cranborne Chase,
All of Dorset apace
A red-and-black-capped hue and crier.

Full six days a week the squire rode
From his Langton, near Blandford, abode;
Clifton Woods, Melcombe Park,
Decoy Pond: patriarch
Of the Noble Science and the code.

At Langton, on the banks of the Stour,
He kept thirty-four hunters, a score
For his tenants and friends;
At Eastbury, made amends
With stabling for fifty mounts more . . .

And seventy-five couples of hounds,
Disported in kennels and grounds;
A fine enterprise
For securing the prize,
Expenditure knowing no bounds.

In that hardy but idyllic clime,
'Mid laurel, laburnum and lime
And short oaks and hazel,
To the song of the ouzel,
He extirpated alopex crime.

JAMES FARQUHARSON

Among Masters the cream of the nation,
No reading-the-riot-act jobation,
He was kindly and courteous,
Considerate and bounteous;
A gentleman to men of all station.

Three times he received testimonial
In argenteous presentation ceremonial,
By admiring subscribers
And besotted imbibers,
And wealthy land-owners baronial.

In the wood centring Badbury Rings,
Where King Arthur in raven-guise wings,
The Old Squire, perchance,
In Valkyrian stance
And knightly court mournfully sings.

A WEAR AND TEAR PACK

Ere Polwhele[6] penned past of the Celt,
Or Lipscomb[7] a fresh pilcher smelt,
Or Pryce[8] made apologia
For Cornu-Archaeologia,
The Four Burrow chased carnivore svelte.

From Scorrier they ran twice a week
To Penzance or Bodmin to seek
The stout moorland fox,
Amid grey, granite rocks,
Gorsey whins or wide grass to far creek . . .

From Hayle to Lostwith'el and Fowey
They roamed with a clamorous joy,
A wear-and-tear pack
In ravage and rack,
A tough, Pompey-Eggesford alloy.

Each fortnight companionable meet:
Hunt dinner at principal seat
Of each member in turn,
Pouring claret from urn;
Loving cup in a friendship replete.

And at Ivybridge for Invitation Week
The Four Burrow were not hard to seek,
Well up with Trelawny
For Dartmoor fox brawny,
Well for'ard of grass-country clique.

When the foxes had all gone to earth
And Bodmin Moor showed a sad dearth
Of vulpecular sport,
The hunt would resort
To hare coursing, with mischievous mirth.

CHARLES TRELAWNY

Then dinner at low, post-change inn,[9]
Roast and boiled with rum toddy or gin,
And tall stories scaring
And anecdotes daring;
Hunting songs to an old mandolin.

When pedigrees and hound genealogy,
And legends from hunting mythology
No longer held sway,
Conversation gave way
To legerdemain or electro-biology.

A waitress of ample proportions
Was urged into curious contortions[10]
To retrieve a half-sovereign,
Titillatin'ly hoverin'
With ingenious but futile retortions.

NOTES ON CHAPTER FOUR

Hayne was a large, quadrangular mansion in castellated, Tudor-Gothic style, seven miles ENE of Launceston, built about 1810 by Wyatville to replace an earlier "castle" gutted by fire. The estate appears to have been sold by the Harris family about 1867. Among three memorial stones was one marking the death of a huntsman killed and eaten by his hounds.

St. Hubert's Hall, an open-air arena at some distance from the house, had seventeen stone seats, lined with wood, and was apparently used for *alfresco* festivities by leading foxhunters during the first half of the 19C. The legend of St. Hubert, a hunter before his conversion, is enshrined in the abbey church in the small Belgian town of that name and attracts an annual pilgrimage in May. A similar legend of a gleaming cross appearing between the antlers of a hunted stag attends the dedication of Holyrood Abbey, founded 1128.

At Ugbrooke, near Chudleigh, seat of Lord Clifford.

Dick Down was huntsman to C. Arthur Harris of Hayne. William Fawcett in his *Sporting Spectacle* records two other cases of hunt servants being devoured by their charges after dark, when they were likely to be unrecognised, especially when out of their hunt livery. They were in Northumberland and Worcestershire. Yet another instance was given by Mr. William Gardiner in describing the Quorn kennels in 1838. He recorded that the joints of six or seven well-hung horses were consumed every week, eaten raw. A bell was rung for dinner and the hounds were called by fours from the courtyard to their stated troughs. Despite their orderly conduct in the presence of a kennelman cracking a whip, a fellow hunt servant who got up in the middle of the night to appease a canine quarrel was summarily devoured by his charges who did not recognise him without his clothes. They picked his bones. W.C.A. Blew, the hunt historian, doubted the truth of the story and of others like it.

Dr. Charles Palk Collyns of Dulverton recalled that the stag was a terror to children who passed through Powderham Park. More than once as a child he was obliged to climb a tree and

stay there for several hours. The death and its cause wa
recorded in the parish register on December 14, 1803, and on
headstone in the churchyard. Lord Courtenay had the de
destroyed.

6. *The History of Cornwall*, 1803.

7. *A Journey into Cornwall*, 1799.

8. *Archaeologia Cornu-Britannica*, 1790.

9. Jamaica Inn

10. Allegedly instigated by a visitor.

WATERMOUTH, NEAR ILFRACOMBE, DEVONSHIRE.

CHAPTER FIVE

THE BEST OF THE REST

SIR WATKIN'S WINNING WAYS

The fate of the first Watkin Wynn,[1]
The first baronet of that kin,
Was somewhat ironic:
Defiance Byronic
Of a prescient plea feminine.

His beauteous and young second wife
Dreamt a dream of a hazard to life;
Begged him not to ride out
To a hunting field rout,
Fearing death-dealing mishap and strife.

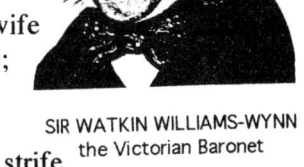

SIR WATKIN WILLIAMS-WYNN
the Victorian Baronet

Sir Watkin half-promised to yield:
Forgo heady joys of the field,
When a well-meaning friend,
Fearing plot to emend,
Warned of future excursions repealed.

So Sir Watkin rode out, had his fun,
Survived an exhilarating run;
Then his horse made a peck,
Broke his master's stiff neck
And his winning ways were undone.

LULLABY AND SWANSONG

When a fleeing fox finds a grave dearth
Of fissures wherein to hide girth,
Too blown to run further,
Unwilling for murther,
He looks for a substitute berth.

A chimney's a favourite place
To counter the ultimate disgrace,
Or a rank, wayside privy
To stifle tantivy,
Secure absolution and grace.

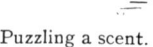

Puzzling a scent.

Such a fugitive in Beaufort's demark,
Run hard from below Stanton Park,
Followed scent of meat pottage
Into Castle Coombe cottage,
Seeking sanctuary in absent babe's ark.

But the fox was unable to bluff
The hounds of the Blue and the Buff:
The fifth Duke, Huntsman Payne,
And the young chatelaine
Saw him routed in riotous rough.

And in Derbyshire, a fox in good style
Set the pace for nigh on twenty mile,
With the hounds neck and neck,
Till there came a sharp check
And compulsion to tarry a while.

The mystified hounds cast about,
Olfactory instinct in doubt;
Then one found a sheep,
An inanimate heap,
Odoriferous within and without.

At last the old hunter gave tongue,
And the fox from the carcass was sprung,
Having ripped out sheep's belly,
There to hide from the melée,
Well-knowing his swansong was sung.

THE BITER BIT

The Old Surrey huntsman, Tom Hills,[2]
Homeward bound and replete to the gills,
Bagfox in his pocket
With Leadenhall docket,
Looking forward to foxhunting thrills . . .

When a voice commands, "Stand and deliver!"
But Tom, though a-shake and a-shiver,
Shows a huntsman's resource
By taking recourse
To the creature a-quake in his quiver.

"Help yourself!" says Tom, feigning disaster,
Vulpine instinct now functioning faster;
"But please leave the pouch,
For the content, I'll vouch,
Is but delicacies for my master."

In plunges the highwayman's hand
In search of supposed contraband,
And the villainous swagman
Is bit by the bagman,
A viciously sharp reprimand.

He hops about, screaming with pain,
Drops his gun in the mud and the rain;
And Tom says, "Good day!"
Is for'ard, away,
The highwayman cursing in vain.

THE TRESPASSER'S BLAIN

Apropos the Tedworth terrain,
A character of muscle and main
Was the Savernake keeper
Of forest and cheeper,
Caleb Simonds, a trespasser's blain.

A fox went to earth in the morning
While huntsman and hounds were still yawning;
The hunt soon retired
But old Simonds perspired,
Digging sand until well nigh the horning.

He stuck at his self-imposed task
For fourteen hours: no-one could ask
For greater devotion
Without thought of promotion;
His reward was the brush and the mask.

Hearing shots, on another occasion,
He needed no moral persuasion
To go out in the night,
Amid wintery blight,
To grapple with poaching invasion . . .

Unarmed save for courage and flail
Against three desperate men to prevail;
They inclined to surrender,
Thinking no lone defender
Would dare their offence to curtail.

Then, finding the keeper alone,
And knowing their cover was blown,
They launched an attack,
But Simonds fought back,
Killing one, the twain to atone.

FOUR OUT OF HAND

Lord Orford's renowned eccentricities
Obscured his inventive propensities,
His experimentation
Confounding the nation,
Despite genius and practical sagacities.

In constant pursuit of good sport,
His body and soul to transport,
He conceived a strange notion
For continuous motion,
Driving four red-deer stags in cohort.

By diligence, discipline and faber,
He fashioned four beasts to the labour
And drove four-in-hand,
In total command
Save for sniggers and sneers from his neighbour.

But, approaching Newmarket one day,
Phaeton drawn by the quadruple trey,
Orford's ears were assailed,
By hounds' cry rudely hailed,
As the pack sensed the cervine bouquet.

As a body the hounds changed direction,
Incensed to a mad insurrection;
With incitement breast high
They drew ever nigh,
In galloping Gilpinesque defection.

So, fearing the ill-fate of Phaethon,
Orford strove to control stag and phaeton,
But the bold charioteer
Could scarce bridle his fear
As the mad *tour de force* swiftly gait on.

But his fiery-eyed steeds, well acquainted
With the nearby Ram Inn, deftly feinted,
The outfit tumultuary
Finding secular sanctuary
In the yard, thence the barn unattainted.

A SPORTSMAN CAUGHT OUT

Able huntsman and cricketer stout,
And a stranger to riot or rout,
Jem Hills[3] wielded willow
Like a boisterous billow
But one day he caught himself out.

With Wyndham's in Sussex he ran
A vixen, with trailed caravan
For more than an hour,
In a progress bizarre,
Round and round on a circular plan.

Jem wearied of vulpine cunctation,
Resolving, with mild imprecation,
To end the impasse
With a requiem mass
After withershins ambuscadation.

Concealing himself in a ditch,
He headed th'importunate bitch,
Then involuntarily caught
The beast as she sought
Safe refuge, in irony rich.

So the huntsman was humbled and hummelled,
The vixen translated, enpommelled,
Carried home as a guest
After death-dealing quest,
Warm-kennelled, cosseted, oenomelled.

THE WILD ONES OF WILLEY

Eft night of comradely carousal,
A four-o'clock, chilling arousal,
Then rare beef and shandy,
Raw eggs beat in brandy,
And out ere the song of the ouzel . . .

Clee Hills, Wenlock Edge to the Wrekin,
Whither Cambrian canine came sneakin',
Squire Forester[4] of Willey,
Like a shrill, boilin' billy,
Tom Moody[5] and hounds gaily speakin' . . .

And Pheobe[6] of Forester's hareem,
Amazonian champion supreme,
In the saddle mad-daring,
For danger not caring,
Whipper-on to feats wild and extreme . . .

George Forester, manorial squire,
Country gentleman, doyen of the shire,
At Tudor-chined hall,
Leaded lights, ivied wall,
Kept free house for mendicant or prior.

They winked at his facile philandering,
Licensed bachelor's convivial meandering:
A lax liberality,
A fond joviality
Not worthy of censure or slandering.

But his paramour's vaulting ambition
Embraced her domestic position;
Loaded gun to his head
In the conjugate bed,
He signed her fiduciary petition.

Tom Moody was whipper-in renowned,
Second huntsman with stout Willey hound;
Only eight-stone but muscular,
Five-foot-six and corpuscular,
With knowledge of venery profound.

A rider of courage and daring,
But civil, good-natured and caring,
He would leap his own height
Without vestige of fright,
Steed mettled and wild, nostrils flaring.

Some said he was too fond of ale
But no-one could bring up the tail
Of processional pack
With his unerring knack;
A Galahad for galloping grail.

Tom Moody's stentorian call,
In the field or baronial hall,
Set joyous hounds singing,
Cups dancing and ringing,
With musical mods to enthrall.

And Tom was a born raconteur,
Of hunt-song a gifted *chanteur*
Himself made immortal
Through Incledon's portal[7]
And Charles Dibdin's verse *par bonheur*.

When Forester gave up the sport,
Relegated his quadruped court,
Tom Moody repined
And swiftly declined,
Prepared for his own sorry mort.

His funeral owed more to the science
Than to staunch Church of England alliance;
Six earth-stoppers bore
Their champion of yore
To the earth, with his wish in compliance . . .

At Barrow, 'neath yew-tree's broad span,
With his old horse accoutred, in van,
With brush, cap, whip, boots,
Four hounds in cahoots,
Then three *view-halloos* partisan.

A SAVERNAKE SWEEPSTAKE

When a chimneysweep's out on his rounds,
Versatility knowing no bounds,
There's luck for a wedding,
Plenitude to plant bedding,
Or assistance to huntsman and hounds.

A sweep widely venturing at Savernake
Encountered a hunt with its prize at stake,
Imprecating in vain
At a fox in a drain,
Refusing his lair to forsake.

The sweep plies his implements and rods,
While the huntsman expectantly nods;
Then a twist and a jerk
While the hounds go berserk,
And some dexterous, horizontal prods . . .

When a brush meets a brush in a drain,
Socializing's a bit of a strain;
There's a *How-d'-ye-do?*
Then a hullabaloo,
Master Reynard emerging *en train*.

A DYNASTY DOOMED

The forebears of famous John Mytton
Pre-dated the first ancient Briton:
Long centuries in Salop
At head of the gallop
Till by folly a dynasty smitten.

Soldiers, sheriffs and squires of high station,
Earning honours and fame, veneration;
Destroyed at a stroke
Like their own sturdy oak:
Dissipated in one generation.

Early fatherless and spoiled by his mother,
The squire had a sister, no brother,
And indulged every whim,
Living life to the brim:
No excess too immoderate to smother.

Expelled from both Westminster and Harrow,
Intemperate, prodigal to the marrow,
He gambled and drank,
Degrading his rank,
Improvident as Biblical sparrow.

He lived in a storm, a commotion,
An urge for continuous motion;
Abhorrence of boredom,
A high-flying whoredom
Of sport and a heightened emotion.

He was headstrong, fanatically zealous,
Greatly daring but prickly and jealous;
He excelled at all sport,
Always first at the mort,
But capricious, impetuous and emulous.

A man with a powerful physique,
Bulldog courage and hot-tempered streak,
He would hazard his all
In a public-house brawl
Or the turn of a card at bezique.

He once gripped a dog by the nose,
A seventy-pound giant in repose;
By the teeth held him up
Like a mewling young pup,
In a trial of strength bellicose.

His craving for constant excitement
Of itself was no moral indictment,
But addiction to drink
Caused the brain cells to shrink,
And bravado to grow with incitement.

On four to six bottles a day
Of vintage port: *felo de se*
Was postponed by fresh air
And exercise whene'er
Fur or feather presented as prey.

He excelled in his virtues and failings,
Intrepid at fences and railings,
And his strong constitution
Delayed retribution
And the need to heed friends' countervailings.

The Squire had few equals astride,
His charger obeyed him with pride;
Though a desperate rider,
Iron grip in downed eider,
Over ditch, drain or fence a sure guide.

On his famous, monocular *Bart*,
He expanded th'equestrian art,
Hunting five days a week
With leadership unique,
Vast muscular force to impart.

He rode at impossible fences,
Ignoring the commoner senses;
Jumped toll gates in tandem,
Risked duckings at random,
Defying all moderating influences.

Impatient for Uppington ferry,
In temper foolhardy and merry,
He swam Severn bore
To far, distant shore,
In contempt for the wharfinger's wherry.

For breeding he had no capacity,
Lacking perseverance, patience, perspicacity,
But kept a fine stable
And hounds keen and biddable,
Spending money with great pervicacity.

He hunted two countries in style,
Keeping thirty-six thoroughbreds the while,
And game preserves handsome
At cost of king's ransom;
Plantation for mile after mile.

Than Mytton was no better shot
For hare, partridge, pheasant for pot,
And on Merioneth moor
Sixty grouse was the score
For his fusillading, duple gavotte.

One winter, with foolhardy pluck,
He leapt from the warmth of his ruck
To lie on thick ice
With his fowling device,
In his nightshirt, to stalk the wild duck.

Impromptu, he'd stage bizarre races:
Waggon horses released from their traces,
Wild leaps over water,
For his friends, madcap slaughter,
And retreat from equestrian graces.

He once took a fancy to flower
As M.P., in abrupt bid for power,
Spent ten thousand pounds
In the Shrewsbury grounds
And sat for a lengthy half-hour.

By way of post-prandial fare
In his salon, he rode a wild bear,
But when playfully spurred,
The animal demurred,
Bit him hard *a l'esprit de guerre*.

Disguised as pecuniary proctor
After dining his parson and doctor,
His "Stand and Deliver!"
With ancient caliver,
Insisted on weighty *crock d'or*.

An unwitting creditor he sent
To lunatic asylum to indent
For instant admission,
Involuntary contrition
For bothering a man overspent.

Stripped finally of pride and caparison,
In durance vile, mayhem and malison,
Too late for amends
And despaired of by friends,
He died in dire penitence and orison.

UP AND OVER

Tom Moody, oblivious of fear,
Surmounter of obstacles sheer,
Pell-mell on wild horses,
Full-tilt at stiff courses
Was a daring and skilled charioteer.

Young Moody, Salopian's pride,
Once ventured severely to chide
A tardy pike-keeper,
An on-the-job sleeper,
And *tanselled* the wretched man's hide.

The next time he happened that way,
Young Moody would brook no delay,
But instead, leapt the gate
In dare-devil spate,
Ignoring the keeper's dismay.

What really gave cause to amaze,
The gate-keeper's senses to faze;
Suspend his belief
And add to his grief:
The horse was attached to a chaise!

At the tenderest touch of the switch,
All three cleared the gate without hitch;
A challenge contended,
Gravitation transcended,
Without breaking a buckle or stitch.

KING OF THE WOLDS

When Yorkshiremen hang out the bunting
For the Father of English foxhunting,
They toast Old Squire Draper,
First to curb vulpine caper
With regular hound-pack confronting.

From Beswick Hall in Holderness Division
Of East Riding, he visited excision
On sheep-killing vermin;
No haberdashing ermine:
King's Huntsman's judicial revision.

His royal insignia were few:
A rust-velvet cap worn askew,
And a broad leathern belt
To hang miscreant's pelt
Round hunting-coat's ill-defined hue.

Ere the weed of the wolds dared to flourish
Or Driffield the sad soil to nourish;
When the elm and the beech
Were rare in vast reach
Of hillside and morasses currish . . .

And pink-corolled ling served the bees
With darkling and ill-gotten lees,
There Squire Draper fed
And diligently bred
His pack of benign Eumenides.

"All the brushes in Christendom" his toast,
 Over succulent ox, salt or roast;
"King and Constitution" first,
 Whetting loyalty and thirst
 And appetite for drolleries of host.

On a paltry seven-hundred-a-year
He contrived fourteen children to rear;
Kept a generous table
And a fine hunting stable,
And kennels and hounds to endear.

His establishment was so much admired
That journeyman-huntsmen aspired
To work without wage
For th'equestrian sage
And for schooling so greatly desired.

In the season the Squire rose at four,
Regardless of snow, ice or hoar,
Himself rousing pack
To mount the attack
On the sheep-killing fox on the moor.

His daughter, the apt-named Diana,
In rare voice, fine form and bandana,
Whipped-in for the Squire
And out, with mild ire,
At close-riding beaux near Nirvana.

So chillingly chaste was this daughter,
No hard-riding male ever caught her;
She died singly blest,
Still fully possessed
Of whole bones and maidenly hauteur.

The huntress lies buried beside
Her father, in fealty and pride;
Both revered by the field
For a bountiful yield
Of sport in that sparse countryside.

PORK PIES AND STILTON

Down from Oxford at age twenty-one,
John White sought the pale, winter sun
Of the Lincolnshire fens
And the taut regimens
Of the hard-riding Squire Osbaldeston.

His apprenticeship quickly complete,
He migrated to Old Melton meet,
Where courage and dash
Over bullfinch and plash
Marked him out as a foxhunter fleet.

CAPT. JOHN WHITE

Stern Master of men of the Cheshire,
He ne'er slackened pace nor the pressure,
Persevering, energetic,
Commanding, Hebetic;
Of the fox, a veritable flesher.

Still vigorous at age seventy-five,
He retained his superlative drive;
And hard-tempered nerve,
Exemplary verve,
Vulpecular transgression to shrive.

So to what did he owe his longevity,
His cast-iron resolve and motivity?
At the Old Melton Club
He eschewed syllabub
And Stilton, debauching festivity . . .

And the contents of best Bordeaux label,
Saint Émilion, Pomerol, wine of fable;
Bumper toast in Medoc
Dispensed round the clock
He steadfastly threw 'neath the table.

Unexpectedly laid to his rest
In the year of the foul rinderpest,[8]
He was destined to die
From a stale mutton pie,
Not sticking to pork like the rest.

A GALLOPING CURE

A *little man* who rode *monstrous hard*,[9]
Oblivious of hunting hazard,
Leaving field far behind
In an envious grind,
Was a sort of canary canard.

For inside the yellow-hued jacket,
As slim as a taper or tacket,
Was a scared jackanapes
Doing jankers for japes
In the stables, and causing a racket.

The monkey was cured of his teasing
And conduct in stables displeasing
By Richmond's enzyme,
Well-fitting the crime,
And his padgroom's anxiety easing.

Near Taunton a hunter, high-born,
Grew restive at sound of the horn,
So his groom led him out
For raddle or rout,
In accoutrements fit for the Quorn.

In the absence of Master or flunkey,
In the saddle he placed a large monkey
Concealed in burnoose,
And turned the pair loose
For performance of dizzard or donkey.

But the animal picked up the reins,
Adroitly negotiated drains:
With dexterity and skill
Was in at the kill,
Amazing amused chatelaines.

CARDINAL VIRTUES

First Master of East Essex Hunt,
Charlie Newman was always up front;
A hard-riding farmer
With a hide tough as armour,
A foxhunter resolute and blunt . . .

He hunted full six days a week,
A man of outstanding physique,
Galloped hunter and hack
Sixty miles there and back,
Retribution on Reynard to wreak.

His leadership sure and incisive,
Of Reynard's resources derisive,
He showed first-rate sport
To admiring cohort,
His victories swift and decisive.

But the Master one day met his match,
A fox he could never quite catch;
A bob-tailed buccaneer,
An audacious compeer,
A creature of skill and dispatch.

He exhausted the strength of the pack,
Set cardinal celebrity aback,
Wore out fancied horses
Over hard-running courses,
Defying the huntsman's best tack.

Admiration soon turned to dismay
As the beast survived, day after day
And the Master lost sleep,
Counting horses and sheep,
And the members began to inveigh.

To scupper the bobtail's *élan*,
The Master evolved a sure plan
On scientific principles:
Twenty couple, invincibles!
And a second horse *pour faire coup de main . . .*

The best from his elegant stable,
Trotted slow by a boy, slight but able;
A Pegasus in waiting,
A prospect elating,
A soaring, Parnassian fable!

His adversary quickly discovered,
The Master, his spirits recovered,
Gave forth joyful whoop,
The pack, poised to swoop,
The thrill of the chase rediscovered.

From covert he shot to first field,
The fate of his quarry near sealed;
No timorous forebodings
As he raced through the Rodings,
But promise of reputation healed.

The scent was breast-high as he rode,
Over meadow and plough fairly strode;
The steed in reserve
Stoutly steeling his nerve
As bliss and adrenalin flowed.

"Old Bellman is tolling his knell,"
 He opined to a fast demoiselle;
"His mask will be mine
 And the brush shall be thine,"
 Said the Master, careering pell-mell.

But the pace was beginning to slow,
Fiddler's elbow to stiffen on bow;
Charlie Newman looked round,
Prepared in one bound
To leap on fresh horse full of go.

But the horse was nowhere to be seen,
Nor padgroom, so youthful and keen:
The lad was quite lost
And the chase! At what cost!
The Master gave vent to his spleen.

The fox races on without reck
But the horses are blown, the hounds check;
The hunt is defeated,
The fox more conceited,
And the Master's bold strategem a wreck.

He rides homeward, crestfallen and pensive,
But for horse's fate, not apprehensive;
Then, quitting a lane,
Oh barbarous bane!
There he lies in demise comprehensive . . .

Within yards of the last fence he leapt
For a rider too thrusting, inept;
The gallant grey steed
Died in reckless stampede
Towards rendezvous that nobody kept.

And what of the fleet-of-foot fox
Which broke horses' hearts and stout hocks?
He was shamefully shot
In his turnip-field squat
By a yokel not fit for the stocks.

ROUGH, ROARING RASCALS

Complementing field-craft erudition,
The North boasted bardic tradition:
Ceremonial exalting[10]
After fatal fox-halting,
And revels in raucous rendition.

When the pack, homeward bound, killed a fox,
'Twixt points of divine equinox,
The hunt formed a quorum
And quaffed a vast jorum
Dipped thrice with the brush and the hocks.*

At Alnwick, keep second to none,
Don Juan, after animating run,
Would wildly regale
With bacchanal tale,
Indulging in venerous fun.

The Duke kept an excellent table,
And his *chef de cuisine,* man of fable,
Had a fox's head devilled,
Though somewhat dishevelled,
For dinner, in sauce nobly sable.

*Pads.

NOTES ON CHAPTER FIVE

. Sir Watkin Wynn was killed in 1749 at Acton, near Wrexham, Denbighshire, the seat of Sir Robert Cunliffe.

. The incident occurred on Streatham Common when Hills was huntsman to Mr. Maberley (1812-20). Hunting bagfoxes bought from dealers was then common. Squire Osbaldeston, hunting in Suffolk in the 1820s, bought foxes at thirty shillings a brace from a dealer in the Tottenham Court Road and had them delivered by the dozen brace in a covered cart.

. Jem Hills, brother of Tom, described himself as "By an earth-stopper, out of a huntsman's daughter." Turned out of home at the age of ten with a suit of clothes and a shilling, he was, first, padgroom to the Duke of Dorset. When the Duke was killed, Jem became whipper-in to harriers in Kent. Later, he was second whipper-in to his brother with the Old Surrey and then, aged eighteen, kennel huntsman and first whip to Col. Wyndham at Petworth in Sussex. There he played in the Sussex XI for eight years, a talented batsman. When William Long became huntsman to the Heythrop in 1826, Jem Hills went to Badminton for five seasons as second whipper-in and spent five more as first whip with the Vale of White Horse, returning to the Heythrop as huntsman for thirty seasons until retirement in 1865. A subscription raised £1,080. Jem Hills was famous as a galloping huntsman who bred hounds for quality and speed. He killed a thousand brace of fox in twenty-five years.

. Squire Forester outlived Tom Moody by fifteen years. He was M.P. for Wenlock for thirty years and raised a company of volunteers during the invasion scare.

. Tom Moody died in 1796.

Pheobe Higgs claimed an increased allowance.

Charles Incledon, a famous Cornish tenor, sang Charles Dibdin's famous song immortalising Moody at Drury Lane Theatre. A party of Salopian foxhunters, in Town specially to hear the song, were dissatisfied with the rendering of the chorus and climbed on to the stage as a body in their scarlet coats and top boots and gave the *view-halloo* in a manner to startle and delight the audience.

8.   Cattle plague of 1866 affecting ruminants.

9.   The monkey was strapped to the saddle of the fastest hunter in the Duke of Richmond's stable in Sussex.

10. The practice of dipping pads and sometimes the mask or brush into a bowl of punch was continued in the North of England late into the last century.   It often included ceremonial and fines for hunt members too fastidious to imbibe the aura of the fox with the liquor.   In some districts the liver was placed in a jug of beer or a gallon of ale poured through the mask to drip from the fox's tongue.   These insanitary rites were accompanied by a "Health unto his majesty", meaning the fox.

UP THE CHIMNEY.

DOWN THE CHIMNEY.

CHAPTER SIX

THOUGHTS UPON HUNTING

COLONEL COOK'S CARNIVORES

Colonel Cook, MFH, wanted blood,
No nipping a kill in the bud
But hounds running tauter
To climactic slaughter;
A gory, vulpecular flood.

Without bloodshed foxhunting would wither,
A hound-pack disconsolately dither,
Irresolute, half-hearted,
From quarry disparted,
Confused, running hither and thither.

Running bagmen was a practice despicable,
Unsporting and barely vindicable;
The wild fox alone
Must to nature atone
As miscreant and creature masticable.

The third deadly sin was uplifting
A slack-snooking pack, vainly shifting
To more promising sward,
A practice abhorred,
The ruck from its true business rifting.

EQUESTRIAN BLISS

Hacking home in the teeth of a blizzard
With nothing to pour down the gizzard;
Twenty miles more to go
Through the sleet and the snow:
The game's for a dolt or a dizzard!

Not a house nor a lantern in sight,
Neither sandwich nor biscuit to bite;
Wet through to the skin
In a fierce, howling din:
The Devil a scene to bedight!

EVIDENCE OF A GOOD DAY

No moon from the heavens condescending,
The road stretches black and unending;
The gale gives no quarter,
The boots full of water;
The breeches are stiff and unbending.

Walk a mile, trot a mile, lead a mile.
A travesty of dawn's dashing style;
The horse is dead beat,
Nearly out on his feet:
Oh for shelter to tarry awhile!

The banshees and buzzards are screaming,
Hobgoblins and witches blaspheming;
The tree branches lashing,
The mud ever splashing,
Oh for supper and hot bath a-steaming!

True bliss on the back of a horse?
Poetic, Parnassian discourse?
Or abusing one's leisure,
Sado-masochist's pleasure?
What folly! What nagging remorse!

MANLY DISPORT.

In *The Kingdom* the Earl of Kintore[1]
Started hunting in late 'Twenty-four:
A connoisseur of hounds
From the best hunting grounds:
Keen student of foxhunting lore . . .

Seeking hounds that would hunt, not mere chasers,
No bow-wowing sprinters or racers;
No flashers or dashers
Or untidy splashers,
But disciplined dogs, steady pacers.

If entered at once to the game:
No schooling with harriers to tame
The young, questing novice,
He'd live up to promise,
Progressing to prowess and fame.

Dissenting from famed Mr. Meynell
On conduct of stable and kennel,
The Earl thought one score
Couple: fewer, not more,
Quite sufficient to sound vulpine knell.

As to humans engaged in the sport,
Foxhunting was manly disport
Giving exercise and health
And spiritual wealth,
The contemplative mind to comport.

All the faculties of man were displayed:
Good sense, fortitude on parade,
From peasant to peer,
Fine men of good cheer,
A uniquely Britannic cavalcade

He deplored indiscriminate hallooing;
No noisy encouragement or wooing,
No lifting of hounds
Save from poor-scenting grounds
Or where cattle forestalled rendezvous-ing.

Lord Kintore admired a good run:
An hour, ere the quarry was won,
At a good holding pace,
The whole hunt to embrace,
No rider too far from the fun.

POINTS FOR WRANGLERS

Generations of Varsity men
Have hunted the Cambridgeshire fen,
Hast'ning slowly o'er plough,
Ne'er desponding at slough,
Stable-minded, of deep-furrowed ken . . .

Jumping ditches obscured by rank grass,
Thorn hedges, in rubrical mass,
Heavy going for most,
With few honours to boast
Whether *alumni* clever or crass.

Whilst Oxford taught riding and style,
High-flying and dilettantish wile,
Cantabrigians soon learned
That the science well-churned
Led to long-lasting, life-casting chyle.

Endurance through flood and field fallow,
No place for the languid or callow
But thoroughbred blood
Over drain and through mud:
A pilgrim's progression to hallow.

PACERS AND CHASERS

Should we take a keen student to task
For innocently chancing to ask,
In the interests of science,
The degree of alliance
'Twixt rider and contents of flask?

Are the sips and the gulps and the swallows
In the nooks and the crannies and hollows
For quenching the thirst
Or for fuelling a burst
Of Dutch courage as brave leader *halloos*?

What tipple or tot or libation,
What noggin or dram or potation
Advances the cause,
Retarding the yaws,
Assisting a man's levitation?

Cherry brandy, sloe gin or beef tea?
Perhaps whisky or rum will agree:
Or *Chateau d'Yquem*,
To banish the phlegm
And the cold and faint-hearted *ennui*.

Maybe brandy and old ginger wine
Or curaçao and whisky combine
After numerous tastings
To soften the bastings,
And render the falls anodyne.

In Yorkshire, a hunting divine,
Eschewing plain spirits or wine,
Supped a nauseous beverage
To bolster his leverage:
Irish whiskey admixed with quinine.

The Reverend George Hustler's home brew
Saved many a man from a stew,
The ghastly surprise
Of his vile merchandise
Reviving them all, save a few.

Mr. Dale thought a flask of light port
Afforded good moral support;
Two sandwiches to munch,
On the trot, for his lunch,
And a piece of cake after the sport.

King George, in a gesture of *hauteur*
To a rider half-dead from the slaughter,
Extracts from his coffers
And generously offers
Not brandy but weak barley water.

Mr. Meynell had excellent runs
On tincture of rhubarb and tuns
Of veal tea and bran,
To stay in the van,
And victuals a slower man shuns.

John Smith, with the Meynell, rode prouder
After taking his famed jumping powder,
Which made him feel taller
And fences look smaller,
And stews look like alcoholic chowder.

Adam Sherwood, the Buckinghamshire sweep,
From a two-barrelled glass flask drank deep;
In one side was brandy,
In t'other, quite handy
Was gin to spur mind-boggling leap.

ALL THINGS TO ALL MEN

What qualities make a good Master?
Not a paragon or saint alabaster,
But a hard-riding man
Who stays in the van,
A leader of men and good caster?

Mr. Trollope evolved an opinion
As to how the best man held dominion
Over fellow enthusiasts
And hunting iconoclasts,
Field servants and lesser hunt minion.

The members should hold him in awe,
No mild eccentricity or flaw
Compromising their loyalty,
Or unquestioning fealty:
An absolute ruler, The Law.

Unscrupulous but honest, despotic,
Approachable but aloof, symbiotic,
Occasional tyrant,
Sympathetic gallant,
Epidermis rhinocerotic . . .

Always tolerant but firmly opined,
To the culpable, cruel to be kind;
Severe but forbearing,
Well-expressed without swearing,
Robust and forthright but refined . . .

Exercising unflinching authority
On the strength of his own popularity,
Both truculent and pleasant
To peer, squire or peasant,
Magisterial, benign omniparity . . .

ANTHONY TROLLOPE

Self-sacrificing, diligent and eager,
A transparently honest intriguer;
Strong in health, heart and mind,
Resolute for the find,
A giant among men, a seven-leaguer.

Stout of purse, economical but lavish,
Open-handed but mean as MacTavish;
All things to all men
And the fox in his den,
And prepared the fair sex to enravish.

Thus defined was the Master utopian,
In paradox profound and Trollopian;
Indelibly stamped,
Although logically cramped,
In opinion and prose cornucopian.

A RACE APART

Dr. Chalmers, the Scottish divine,
Pondered much on point, angle and line;
Mathematician and teacher,
Zealous minister, powerful preacher,
He scented the Grander Design.

An allusion to Fife hunting field
From the Kilmany pulpit could yield
A rapt *View halloo!*
Indecorous! Taboo!
When hunt metaphor aptly appealed.

Sagacious, gargantuan *Wee Free*,
Dr. Chalmers, the economist, could see
The hunt's contribution
To rural absolution,
And the moral uplift to the lea.

He described devotees of the chase
As a separate and outstanding race,
Arrayed like a *wapin-schaw*,
With a dash of the outlaw,
And recklessness plain on the face . . .

Admiring dexterity in danger,
Audacious and daring free-ranger;
A race *unco' braw*,
Somewhat arrogant and raw,
Not entirely unkind to the stranger.

THE MILLIONAIRE MISER

John Elwes, the millionaire miser,
Ruled his roost like a Teutonic Kaiser,
Requiring his tenants,
Under pain of dire penance,
To board hounds like an unpaid franchiser.[2]

In a style parsimonious, austere,
He ran hounds on three-hundred-a-year,
With his man-servant, Thomas,
His huntsman from Hallowmas
And domestic in bondage severe.

With never a thought toward treason,
He was kennelman and groom in the season,
And milkmaid and butler,
And valet and sutler,
And abused like a dog, without reason.

Long-suffering but willing and meek,
Idle dog amid Augean reek,
Old Thomas stayed loyal
On weak pennyroyal
And reward of but eighteen pence a week.

A RURAL ECONOMY

Lord Mayo, with courage and flair,
Led the field with the doughty Kildare;
Fearless man on a horse
And a strong, driving force,
He essayed what no other would dare.

In field as in politics commanding,
With stature and intellect outstanding,
Perception adroit,
No dawdling introit,
Strategic appraisal demanding.

In Kildare, a *ticht* boy called Mick,
Foot-runner, obliging and quick,
A chirruping cricket
In an obscurant thicket
Ran with Mayo o'er broad bailiwick.

Never seen to do a day's work,
Yet never appearing to shirk,
He was cheerful and true
To the hunt *view halloo*,
Running miles without payment or perk.

Gently chided one day by the Peer
For wastage of energy severe:
Not tending his 'taters
But chasin' rank craturs,
He countered with innocent cheer:

"Me Lard, what ye say must be true;
Oi'm a fool to do what Oi do,
But 'av fools there was none
From Naas to Dublun,
Foxhunters would be sorra few."

A NOBLE APPORTIONMENT

Mr. Dale was an Oxford M.A.
And an erudite man in his way;
Historian and writer,
Illumining, none brighter,
The manners and men of his day.

Not to mention the horses and hounds,
The Masters and fine hunting grounds;
The kennels and coverts
And haunts of horse lovers,
Blandiloquence knowing no bounds.

For Goosey, Goodall and Gillard,
Dale nurtured the highest regard,
Admiring their knowledge,
Uncluttered by college
Or other progressive canard.

FRANK GILLARD

He deplored a boy's gifts' dissipation
By the influence of State education,
Believing that lads
Ought to follow their dads,
Not despising their menial station.

He extolled the simple requirement,
Deploring irrelevant acquirement;
Praising minds undistracted,
Field craft unredacted,
Single-minded pursuit of the scent.

A man well content with his portion
Would achieve his success in proportion,
Leaving learning and wife
For the task of his life
As a huntsman. What nobler apportion!

THE FIRST COMMANDMENT . . .

In defiance of sporting epistle,
First commandment of unwritten missal,
A man shot a fox
Chased by Brocklesby hocks,
From his boss earning instant dismissal.

But Lonsdale, a Lord of Creation,
Prime arbiter of sport for the nation,
Shot a fox for a joke
Designed to provoke
Lady Grace to abashed consternation.

LORD LONSDALE

To the Bicester a cleric complained
That a nocturnal visitor distrained
On the best of his flock:
The woollier stock,
And asked that the beast be constrained.

He was counselled to shoot the sheep worrier
And dispose of the fur to a furrier;
So he lay out at night,
Letting go left and right,
Despatching the Master's prize terrier.

The villainous cleric, Jack Froude,
Confessing his henchman, allowed
That Babbage[3] had sinned
When vicariously twinned
With himself, in mayhem advowed.

And, lacking commandment unbroken,
Parson Froude struggled hard for a token
Of redemptory grace
With which to save face,
And absolution freely betoken.

At last came divine inspiration:
For sin an appropriate oblation;
"Hast thee e'er shot a fox?"
Asked the priest heterodox,
Thus saving sad soul from damnation.

LAMENT FOR THE FALLEN

In the hunting field is there indifference
To the fate of the fallen? A nonchalance,
A sad lack of charity,
A coarse jocularity,
A regrettable and culpable ambivalence?

When a chap falls a bit of a cropper
At a bullfinch or almighty stopper,
There's no need to stop
To examine the drop,
Nor the mud on a sadly-crushed topper.

When a parson falls hard on a Monday,[4]
A hard-riding, very-fast-run day,
Lying prone in a ditch,
The cruel passing rich
May opine, "He'll keep until Sunday!"

Hely-Hutchinson, Barnard and Farrel,
The last in funereal apparel,
Were jumping high fences,
Defying the senses:
Three stag-hunting jumpers non-pareil . . .

When the first made unspoken farewell,
No harbinger tolling the knell:
Said Barnard, on the thump,
Lining up the next jump,
"There's a job for you later on, Farrel."

FEAR AND FANCY

Does the wild stag or paddock-fed deer
Experience positive fear
When chased by the hounds
Over limitless bounds
Of indigenous moorland and mere?

Fox Russell[5] deplored the promotion
Of a guilelessly ignorant notion:
He could not recall
Any case to appall
Of fearfully fast locomotion.

Of the hounds, a paddock-fed deer
Never showed any panic or fear
And, indeed, when enlarged
Or explicitly discharged,
Would linger and graze in good cheer.

When purposefully driven away
By huntsman or raucous hounds' bay,
He would start at a trot,
Hardly caring a jot,
Indifferent to threatened affray.

The author recalled a deer chase
Where the quarry, with dignity and grace,
Would jog to the meet,
Hounds and horses *en suite*,
Run his line, then return to his base.

In the case of the wild, moorland deer,
He opined that the palpable fear
Was most seen 'mongst the hunters
And incautious punters
Who tackled the fierce mountaineer.

And a sportsman-historian[6] surmised
That a deer was by nature apprised
Of the predator's role
In taking his toll,
In ecology non-moralised.

Whether hunted by carnivore or man,
By instinct and impulse he ran,
A pre-destined quarry,
Proud-mantled, not sorry,
Majestic in Nature's vast plan.

And a Colonel Robertson-Aikman,[7]
A field, forest, prairie and lake man,
Called for sense of proportion
And lack of distortion
By shrill, bleeding-heart, ache and wakeman.

Inflicting unnecessary pain
Was a true sportsman's ruin and bane;
Although Nature was cruel
In uneven duel,
Beast and bird of prey gory in stain.

Since Cush begat Nimrod man hunted
Without conscience or sentience blunted,
And venery in vogue
Was swift to prorogue
The poacher or cruelly wonted.

Did those who the sport would decry
Never eat a veal and ham pie?
Did the calf and the pig
Really not care a fig
About when, where and how they would die?

Deer, fox and hare all had a chance
To evade the enemy's advance;
Ample warning or "law"
To widen the yaw
Of the hunt in its ponderous perchance.

So, if humans from hunting forbear
In pathos fallacious, false care
For the fox or the deer,
And a glut should appear,
We must bring back the wolf and the bear.

AN INVERTEBRATE CHIROPRACTOR

In scarcity, the medical profession
Provided a useful succession
Of hunters and chasers
And hurdlers and pacers,
Promoted from menial oppression . . .

CASTRATOR, after
Giovanni Croce, 1573,
chirurgeon, Venice

'Twixt the shafts; and suitably named,
Their origin boldly proclaimed
In exercise prolusory
And aperients illusory,
And instruments jocundly defamed.

Thus *Scalpel, Forceps* and *Dilator,*
And *Lancet, Retractor, Inspirator,*
And cathartics renowned
Thronged the late hunting ground,
From the stables of apt nomenclator.

One such was a horse called *Bonesetter,*
Whose owner might well have known better;
He bolted on ice,
Threw his man in a trice,
Crushed his skull like a folded biretta.

CHACUN A SON GOUT

Charles Apperley, the veteran, averred
That the foxhunter, booted and spurred,
Though robust with true grit
Must needs ride fighting-fit
To conquer the folds and wolds shirred . . .

And the hazards, the knocks and the bruises,
The ditches and drains and the oozes,
The gateposts and branches
And stone avalanches
And quadrupeds' near-lethal ruses . . .

Although one-armed men, single-eyed horses,
Oft traversed the stiffest of courses,
Like Nelson, elided,
But never derided,
In manly pursuance of torses.

The chroniclers omitted to tell
What singular mishap befell
A seafarer brave
On broad, ocean wave,
One-legged, skew-skegged Cap'n Pell . . .

Who, *sans* scissor-like grip at the thigh,
Cut a dash erratic and wry,
Holding on to the pommel
While queer, hapless hummel
Skew-arched over fences too high.

Most common of handicaps was gout,
But nary a victim thrown out,
The *urate of sodium*
Ne'er leading to odium
Nor inflaming the wrath of the stout.

CHARLES APPERLEY

A Yorkshireman crippled with gout
With Lord Derby's hounds bravely rode out,
Lifted into the saddle
To brave timber or raddle,
Riding hard as an Indian scout.

And in Devon, Mr. Westlake, the skipper,
Rode shod in an old carpet slipper:
"Mind my leg!" was the shout
From the martyr to gout
To thrusting or close-riding tripper.

And gracing the Beds. covert-side
To the Oakley's endearment and pride
Was the Hon. Samuel Ongley,
Fate's decree thwarting strongly
With gout-swollen feet firm astride.

Like Lazarus he rose from his bed,
Preferring the quick to the dead,
No man riding harder,
Pain conquered by ardour
In tribute to sportsmen true-bred.

In a right royal progress through Lancs.,
James the First[8] gave enthusiastic thanks
For venery and victuals,
And sirloin and skittles,
And claret and succulent sheeps' shanks.

When His Majesty had a bad twinge,
His royal indulgence to swinge,
He plunged both his feet
Into broken stag's heat,
The rheumaticky pain to impinge.

SOFT GOING IN THE NORTH

The Carlisle and Newcastle line
Offered those in equestrian decline
A sixty-mile point
To rendezvous conjoint
With the Bewcastle, Haydon and Tyne.

To compensate the coachmen and guards
Made redundant from highway hazards,
The company employed them,
And skilfully deployed them
On the trains and at stations and yards.

Ex-coachmen, still nimble and quivery,
Were adorned in white hats and hunt livery,
And postboy and varlet,
Resplendent in scarlet,
Were poised for adroit mail delivery.

The train, at a mighty fine clip:
Six hours for a spanking round trip
Drawn by sturdy steam horse,
Over picturesque course,
With the Master up front, letting rip . . .

But stopping at every station,
In deference to urban creation,
Where whipper-in scurried
To haste the unhurried,
And press on to great conurbation.

To Wetheral and ninety-foot leap
Over Eden, fast-flowing and deep,
On to Head's Nook, scream shrill,
Grinding slow past How Mill,
Thence to Brampton and Hadrian keep.

Through Naworth and Low Row they ambled,
Through Gilsland salubriously rambled,
Where Scott tufted bride
From Arcadian hide;
Thence to Greenhead and Haltwhistle wambled.

On to Bardon Mill, Haydon Bridge, Hexham,
No ticklish scent e'er to perplex 'em;
No chafing astride
But a soft-going ride,
Neither bullfinch nor rasper to vex 'em.

A STEELY RECOURSE

On a jade in non-dynamic cycle
With the East Kent, 'mid hoar frost and icicle;
How to finish the chase
As a masterful ace?
Mr. Selby Lowndes[9] borrowed a bicycle!

And his lady-wife, no less resourceful,
Supportive and madly endorseful,
Used a perambulator,
A make-shift incubator,
To air puppies and babies discourseful.

A MUTUAL AGILITY

At Stratford, Mr. W. Barke,
Prize-fighter and rider of mark,
Jumped a high turnpike rail,
Mounted facing the tail
Of his pony, by way of a lark . . .

H. W. SELBY LOWNDES.

And to prove the animal's docility,
And remarkable jumping ability;
And justify the price,
He did the trick twice:
Fifty guineas for mutual agility.

NOTES ON CHAPTER SIX

. Lord Kintore was admitted to the Fife Club by ballot in September, 1825. The royal burgh of that name in Aberdeenshire gives the title of earl in the Scottish and baron in the English peerage to the head of the Keith-Falconer family.

?. J. Fairfax Blakeborough recorded that on many estates in Yorkshire the tenant was commonly required to keep a hound for the landlord "free of all expense, one dog, bitch or puppy," during the tenancy. He was further required not to allow any "disorderly, debauched or criminal characters" to frequent his house, and to live "Godly, honestly, and willingly" in that station to which he had been called.

. Mr. Froude's servant and conspirator in mischief recovered from his death-bed illness and continued in his wild ways.

. Believed to be the Rev. William Pochin of the Cottesmore.

. Fox Russell, author of *In Scarlet and Silk*, quoted by Sir Reginald Graham Bart., Master of the Tedworth, 1879-82.

. W. F. Collier in a paper before the Devonshire Association for the Advancement of Science, Literature and Art at Okehampton, 1895.

. Col. Robertson-Aikman, old Etonian who won numerous prizes for harriers at Peterborough Hound Show in his time. By 1921 he had been Master of Foxhounds for five years and Master of Harriers for twenty-two years. He ran, as a boy, with the Eton College Hunt.

a Lord Ribblesdale, who was Master of the Queen's Buckhounds (1892-95), confessed that he never knew what a carted deer would do when turned out. It would run up and down fences, stand in the corner of a field looking at him, trot back down a road into the pack instead of galloping away from it, and altogether behave in "a most un-Landseer-like way".

> Mr. T. Neville of Chilland recorded in his journal in 1870 that he tamed a red deer presented to him by the Duke of Beaufort which, after being turned out and chased by the hounds and

going to bay, would respond to the owner's call and trot hom alongside his horse. He once took soil after a chase but left th pool with a great bound on being called. A fallow dee presented to him by the Earl of Portsmouth, althoug frequently chased by the hounds, would come up at feedin time and eat meal out of their trough. A jackal given to him b a friend from India followed him about like a dog, rompe ahead in the fields and returned on being called. Mr. Nevil repeatedly hunted him with his bloodhounds. If cornered h would bare his teeth to keep the hounds at bay until his owne rescued him.

8. King James revived the sport of hunting throughout Englan holding the running of hounds to be the noblest sort, an shooting with guns and bows to be a thievish form of sport. H hunted the Holcombe country in 1617, being lavishl entertained by Sir Gilbert Hoghton at Hoghton Tower, an piloted by his son, a Court favourite. It was here (among oth places) he was said to have dubbed surloin, *Sir Loin*, in tribu to a bounteous festive board. The King killed five bucks c August 13, in the company of knights and squires from mil around, resplendent on caparisoned steeds. He admired th Holcombe hounds so much that he granted their owner a roy warrant to hunt over twelve municipalities, wearing the king scarlet livery.

9. Mr. H. W. Selby Lowndes resigned the mastership of th Bilsdale (1897-1900) to hunt the East Kent, which he did wi distinction for thirty years. His unorthodox steed did duty in great run during the 1905-06 season.

10. Mr William Barke was the proprietor of the White Lio Stratford-on-Avon, where the Warwickshire Hunt Club he their fortnightly dinners. He was a welter-weight boxer and noted equestrian. He sold his pony, *Milcote*, to a Mr. Zouc for the asking price without further demonstration.

CHAPTER SEVEN

HUNTING PARSONS

CURATIVE QUALITIES

Should a clergyman follow the hounds?
Should he gallop o'er foxhunting grounds,
Throwing cares to the wind?
Who's to say he has sinned
When his *view halloo* joyfully sounds?

A primitive, coursing emotion?
A vulgar, ungodly devotion?
Or a hymn to the Deity,
Translating corporeity:
A sermon in music and motion?

Must a knee-breechèd Anglican ordinand
Ape a feeble, effeminate Ferdinand,
Never mounting his mare
For chase of the hare,
But mincing and prancing the saraband?

Did Orders denote the effeminate?
Confine social grace to the geminate?
Turn manly hirsutes
To girlish pursuits,
The better the Word to disseminate?

What a muscular parson obdurate
Desired in a suitable curate
Was a strong constitution,
A leaping locution
And a seat and a conscience indurate . . .

A fondness for horses and dogs,
A hatred of pale pedagogues,
A passion for sport
And post-prandial port,
And indifference to falling in bogs.

No matinees admiring the ladies,
No rescuing of Judy O'Gradys,
No proffering the bouquet,
No dawdling at croquet
But taking *a man's road t*o Hades.

When Russell purported to choose
A curate of orthodox views,
He meant a divine
Who rode a straight line,
Impervious to injury or bruise.

The incumbent was truly irate,
Dismissing an aspirant mate
Full of suave airs and graces
Who, put through his paces,   JACK RUSSELL
Couldn't rise to a lowly farm gate.

KEEPING BODY AND SOUL TOGETHER

Bishop Phillpotts detested "the science",
That biped and canine alliance
Which drove brethren clerical
To joy near-hysterical
And neglect their weekday compliance.

In the diocese of Exon alone
A score of incumbents would own
A large hunting pack,
An ungodly claque,
In defiance of bell, book and throne.

Such a one was the Reverend John Froude,
With Knowstone and Molland endowed,
A hard-riding minister,
Unruly and sinister,
Unspeakably arrogant and proud.

Said his Lordship to hare-hunting Jack,
"They tell me you keep a large pack."
"'Tis the hounds that keep me!"
Replied Jack with some glee:
"For conies my table don't lack!

BISHOP PHILLPOTTS

"There bain't be no butcher for miles,"
Rejoined *Passon Vrowd*, full of smiles,
"So we'm 'bliged to eat hares,
And us won't use no snares,
So 'tis harriers the soul reconciles."

HOSPITABLE DISCOURSE

If Russell was one of the best
Of the hunting divines of the West,
Then Froude was the worst,
A cleric accursed,
A clergyman worse than a jest.

A man of good fortune and family,
But a stranger to virtue and homily,
Froude shook on a deal
With the Devil's own seal:
The hand of deceit given clammily.

If scheming to sell a dud horse,
He'd engage in hospitable discourse;
His customer regale
With strong, home-brewed ale
Till he settled the bargain perforce.

Too fuddled to mount the sad beast,
The stranger was readily fleeced;
Then Froude would lie low
Till the copious flow
Of angry remonstrance had ceased.

If a vendor declined to endorse
A low price for a coveted horse,
Parson Froude's threats of mayhem
And promise of requiem
Soon persuaded a man his best course.

THE FESTIVE BOARD

A day in the saddle complete
After Chulmleigh or South Molton meet;
Mr. Russell and friends
Having made their amends
To the inner man, cheered and replete . . .

And then the *badinage* flows
With the port and the punch-bowl: *bons mots*
Wicked wit, playful sallies,
Racy yarns, classic rallies,
Tall stories and purple-pink prose.

The after-dinner proceedings
Are impromptu: no warnings or heedings;
A well-fancied mount
Is brought to account
At auction: no promptings or pleadings.

Any member might name a friend's horse,
The owner then having recourse
To only one bid
To get himself rid
Of the fancier and the remorse.

A gentleman dining too well,
And bound by the auctioneer's spell,
Might find he had bought
An animal fraught
Which he couldn't subsequently sell.

Parson Russell went early to bed,
Preferring to keep a clear head,
Not coveting a steed
His neighbour might need,
And knowing where avarice led.

A BIPED TRANSPORTED

To stay in the saddle all day
As a self-imposed rule, come what may,
Is hard on the horse
And the rider, of course,
Not to mention the fugitive prey.

The Reverend Jack Michell's stern code
Was the rule at his Cotleigh abode;
He would not alight
For respite or bite
Till reaching the end of the road.

A twenty-mile point was no strain
To this stalwart of vigour and main;
From Cotleigh to Taunton,
A run not to daunt 'un,
Nor clerical fervour constrain.

While the marathon courses he durst
Brought on a great hunger and thirst,
He contained his desires
Till the church tower and byres
Spurred a home-coming joy fit to burst.

HEARTS AND MINDS

The zeal of the Reverend John Bower
Engendered a singular power
O'er the souls in his cure,
In a parish obscure,
In Ebor's penurious dower.

A stout-hearted English divine,
Hard-tempered in Bridlington brine
Craggy-visaged and slight,
Luminary unbright,
A preacher not destined to shine . . .

But in leggings and clerical stock,
Austere in funereal frock,
On a thirty-pound jade,
A one-man cavalcade,
Mr. Bower was loved by his flock.

Rough rider from meanest abidings,
Hardest horseman and first in three Ridings
Through hedge and o'er drain,
Like a black hurricane,
To Reynard to bring the ill-tidings.

A notable Yorkshire divine,
His soul and his saddle to shine
As East Riding rector
And Hurworth Hunt lector,
Charles Atkinson rode a straight line.

From Holderness, vindy and vasty,
Via Hurworth, Bedale, York and Nasty,
O'er stern Bramham Moor,
He followed the spoor,
With energy, prayer, port and pasty.

In his eightieth year he revealed
A desire to expire in the field
And, ten minutes later,
His horse hit a crater
And seat over apex he keeled.

The Archbishop, in tribute, opined
That foxhunting broadened the mind,
Enhanced human nature,
Encouraged adventure
And comradely courtesy refined.

Spontaneously and simply it drew
Rural classes to uniform view
Of the verities of life,
Without conflict or strife,
By the death of the creature they slew.

HIGH TABLE

In describing the fox as inedible,
Oscar Wilde voiced an adage incredible:
While the hunt may retreat
From consuming such meat,
To the hound it is flesh highly edible.

A Colonel John Reeve[1], Squire of Leadenham,
Was reputed himself to have fed on 'em;
He'd a fox served for dinner
By his butler, one Skinner,
Consuming the qualities bred in 'em.

He once served a parson fox tongue,
Well garnished and very well hung;
His guest, fit to choke,
Not deceived by the joke,
But its *haute-cuisine* praises were sung.

When the Cloth asked the Colonel to dine,
Desiring the score to align,
By way of do-gooding
He served "tapioca pudding"
Made of frogspawn and nautical twine.

A BIRD ON THE WING

Scarce-known to the Devon ornithologist,
A soaring, itinerant liturgist,[2]
A black *rara avis*,
A raptorial mavis,
Diverted South Devon ecclesiologist.

Bestirred from his Jacobean bower,
Six bells roundly rung from the tower,
Our white-throated throstle,
High-flying apostle,
Flew off, vulpine prey to devour.

Short of leg and perched high on tall horse,
He stuck to a straight, narrow course,
Leaping hedges and ditches,
Bidding fair to split breeches
Due to animal's stringhalted torse.

When he came to a difficult bank
He would slide down the animal's shank,
Adroitly avail
Himself of the tail,
Holding hard with half-nelson to hank.

A PEASANTS' REVOLT

Bill Chafin of Chettle once rated
Prince Cambrian for code violated
In crying the hue
Of a fox in a stew
Whereby Charlie and chase were truncated.

The Prince made amends, offering dinner
To mollify the reverend man inner,
But he turned up with bitches,
Old boots and torn breeches,
A social and sartorial sinner.

Mr. Chafin was Lord of the Chase
At Cranborne, where deer roamed apace:
Woodcock and wild fowl,
Hare, rabbit and owl,
To boscage and verdure gave grace . . .

Of Lydlinch, in Dorset, the Rector,
For souls, an unlikely prospector,
But of peasants and poachers
And forest encroachers,
A mighty and jealous corrector.

As Ranger, his rule was supreme:
Neither sovereign nor noble might deem
To order his days
Or question his ways,
Hunt a hart, start a hare, fish a stream.

Rights of venison and vert were sole vested
In the Ranger: infringement contested
By forest law or court,
Where illicit mort
By penalties severe were behested.

But commoner and cottier found ways
Both devious and cunning to faze
The keepers and Ranger
And dutiful granger,
In silent, unsung *Marseillaise*.

Despite censure, deer-stealing was rife:
A male blooding, a brave way of life;
Save a hunter, no youth,
Howe'er manly or couth,
Stood tall or commanded a wife.

GOD AND MAMMON

THE BELVOIR HOUND VAN.

With the Belvoir rode Mammon and Church,
Neither riches nor rites to besmirch;
Each an hon. whipper-in
Of sanctity and sin
'Mongst the black and tan hounds in late search.

Banker Hardy, Parson Newcombe[3] together
Braved nightfall and inclement weather
To seek missing hounds
Twenty miles out of bounds,
Late scenting, seceding from tether.

No day was too long for John Hardy,
No slow-feath'ring foxhound too tardy:
The pack was his treasure
With heart in good measure;
Chiennes courantes his *bichettes mal gardées*.

And likewise, silent-horned, doing alms,
Billy Newcombe, darkness lit, singing psalms,
Served Deity and Master,
Upstanding pilaster
Of Godhead and hunt, without qualms.

A CURE UNPROPITIOUS

Keble Martin,[4] a bright, budding botanist,
Bird-watcher and keen lepidopterist,
Drew the line at affray:
Any creature to slay
Was disgrace worse than death to a naturalist.

At Dartington, on warm, sunny day,
He'd watch fox-cubs at innocent play,
Rejoice in their frolics
With pastoral bucolics
And peacefully pass on his way.

Fledgling curate at Beeston years later,
He was wired by his old Alma Pater,
Benign Bishop Ridding,[5]
Peremptorily bidding
Attendance in knickers or gaiter . . .

To birds-nest at Thurgarton Priory,
The seat of his lordship's seignory;
His vicar agreed,
Off he cycled at speed
For high-blown, encyclical afflatory.

Emerging from boscage and bestiary,
The bishop and obedientiary
Spied a fox which, alack!
Had a cock on his back:
No gentle, reformed penitentiary!

On an impulse the priest hurled his stick,
A naive, non-Franciscan trick,
Striking fox on the neck,
An uncurative check
Cutting prospects and fox to the quick.

SPIRITUAL REALIGNMENT

Sporting vicar, when taken to task
By his bishop, was driven to ask
Why tandem progression[6]
Invoked intercession,
Though his lordship should supinely bask . . .

In a self-righteous, Gileadic air
When driving a carriage and pair;
Why two mares abreast
Were episcop'lly blest:
Fore and aft, a mode to forswear.

His lordship rejoined with a parable,
Neither finny, nor vinic, nor arable,
But in logic composed,
Apposite and well-nosed,
Both dextrous and prayerf'lly comparable.

The Rector of Ford, Thomas Knight,
Apt student of foxhunting rite,
A rider to hounds
In Northumberland grounds
In his youth, a keen acolyte . . .

Forsook the straight cross-country point,
Endeavoured his soul to anoint
With Puseyite[7] polish,
His guilt to demolish,
Renouncing the call counterpoint.

When reivers invaded his bower,
His spiritual pride to deflower,
He set them at nought
And invoked higher thought,
Viewing keenly from soaring church tower.[8]

DR. PUSEY

A PASSIONATE PARSON

When Harriet Beecher Stowe stayed
With the Kingsleys, they dutifully prayed
For the health of the weald
And the beast in the field
And the fox in his frolicsome glade . . .

Which embarrassed the children who knew
That their father, though good man and true,
Rode hotly to hounds
In the hale, Bramshill bounds,
And the gallant, dumb animal slew.

CHARLES KINGSLEY

He'd abandon a hot, steaming dinner
To don mantle of rough-riding sinner,
In sacrificial rite,
An unholy sight;
Kind to horses but sharp-chiselled whinner.

He studied the minutest particle
Of Faith and the Thirty-seventh Article,
Crossing swords with John Newman
With critical acumen,
Not neglecting the smallest appendicle.

To the Church he devoted his life,
Toiling hard in a vineyard of strife,
But tickled brown trout,
Was for blood-sport devout,
And passionately fond of his wife.

Ensconced in his glorious Devon,
Ecstatic love further to leaven
He pictured them both,
Rudely plighting their troth,   CARDINAL
In situ, ascending to Heaven.   NEWMAN

A BLITHE SPIRIT

Lord Grafton,[9] thrown into a ditch,
Lying prone like a filleted flitch,
Was adroitly o'erleap'd
By a curate adept,
Crying, "Lie still, my Lord," to bewitch . . .

His Grace by a spirited ardour,
A conscience indurate and harder;
Hunting zeal far transcending
Samaritan bending
Of obsequious, Christian tabarder.

Hauled out of the ditch by attendant,
Admiration o'er injury ascendant,
He swore the first living
To fall to his giving
Would go to the spirit transcendent.

NOTES ON CHAPTER SEVEN

1. Col. Reeve lived at Leadenham Hall, twelve miles south
   Lincoln. The Rev. Thomas Heathcote, Squire of Folkingha
   got the frogspawn from his pike pond at Lenton Vicarage,
   miles East of Grantham, Lincs. Three years later, in Decemb
   1881, Heathcote met with a serious accident when his horse f
   at a fence and broke its back. The vicar's own spine was
   badly injured that he died from the effects eighteen mon
   later, then aged seventy-four. The horse involved w
   Glenhorne. He was bought by Heathcote without inspection
   an auction sale of Sir Thomas Leynard's stable at Belhus P
   for £170. When the hunter arrived at Lenton Vicarage, t
   purchase was deplored by the five other members of the fam
   who rode to hounds. The horse had few points to comme
   him. He had a big, fiddle-shaped head, a long neck, sm
   quarters but a good shoulder. However, he proved to be a go
   hunter and carried the ladies of the family well. One of
   forefeet, mounted in silver and fashioned as an inkwell, was us
   by Frank Gillard, huntsman to the Dukes of Rutland, in writi
   his reminiscences.

The Rev. George Bird of Christow, Devon, in the winter of 1880-81 which was exceptionally cold.

The Rev. W.C. Newcombe (1813-96), an Old Etonian, was Rector of Boothby, Lincs., and a stalwart member of the Belvoir Hunt for more than half a century. He was a spirited, if not polished rider, with iron resolve and had some bad falls. Mr "Banker" Hardy was hon. secretary to the

BIRDS OF PASSAGE.

hunt for many years. Neither of them ever went home before the hounds, Parson Newcombe's hunting boots were often to be seen beneath his cassock at mid-week weddings and funerals.

As a member of the Oxford Volunteer Corps and of the University Rifle Eight, Keble Martin wished to volunteer for the South African war but his father told him he must choose between soldiering and ordination: the two aims were inconsistent. Martin chose ordination but was an Army chaplain in the First World War when the nearest he got to marksmanship was carrying the rifles of exhausted soldiers.

George Ridding, former headmaster of Winchester, and first bishop of Southwell, ordained Martin deacon in 1902 and priest in 1903. His first wife was Martin's mother's sister. There is a bronze effigy in Newstead Abbey, Notts.

Double-harness was a commoner method of driving than tandem, where the reins lay nearly parallel one above the other, compared with the greater spread in front of the hand with the former. The leader in tandem is entirely independent, being unrestrained by a partner, and can turn about to face the driver unless promptly controlled by a cut with the thong of the whip on the side to which the horse is turning. If that fails the only remedy is to turn the wheeler also and then to resume the original direction. Thus it is unsafe to harness a tandem to a four-wheeled vehicle. If the wheeler should be turned too sharply, the front wheels may lock and overturn the carriage. Tandem driving required more nerve and skill than double-harness and might have been thought too ostentatious for a clergyman.

7.   Canon Pusey (1800-82) of Christ Church, Oxford, preached fo
        a revival of Catholic doctrine in the Church of England.

8.   Another former rider to hounds who viewed the hunt keenl
        from a tower, when too infirm to hunt, was Lord Rancliff
        (d.1852). He rode with the Quorn for many years and kne
        every fence in the country. He lived at Bunny Park, 6½m. S. c
        Nottingham. The tower, close by the hall, was built by his grea
        grandfather Sir Thomas Parkyns who, with his wife, "enjoyed
        day's hunting" from its summit.

9.   The Duke of Grafton, who hunted mostly in Suffolk an
        Surrey, was out with the Charlton, near Goodwood, under th
        patronage of his cousin, the Duke of Richmond, in the 18C
        Peter Pindar described how George III at Windsor knew bett
        than to stop and shed a tear when old Parson Young, whom th
        King had cajoled into riding his blind horse to hounds, fell an
        broke his neck when the horse stumbled.

The Duke of Richmond's Dog Kennel at Goodwood in Sussex.

Publish'd according to Act of Parliament by J.Wheble, Warwick Square Octo.1.1793.

CHAPTER EIGHT

HARDY HOUNDS

A LACK OF HINDSIGHT

The Bedale, in epic of yore,
'Mid rank, marshy swale of the moor,
Unkenneled incumbent,
Devoutly recumbent,[1]
With a *view halloo* to a score.

At Smearholmes the fox went to ground
And *Rambler*, the keen, leading hound,
At once got stuck in,
Wedged tight, when his kin
Attacked their poor comrade, fast-bound.

Jack Robinson was first on the scene,
Not suspecting behaviour obscene
But cheering them on
To where light never shone,
Till suddenly he kenned the *cuisine*.

But before he could utter his name,
The hounds had compounded their shame,
Devoured tender haunches
With cruel, canine craunches;
Sad-sullied their title to fame.

A SOARING SUCCESS

When John Corbet succeeded John Warde,
Over fast-running Warwickshire sward,
He brought a fine hound
To the classical ground,
To earn universal accord.

For eight seasons he ran without fault,
Never lame, never coming to halt;
The best in the pack,
Full of speed and attack
And renowned for capacity to vault.

From a Gothical peak of esteem,
Both Master and hound led the team
With *Trojan*, the hero,
A soaring torero,
And Corbet, the Master, supreme.

A SOARING TORERO

At Chillington,[2] a wall of great height
Halted all save the *Trojan* delight
Who, with one massive bound,
Cleared the wall and was found
With the quarry at bay in a bight.

A North Shropshire type.

And at Perry Woods, a matching exploit
Proved *Trojan ballista* adroit
Over towering brick wall,
After fox, to enthrall:
A high-flying, self-propelled quoit.

The field and the rest of the pack,
Lacking courage and baladine knack,
Perforce used the gate
To Lord Dartmouth's estate,
And the same again on the way back.

A Warwickshire type.

Trojan carried the scent on his own
To the wood where the miscreant had flown;
Then the pack, joining cry,
Vainly sought to outvie
His prowess in muscle and bone.

Then on Hagley to Halesowen tack,
He cornered the fox for the pack,
His consummate skill
In achieving the kill
A marvel to huntsman and hack.

HEAVYWEIGHT CHAMPIONS

When a man rode at twenty-two stone
With the Pytchley, he travelled alone
Unless, like John Warde,
Commanding the sward
With leadership, muscle and bone.

Pytchley Potentate, 1897.

His hounds were built big like their Master,
Kept big lest they ran even faster;
More like mastiffs, 'twas said,
Though not big in the head,
And not at all prone to disaster . . .

Though sometimes attracting derision
From men of another division,
Who called them *jackasses*
Though, high in the grasses,
They ran with the greatest precision.

At twenty-eight inches, renowned
For sport in the Northampton ground,
They were finally sold,
When the Master grew old,
To Lord Althorp for one thousand pound.

NO PATH TO GLORY

When a gentleman's chimney needs sweeping,
A small boy, unwillingly creeping,
Or a man with a brush,
Must effect a dry flush,
While the household is blissfully sleeping.

If a fox does the job free of charge,
In an effort to gain its discharge
From domestic confinement,
As a basket consignment,
It should be left free to run large.

Mr. Vyner left fox overnight
In that sooty, combustible plight:
When an ignorant maid,
Morning fire having laid,
Opened shutters, the fox saw the light.

Through the window it went like a rocket,
Leaping shrubs like a gamboling brocket:
Through ankle-deep snow
And winter-wind blow,
Not caring for tame bagman's docket.

Quickly donning stout top-coat and boot,
Mr. Vyner set off in pursuit
With huntsmen and hounds,
Through the virgin-white grounds,
Swiftly finding the scent and the soot.

The pungently-carbonaceous trail
Led them straight to vulpecular tail;
They mobbed the poor beast
In an unseemly feast,
Disregarding the devilish veil.

If moral there be to this story
Of vulpicide, unsporting and hoary,
It's that taking a brush
In a Gadarene rush
Is no path to foxhunting glory.

A LOWER CALLING

George Cross had the horse-sense to burgeon
As a talented veterinary surgeon
And qualified at college
In a wide range of knowledge
From hunters to falcon and sturgeon.

A farm bailiff's son from Kincardine,
He was keen as devoted St. Bernardine
On the cure of diseases
From coughs, colds and sneezes
To distemper or minuscule muscardine.

But his passion for hunting and hounds
Was excessive and got out of bounds;
He abandoned his calling
For the whelping and bawling
And chores of a kennelman's rounds.

As whipper-in or huntsman he served,
Horses treated and foxes conserved;
A successful hound-breeder
And fond Surtees reader:
Every aspect of hunting observed.

A man for all seasons and ages,
He cared not for money or wages;
He went soft in the brain,
Became somewhat profane,
Going mad in perceptible stages.

AFTER THE DAY'S WORK.

A CAPITAL OFFENCE

When foot-soldiers, faithful and true,
Run amok, like a rioting crew,
Wreaking mayhem and slaughter,
Without mercy or quarter,
The Colonel[3] knows what he must do.

First gather the evidence shaming,
Assemble the witnesses claiming
That unlovely crime
Has sullied the cyme:
Then the charges set out, firmly framing.

No glorious first day of June,
That 'Ninety-four-boding forenoon,
But senior redcoat,
Grim-faced, tight of throat,
Presiding: a black-capped dragoon.

Notwithstanding the *Riot Act* read,
Much bloody gore having been shed
And murder committed;
No culprit acquitted:
The verdict delivered in dread.

Then the twenty-four culprits troop out,
Their fate is no longer in doubt;
After trial by court-martial,
Heavy-hearted, impartial;
A sad end for fighting lads stout.

The culprits' unspeakable crime
That summer, in fair Exmoor clime?
The killing of sheep
On the hills, green and steep,
Of that staghunting country sublime.

'Twas pleaded in strong mitigation
That the hounds, on close season vacation,
Were unfairly repressed,
Constrained and oppressed;
In a state of extreme titubation:

That lack of exercise had led
To a rush of hot blood to the head,
To a false disposition,
An unnatural condition,
A predictable consequence inbred.

Moreover, the apologists dissembled,
The scent of the sheep much resembled
The scent of the deer,
To the brave mountaineer
With his olfactory senses a-trembled.

Such debate swayed the court not a jot,
Though the guilty were spared the garrotte;
Sheep **must** safely graze,
Despite hounds' questing craze:
Twelve couple were summarily shot.

WINDING A MORT

Lady Pembroke, first woman high sheriff,*
Described, in a **Gothic sans serif**,
How a hound ran a stag
Over moorland and crag,
At a morbidly mutual tariff.

The singular greyhound, named *Hercules*,
Chased an ungulate designate *Hart-a-greese*,
Sixty miles there and back,
Over borderly track;
Whinfell Park[4] to Red Kirk,[5] just to tease.

*Countess of Pembroke, Baroness Clifford and hereditary sheriff of Westmorland (1590-1676)

The stag leaped the park pales and died,
And *Hercules* gallantly tried
To emulate the beast,
And consummate the feast,
But fell dead on the contrary side.

So the hound wound a mort for the stag,
And the hart scored a posthumous bag;
But Herculean task
Was too much to ask
For a tail at the end with no wag.

AN ILL-MATCHED ASSORTMENT

Braes of Derwent dog foxes and vixen
Were hunted by old Siddle Dixon,
A publican by trade,
On an ill-gotten jade,
From a kennel resembling a mixen.

Thirteen ill-matched couples included,
In that filthy establishment secluded,
Two couple bloodhounds,
Maintained on the grounds
Of good sport in country well-wooded.

Colonel Cowen,[6] the Master, intended,
If the over-large hounds condescended,
To cross the whole pack,
A rude-beam attack,
Anent which, the least said, soonest mended.

Braes of Derwent could show a long tail
When following vulpecular trail,
But although never swarming,
Ill-assorted, non-conforming,
Showed sport over woodland and swale.

LONGEVITY IN LAKELAND

A hard-bitten hound y-clept *Cleaver,*
Of fox an inveterate reiver,
Would jump more than nine feet
Over kennelyard mete;
'Mid the Lakes, a high-flying achiever.

His face bore fine etching, bold scar
From battles with dog-fox afar,
And precipitous falls
In vulpecular mauls,
And blastings mid borrans bizarre.

Twelve seasons he ran in the lead
With pluck, perseverance and speed,
Always in at the death,
Always game to last breath;
Intelligent, the best of his breed.

He ran with the Ullswater pack,
An harmonious symposiac[8]
Of the long-standing Patterdale
And the Bald How or Matterdale,
Each hunting a mountainous track.

With kennels at Patterdale Hall,
Twenty couple would skilfully trawl
The barrows and binks
And the borrans and brinks
Of the fells in a clime to appall.

They were musical, hardy and fleet,
Resourceful, hard-working and neat,
Oft laying out all night,
Despite rheumatic blight
From exposure to wind, snow and sleet.

The flower of the pack could die young,
From nab, knott or ness rudely flung,
Or cragfast in rock
For sly Reynard to mock,
Or drowned, silent heroes unsung.

So *Cleaver's* astonishing longevity
Defied Lakeland's searing severity;
A lion-hearted king
With a tiger-like spring,
He decreed fox's fate with legerity.

A NOSE FOR CRIME

As a hunter will leap daunting fences,
So a gun-dog's olfactory senses
Will make giant strides
To discover the hides
Of prey whose effluvia incenses.

Mr. Berkeley, on Holmsley with gun,[9]
In a favourite New Forest run
Of the fleet, fallow deer,
In a hard winter drear,
Killed a doe under wan midday sun.

Having noted on keen mental chart
The place, he continued his art
After woodcock and rabbit,
As befitted his habit,
While the woodman was gone for a cart.

In that valley of hunter secluded,
His canine entourage included
A Scotch deerhound and
A black Newfoundland,
With their master in killing colluded.

On climbing a neighbouring hill
And turning for view of the kill,
Berkeley failed to discern
Any corpse in the fern
Or the gorse and bog-myrtle and quill.

Three men were dispatched to high ground
To scan the horizon around:
All three who had been
At the death-dealing scene,
Dragging carcass from bog to dry mound.

The doe had been spirited away:
No trace on that hard winter's day
Of a thief's bivouac
Or a deer stealer's track;
No plundering gang to belay.

The deer hound was ordered to snook
For ungulate's sanguinary peruke,
But spoke not to scent,
A nose indigent,
Heeding neither kind word nor rebuke.

Then retriever took leave of his master
To try and avert a disaster;
Put his nose to the ground
And went off at a bound,
A singular novitiate caster.

Where the three men had parted he checked,
Trying each track in turn and then trekked
Along a new line
Down a gentle decline,
In a manner discreet, circumspect.

He came to the railway and halted,
Looked each way and then back, as if faulted;
But when master arrived,
His snooking revived:
He went on, the fence having vaulted . . .

Down the line, towards plate-laying gang,
Where hammer on metal road rang,
But soon turned about,
Employing his snout
With his back to the clatter and clang.

He then crossed the rail to far side
Where his master's keen eye soon espied
A print in the sand,
A neat ampersand
Deeply etched, linking criminals with hide.

The pair owned the scent, padding on
Towards Burley where poachers had gone;
The dog ran ahead
And then joyfully led
His master to prize amazon.

So the dog resolved complex confusion,
Indicated the railmen's collusion;
Recovered the prize,
Led the thieves to assize,
Exploding malign circumclusion.

A triumph of canine sagacity
Combined with olfactory veracity,
For he ne'er before ran
Scent of quadruped or man,
Least of all in faint-blooded pervicacity.

OUTLAWS AND BYLAWS

> Seeking sanctuary or temporal deferment
> Of death and a sacred interment
> In a Torquay churchyard,
> A fugitive Reynard
> Was saved by municipal averment.

> As the South Devon in blasphemous din
> Rushed forward with slavering grin,
> The custodian rushed out
> With a horrified shout:
> "Oh, Gentlemen! **DOGS aren't allowed in!**"

NOTES ON CHAPTER EIGHT

1. The hounds found in Vicar's Moor, near Maunby. John Thomas Robinson came from Leckby.

2. Chillington, Staffs. and Perry Woods, near Birmingham.

3. Col. Basset of Watermouth, near Ilfracombe, who was Master of the Devon and Somerset Staghounds in 1794.

4. Whinfell Park, 6m. NE Kendall.

5. Red Kirk, near Annan, Dumfriesshire, approx. 46m. by post road.

6. Col. J.A. Cowen, Master (1868-95).

7. Cleaver was reared at Grayrigg Hall, near Kendall, and was the favourite hound of the huntsman, Joe Bowman. The hound's death was announced at a Patterdale puppy show. Bowman was credited with killing the biggest fox ever dispatched in England. It was a greyhound fox weighing 23 pounds and measuring 52 inches from nose to end of brush.

8. The packs were amalgamated in 1873.

9. The incident took place near Burley, Ringwood, in 1852. The
    Duke of Cambridge, Ranger of the New Forest, had license
    Berkeley to shoot does and distribute the bounty to the poor. He
    later got a warrant to shoot bucks but said it took him nearly seven
    years, summer and winter, to reduce the royal deer "by royal
    command". Two "notoriously bad characters" were jailed for
    two months for stealing the carcass. *Tramp*, the retriever, was
    found one day on the railway line, decapitated. He was then close
    to old age. Berkeley held that no one species of dog was more
    intelligent than another. The development of mental capacity
    depended on habit and education. Berkeley recalled how an
    intelligent and well-trained pointer owned by his father, the Earl,
    saved the life of his sister, Lady Granard. They had driven from
    London to the Earl's seat, Cranford House, for the weekend, with
    no additional servants. The pointer, *Doll*, a stranger to the servants
    at Cranford, retired for the night with her master. Lord Berkeley
    was asleep with *Doll* on his bed, when awoken by stealthy
    movements. He seized a loaded pistol from his bedside chair in the
    pitch-dark room. The door opened slowly and the intruder moved
    towards his bed. Wondering at the silence of his house-dog, he
    stretched out his left hand to find her awake and aware of the
    presence of the visitor. Her head was erect and her ears up. Lord
    Berkeley knew she would have flown at any stranger. Suddenly
    Doll relaxed and her tail thumped the bed clothes. Lord Berkeley
    replaced the pistol and grasped the arm of his sleep-walking sister.
    But for the dog and Lord Berkeley's knowledge of her fidelity
    and intelligence, he might have shot his sister.

Cranford House, near Heathrow, was demolished in 1939.

OSBALDESTON'S SIRE *FURRIER*

CHAPTER NINE

MAIN AND DRAIN

THE HEXHAMSHIRE FOSSE

Returning one night from a kill,
Despite warning from loft *whippoor-will*,*
George Cowing tried to cross
The Hexhamshire fosse
At the ford below old Bardon Mill.

A sudden *fresh* rattled his horse,
Which floundered in treacherous course;
Though in horsemanship sound,
The rider was drowned,
To the hunt's and the widow's remorse.

Few huntsmen would dare swim the Tyne
For fear of a torrent malign,
And dire, rapid flooding
And huge boulders scudding
As the hills fulfilled Nature's design.

One visitor, unsuspecting and bolder,
And schooled in a climate much colder,
Met a mouldering end
'Cross the sea at Ostend,
His horn still slung over his shoulder.

*nightjar

A DEVILISH FRIGHT

With a view to the hunters' sport spoiling
And pursuit by the hounds neatly foiling,
And to cure his fatigue
And by way of intrigue,
A stag will resort to deep soiling.

Thus lying-up under the snarl
Of a bough in a bend of the Barle,[1]
One such astute beast
Escaped huntsman's sharp priest
In the soiling-pit water and marl.

Secure in his watery redoubt,
Concealed save for antlers and snout,
The stag cooled his hide
Till the hunt should decide
To call it a day, turn about.

Come twilight, a rude, labouring man
Seeking trout for his wife's frying-pan,
Cast a small-mesh Seine net
From the broad parapet
Of the o'er-hanging elder-tree span.

The stag, swimming out from his hide,
Caught a leg in the net as he tried
To reach the far bank,
Giving poacher a yank
From the tree into swift-running tide.

Deeply shocked by the sudden immersion
And the rapid, impromptu excursion,
He feared for his life
And the fate of his wife,
Suspecting supernatural subversion.

At the height of his horrification
And the need for divine explication,
He espies *cloven hoof!*
Oh ghastly reproof!
Excruciating horripilation!

He struggles across to the bank,
Finds the foliage stinking and rank;
Staggers home, wet and shivering,
Scared to death, pale and quivering,
Old Hornie's vile stench at his flank.

His wife sends for local physician,
Deploring her man's dire condition:
'Er looked prapper wisht
An' purty nare disht;
'Er veared 'er waz gwain tu perdishun!

Dr. Collyns diagnosed severe fright:
A pseudo-demoniacal blight;
Demonstrating, next day,
The tracks and the trey
Of the ill-smelling quadruped sprite.

SIR CLAUDE DE CRESPIGNY'S IMMERSION

An unusual resort for a fox,
Pursued by East Essex red frocks,
Was a Blackwater salting,
Which led to the halting
Of horses and hounds on the rocks.

The fox was first found in retreat,
North-west of Sir Claude's country seat,
Namely Champion Lodge,
For the hunt to dislodge,
Making off for the Goldhanger leat.

One seventh of a mile from the bank,
Succeeding the hounds to outflank,
The fox was espied,
In its impudent hide,
Like a puppy enjoying a prank.

Undaunted, Crespigny swam out
To the fox's estuarial redoubt
With most of the pack
Swimming close at his back,
Expecting a watery rout.

A black and white stallion hound
Called *Finder* soon had the fox drowned;
Sir Claude took a dive
Posthumously to shrive
The beast for a feast on dry ground.

CRESPIGNY.

With the carcass *broke up* on the salting,
Sir Claude and the hounds all exalting,
Aquatic prowess
Achieving success
Over vulpine sagacity o'er-vaulting.

SWAN LAKE

To fall twice in a field of just five
And, nevertheless, to survive
To capture the race,
At a rocketing pace,
Seems a marvellous feat to contrive.

Claude Crespigny went down and got up
With the alacrity of a pup,
And minor abrasions,
On two brief occasions,
In an Essex and Suffolk Hunt Cup.[2]

It seems only fair we should mention,
To avoid any bone of contention,
That three more of the five
Took a similar dive
At least once at that watery convention.

Crespigny, at six to four on,
Was clearly the favourite swan;
He won by a distance
With *Brown Tommy's* assistance,
An aquatic phenomenon!

A PLUCKY ANIMAL

To follow a fox all the way
From the Forth to the banks of the Tay,
In a hard-riding run,
Was superlative fun
But not capital sport on that day.

The meet was at Lundin Links Station,
Of *The Kingdom*, the cream of the nation:
Col. Thomson supreme
In the members' esteem,
And the whole in rapt anticipation.

By the hounds there was covert inspection,
Then a flash in wrong-headed direction
After transient hare,
Disturbed in its lair,
But no danger of real insurrection.

Then a note from the Master's horn sounds,
From the wood stream the spirited hounds
After promising scent,
With November air blent,
Running fast for the Durie coal grounds.

The heart of the master rejoices
At the colourful scene and the voices
Of fast-running hounds,
As horse's hoof pounds,
And laggards lament Hobson's choices.

Then the melody suddenly ceases,
The harmony abruptly decreases:
Pack rushing amain,
Halts mute at a drain,
And speculation increases.

Cold water precipitates ejection,
The fox giving up his protection,
Refreshed by his bath,
He takes a new path,
Eighteen couple resuming prospection.

Torloisk is the quarry's next point,
Reached in safety for fox to anoint
The welcoming covert,
But is it another
Whose scent is now run counterpoint?

No matter! They stick to the line,
Whatever the hunt may opine,
To Rameldrie racing,
Through gorse and broom pacing,
Intent on a punishment condign.

Then suddenly our Reynard turns North,
Abandoning return to the Forth,
And only a trio
Of riders, *con brio*,
Are left in pursuit on that swarth.

They follow the hounds to Ramornie,
Like skirmishers chased by *Old Hornie!*
The fox keeps on running,
Straight-necked and still cunning,
Through Melville Woods: On with the tournie!

Lindores, Dunborg and Glenduckie,
To the banks of the Tay he was lucky;
But what happened then
Was beyond human ken . . .
The fate of that animal plucky.

A SOARING SPIRIT

As the day was beginning to yawn,
Mr. Lycett Green,[3] riding *Grey Dawn*,
At Derring's Wood found
A fox to expound
The best of vulpecular brawn.

York and Ainsty set off in pursuit,
Determined on sanguinary moot,
Jumping thorn fence and drain
On that clay-clogged terrain:
For danger not giving a hoot.

They came to the flooded Alne Beck,
For the timorous a formidable check;
The hounds go across
But seven men take a toss
Into cold water up to the neck.

The far bank was vertical, sheer-sided,
By mountebanks only derided;
So the floundering horse
Took the easiest course,
Returning to nearside, elided.

One rider got in and rode out
Of that icily forbidding redoubt:
A lady sedate
Whose neat featherweight
Ensured an adroit turnabout.

One tyro rode hard for the drain
But his horse, on the brink of the main,
Changed his footing, stopped short,
Propelling consort
To far bank, as *arriviste* arcane.

Mr. Green, verdant-hued at the ghyll,
But game for a watery spill,
Made a to'gallant leap
Over chill, vasty deep:
More than twenty-seven feet, with great skill.

THE ULTIMATE POINT

Colonel Thomson of Fife, coursing questor[4]
For fox all points South via Leicester,
Found a Logan Rock meet
Rather less than a treat
In a roarin' and ragin' Sou'wester.

Voices drowned in the wind and the waves,
Foxes fast in the rocks and the caves;
The huntsman imploring,
Flapping arms, semaphoring
In a country of crazed architraves . . .

Nature's *blitzkrieg* at Ultima Thule,
No place for a rider unruly,
So the hunt trots inland,
A defeated command
But avoiding disaster and *doolie*.

A SINGULAR ENCOUNTER

Extraordinary and singular luck,
A deft horse, clever riding and pluck
Spared a hunting man brave
From a watery grave
Off the horn of belligerent buck.*

Sidney Tucker, doyen of the chase,
The Devon and Somerset ace,
Had hunted the stag
With the singular knag
To Glenthorne's precipitous face.

From cliff-top on two-counties border,
Descending the path in short order,
From eleven-hundred feet
Down the narrow estreat
He confronts the reluctant seaboarder . . .

In retreat up the zig-zagging path,
Eschewing estuarial bath:
Stag lunges at huntsman
But Tucker, fine stuntsman,
Leans seaward, a neat allopath.

The antler-less side of the head
Merely grazes the horseman instead
Of pitching the horse
Into aerial course,
With hunter and huntsman soon dead.[5]

Mr Jorrocks, in sentiments crass,
Thought a deer chase like " 'unting a hass",
Though a stag's perspicacity
Match staghound's audacity
On stickle, in rake or morass.

*stag

To outwit a following pack,
A veteran will quarter and tack
To a somnolent herd
Where a brother, bestirred,
Must run before pending attack.

Dr. Collyns recalled an old stag
Which, thrice in one chase, 'scaped the bag
By turning out deer,
Like a rude buccaneer,
Commandeering a lair in the quag.

But the huntsman was equally clever,
Discerning his quarry's endeavour,
Returning each time
To the beast in his prime,
Frustrating the bid to dissever . . .

The hunt and the hounds from their prey;
But the wily old stag got away,
The scent neatly foiling,
By sinking and soiling
In a pool for a cool matinée.

RUNNING AWAY TO SEA

Stout burghers of Sunderland Hunt
One Monday, for such was their wont,
After draining a pottle
Turned out, at Newbottle,
A bagfox some yards to the front.

As the hounds harked to huntsman's *halloo*,
A hare promised *jellied ragout*,
Starting into their path,
Courting hounds' scissored snath,
The interloper slaughtered at view.

Then, again on to carnivore scent,
Twelve miles, with felonious intent,
When he leaps into quarry,
A lime-burner's corrie,
Creeping out at the eye, nearly spent.

Once more the hounds latch on to foil,
Then the fox enters conduit to spoil
Their olfactory joy
And, in dexterous ploy,
Takes to river, pursuers to moil.

No takers for watery chase,
He comes ashore, quickens the pace
For fourteen miles more,
Keeping close to the shore,
The Sunderland pack to abase.

Then on shipboard he calmly embarks,
While the pack disconsolately barks,
High and dry on Ayres Quay
As the ship puts to sea,
And Reynard with sailors skylarks.

A NAUTICAL POINT

Soltau Symons's Chaddlewood seat,
Scene of salt-horse's disjointed meet,
Found Vice-Admiral Parker
A dim-beamish marker,
Flag officer adrift from his fleet.

ADMIRAL PARKER

Frost and snow spoiling scent to the North,
The Dartmoor cast South to green swarth,
Found a fox and gave chase
At a spanking good pace,
Pressing onward to piscary forth.

On to Kitley the sturdy fox beat,
Seeking sanctuary at silver-grey seat:
But no haven on hard
Of Baldwin Bastard
So, swift through the woods to Cofflete.

KITLEY, S. DEV

With the tide in the estuary high,
And the Admiral's harbingers nigh
And singing of slaughter,
He leaped for the water,
Swimming strong, seeking death to defy.

The hounds in a clamouring clique
Plunged into the tree-shrouded creek,
Panting hard for the kill
In the ravening rill,
Fast-fixed on vulpecular reek.

To the boathouse young Bill Adams flew
For a row-boat or Carib canoe,
And with Will Boxall dashing
And Collins-Splatt splashing
They launched with a joyous *halloo.*

Then a fearless Lieutenant R.M.
Grasped firmly a second boat's stem,
Assuming command
Of the nautical band,
Without burgee or gold diadem.

The Master, nigh on seventeen stone,
Steamed up on leviathan roan
To weigh up the action,
Amphibious infraction:
Intrepid but *lacking in tone.*

A praam on the Yealm? A mere mere!
No main-sheet but watery bier!
A red-duster Master
Courting shame and disaster?
The Vice-Admiral retired to the Rear.

Downstream to the confluence they rowed,
Landlubbers lamenting the mode:
Redjacket flotilla,
Of shame no scintilla,
Sad-mocking the Admiral's code.

From the vantage of neighbouring heights
And sundry estuarial bights,
Both gentry and yokels,
Some armed with bifocals,
Viewed the prospect of terminal rites.

But the gallant, high-tailed carnivore
Swam nigh on half-mile to far shore,
Went to earth on home ground
Undefiled by moor hound:
Lived to roam o'er his Eden once more.[6]

TRAGEDY AT NEWBY FERRY

York and Ainsty, one bright, sunny morning,
Brisk and cheerful, no Delphic forewarning,
Rode out for the chase,
Dire fate to embrace
And plunge the whole county in mourning.[7]

Sir Charles on *Saltfish*, seasoned steed,
Lords and ladies, the best of the breed:
The finest and bravest
The Lord ever gavest,
Vulpecular pride to impede . . .

In that country of sycamore and wych,
Stiff thorn fence and death-dealing ditch,
Where a hammal, half-tired
Would be quickly retired,
If not killed in precipitous pitch.

The home covert put to the test
And found blank, they rode a mile west
And at Cayton Gill found,
In slumber profound,
The first victim of sorry day's quest.

Greenwood's whin saw a fox go away,
Fate's lure on that ominous day,
Double circle describing,
Geometrically gibing,
Transposing the hunt and the prey.

Sir Charles was convinced he had found
The same fox before on that ground,
Which steeled his resolve
The mystery to solve,
And the felony not to compound.

Spurred on by the Master's own zeal,
Ripon rowels dug in at the heel;
Though Devil's darts pointing
To watery anointing,
Caution thrown to the wind in trust leal.

The hunt careered on, ever quicker,
Each man like a sharp, border pricker:
Single-minded pursuit
Of the quarry hirsute,
And death for the two-timing slicker.

The fox ran two miles to the Ure,
Swam the swift, swollen tide to secure
Safe lair in the cowberry,
While the hunt at the ferry
Prepared their best men to immure.

No inkling of tragedy foreboding,
Scant thought to the gross overloading:
An impatient throng,
Ever pressing, headstrong
For the chase, incessantly goading.

Thirteen men, eleven horse in the boat,
Over-freighted, she scarce got afloat,
Began to careen
And then dangerously lean,
Frighting horse and alarming redcoat.

Captain Key, sensing trouble, leaped out,
Avoided the punishing bout;
Made his way by the chain,
With composure urbane,
To the bank, with a cautionary shout.

Saltfish jumped, caught a leg in the chain,
Sir Charles clinging fast to the rein:
Then into the cauldron
With best of brave squadron
And never glad morning again.

Sir Charles seemed to swim for some trees
O'er-hanging far shore like a frieze,
But a bystander there
With a mesmeric stare
Failed to answer the rescuers' pleas.

Mr. Thompson of Kirby swam out,
In a lone rescue mission devout,
But the tide took the Master
Ever on to disaster
In that perilous, Charybdian rout.

The river, in spate, sped him on,
A rare, racing, cruel Rubicon;
Then *Saltfish* broke free,
Set a course, bent his knee,
As if to deliver doomed don.

He swam to his master in pride
But Sir Charles, reaching up on nearside,
Grasped his faithful nag's bridle,
In hope and prayer idle,
Both sinking in ravenous tide.

The boat now turned over, capsized,
Men and horses peremptorily excised,
Pitched into the water
In murderous slaughter,
Bowed, battered and bloodied: demised.

From the banks, knotted whips proved too short
Calamitous wake to abort,
Wakeman waking too late
The ruin to abate,
Sadly sounding a requiem mort.

Major Mussenden, a dashing Hussar,
Escaped in a sequence bizarre:
He sank and rose twice,
Then, in more than a trice,
Was plucked clear of the milling bazaar.

'Cross country, a fine, fearless rider,
But on river, no confident eider,
Mr. Robinson, non-swimmer,
Took fright at the shimmer
Of water; sat tight, no backslider . . .

Putting faith in the skill of his steed
Over drain or through flood to succeed;
Not dismounting on ferry,
Trusting quadruped equerry
To rise buoyant at moment of need.

Poor Robinson sank with his horse,
Rose again in the buffeting course,
Then his mount, badly blown,
Swiftly sank like a stone,
And he drowned with shrill cries of remorse.

Mr. Lloyd, a champion swimmer
At Eton, when vigorous and slimmer,
At a round sixteen stone,
Was soon to atone
For many a hunt supper brimmer.

As cheerful a man as e'er breathed,
Though in aural perversity sheathed;
Early riser for sport,
A skilled rider, good sort,
Now by quarrelsome aquosity bewreathed . . .

He bravely struck out for the shore,
Oblivious to Ure's thunderous roar,
But his boots and his coat
Made his chances remote:
Dragged him down in the ravaging bore.

Both Vyner and Ingleby swam out,
Planning rescue, mid rabble and rout;
Seizing hold of poor Lloyd,
Hands on shoulders, gently buoyed
Their companion, in heart and hope stout.

Then, almost in reach of the bank,
The gallant dragoons at each flank
Themselves near-succumbed,
Exhausted, benumbed:
Valiant Lloyd released hold, bravely sank.

Five men stood erect on the keel,
Five men made of muscle and steel,
Five men who survived
The manslaughter connived
By the Ure, in its rampaging reel.

Sir George Wombwell, Clare Vyner, Mr. White,
Captain Molyneaux, Major Mussenden: contrite,
Gaunt-visaged in shock
Like heads on a block,
Appalled by Fate's violent indict.

Three others expired on that day,
To the widows' and orphans' dismay:
Mr. Orveys, first whip,
Crop still in his grip,
And the ferrymen, *sans* signs of affray.

No hunt more outrageously riven
Nor Master, than Slingsby of Scriven;
No élite, leading trio
Sent to limbo, *con brio*,
More untimely, unjustly, unshriven.   SIR GEORGE WOMBWELL Bt.

All Yorkshire in horrification
At the Rhadamanthine defloration:
A shock-horrent shiver
Cocytian river
Of tears and profound lamentation.

NOTES ON CHAPTER NINE

At Perry Farm, above Exbridge, in 1839.

Over a waterlogged course at Colchester on May 3, 1888.

Mr. Lycett Green was appointed Master towards the end of the 1885-86 season in succession to Col. York who died in office.

With the Western from Madron, near Penzance, on March 8, 1872. The field included two Trelawnys and five Bolithos.

The incident occurred in 1903; Sidney Tucker was huntsman, 1901-18.

With the Dartmoor Hunt, November 9, 1878. The fox went to earth at Newton Wood.

The disaster occurred on February 4, 1869. The Hunt, under Sir Charles Slingsby, met at Stainley, near Ripon, at 10.30, some members arriving by a special train from York.

THE HUNT SPECIAL.   SIR CHARLES SLINGSBY.

CHAPTER TEN

HALTER AND ALTAR

BOWLING THEM OVER

A Lancashire lass, name of *Skittles*,
Set 'em up for a ha'porth of vittles:
By no means was she shy
But in ample supply
Of all that the male fancy kittles.

She blossomed to ride with the Quorn,
Obedient to Master[1] and horn;
Her name was Miss Walters,
A stranger to altars:
To some ladies, a creature of scorn.

Meet and covert, she managed to shun,
But appeared in the course of a run,
Going well with first flight,
A breath-taking sight,
Seat and superstructure second to none.

A very fast thing across country,
Though never a hint of effrontery,
She was toasted by men
A-gley in a glen,
And enjoyed a deft touch of knight-errantry.

A DASHING HUSSAR

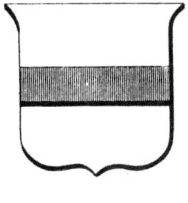

A visiting Baron from Hungary[2]
Experienced a curious vagary
While the guest of a squire,   BACHELOR
An M.P. for his shire,
Whose manner turned distant and vinegary.

By a peccable paradox it chanced
That the nobleman's fame was enhanced
By a scurrilous rumour,
Put about in good humour,
Of a regicide emprise perchanced.

This phenomenon, both subtle and arty,
Served to make him the soul of the party:
'Mongst the ladies a *beau*
And prize catch, even though
Franz Joseph was still hale and hearty.

The next rumour to cause a sensation,
And sweep through a gullible nation,
Alleged criminal congress
With a young married Princess,
An elopement, a duel, sequestration!

Thus promoted to highest society
By repute of condign impropriety,
The resplendent Hussar
And penniless Magyar
Sought a wife of abundant quotiety.   HEIRESS

The Baron espied a clear entry
To the ranks of the old landed gentry:
A beautiful wife
An indolent life,
And all for a pose of knight-errantry.

Honoured guest at first meet of the season,
County wealth, sporting buffs in cohesion,
He presented the brush
To maiden ablush:
No hint of the imminent treason.

At the board of his host: country squire,
Man of wealth, MFH, valiant sire,
A large party assembled,
The Baron dissembled,
And the blush of the heiress grew higher.

Interrupting the Magyar's ingestion,
A young baronet put a question
In the candlelit gloam:
"D'ye hunt foxes at home?"
The riposte brought dire indigestion!

Gnashing teeth on the chef's *marrons glacés*,
On the instant, the guest, Baron *passé*,
Outrage, disbelief,
Purple faces, ladies' grief:
The questing Hussar was *déclassé!*

The Master, apoplectic, aghast,
'Mid the ruins of his sumptuous repast;
His daughter in tears
At the base buccaneer's
Betrayal of honour and caste . . .

In silence, the ladies trooped out:
The gentlemen distraught, put about
By the sad malversation,
Resumed conversation
But not with the ignorant lout.

The Baron left early next day,
No warm farewells gracing his stay;
But icy demeanour
And feminine dolour
Ensuring departure straightway.

And the answer which caused such dismay?
Wrecking foxhunting folks' roundelay,
Humiliating host
By barbarous boast?
"I have *shot* five or six in a day!"

ARDOUR QUENCHED

Colonel Fane,[3] of Fulbeck in Lincs.,
Not one of your pale parlour pinks,
Always up before dawn,
With never a yawn,
Inspecting the coverts and sinks *. . .

Of disposition cheerful and vernal,
Nothing daunted the hard-riding Colonel;
Energetic and venturous,
Much travelled, adventurous,
And true to the verities eternal.

Long famous for sport and stiff fences,
Stubton country elevated the senses;
High hedges, wide ditches
Splitting hotheads and breeches,
And a river to cure indolences.

The Colonel one morning got wed,
Rode to hounds ere the wedding guests were fed;
Got ducked in the Brant,
His zeal to decant,
And the same day to India fled.

* Drains

A PASTORAL ID ILL

Peter Beckford, whose innermost *Thought*
Upon Hunting was eagerly sought
By novice and Master,
And hound medicaster,
Experienced a chase sadly fraught.

His hounds were impeccably bred,
Selected and managed and fed;
Their ailments well physicked,
The heretics inquisicked;
By Master and huntsman well led.

PETER BECKFORD
after John Smart,
1779

But our erudite King of the Sport
Endured a marked lack of rapport
From his Honourable lady,
In *Darset gleäd* shady,
Her social and spiritual mort.

A creature of infinite charm,
Vivacity and leavening barm
In capital society,
High-living ebriety,
She wilted in mode to alarm . . .

WILLIAM BECKFORD

When confronted with foxhunting squire,
Or clodhopping dame from the byre,
The farmer's wife stolid
From dank barken, olid;
Gilcup tutty from bucolic mire.

She sought solace in wild, Gothic folly:
Fonthill Abbey and millionaire molly,
Cousin William, aesthete,
A psychiatrist's treat,
All vapours and pillow-made *trolly*.

FONTHILL ABBEY

His wife's *tria juncta* histrionics
Led Peter to Italianate tonics;
To cure passions incontinent
They toured on the Continent,
Amused by Casanovan Goldonics.

Fair Florence found balance restored,
Affection and marital accord;
But the lovely Louisa,
Now leaning, like Pisa,
Lingered long on a perishing sword.

A FATAL ATTRACTION

A foxhunter's love-hate affinity
With the quarry: a curious confinity,
Spending money and skill
On preserving to kill,
May lead to a dire consanguinity.

Lord Doneraile, the Duhallow Master,
Of distemper, allegèd broadcaster,
Kept a fox as a pet,
A sort of *coquette*,
Unknowingly courting disaster.

He took the tame fox in his brougham
And, in the interior gloom
Of the coachwork japanned,
The beast bit his hand,[4]
Thus sealing the nobleman's doom.

His lordship went down with sitophobia,
Combined with severe claustrophobia;
The fox first got scabies
And then died from rabies,
And the peer from acute hydrophobia.

DROPPING THE PILOT

A high-leaping, capriole-prance?
Haute école and *hauts faits* at a glance?
A pair finely matched
In a dream briefly snatched,
A soaring, equestrian romance?

The Empress of Austria aspired
To an idyll on horseback, gay-squired
By her garlanded "Bay",
In chivalrous essay,
Chaste-galloping to climax inspired.

Captain Middleton, ex-lancer, still thrusting,
For favours and foxes firm justing,   ELIZABETH
Pressing on, fleet and hard,
Parnassian bard,
Admiration and charm freely gusting.

Like a civilised Barbary Bey,
Fine-mettled for fun or affray
In a land of the dates,
Passions, intrigues and hates,
He piloted enwrapt *protégée* . . .

With exemplary verve and panache
And extraordinary nerve, cut a dash
O'er Leicestershire timber,
Stouthearted and limber,
And through dense, Pytchley bullfinch and plash.

Elizabeth followed, entranced,
Her jumping skills subtly enhanced
By her mesmeric leader,
Singing rich, hunting lieder,
Lèse majesté boldly perchanced.

In Erin they romped with the Meath
Over grasslands and emerald-green heath,
Enthused over hunters
And highstepping stunters
And the state of the animals' teeth.

A high-born and Catholic Empress
And a Protestant of lowly address
Drawn together by horses
And challenging courses:
Magnetised by a sporting *noblesse*.

And flouting dictates of society,
Though observing the rules of propriety;
Six seasons of riding,
Chaste passion abiding,
Tight-reined to a soulless sobriety.

Flirtations with corries Hiberian
Mired Anglo-Celt tensions agrarian,
And snubs to Victoria,
In excelsis sans gloria,
Bogged buffers Anglo-Austro-Hungarian.

CAPT. MIDDLETON

So her wish to return every year
To Erin and winter days' cheer
Was sadly frustrated:
Abruptly abated
By Franz Joseph's diktat severe.

Banned from Isles of her spiritual birth,
She grieved in equestrian dearth;
And Middleton, mourning
His "Sisi", *mavourneen*,
Rode out his Kildarean mirth.

Deprived of her catalyst, Bay,
She wilted and wasted away,
By an anarchist killed,
She died unfulfilled:
Heart and soul, a sad *émigrée*.

And Middleton, who married for money,
Lost to pastures of romance and honey;
Ne'er again winsome ace,
Broke his neck in a race:
Fate's practical joke less than funny.

A STARK CHOICE

When a hunting man's thoughts turn to marriage,
His in-laws-to-be may disparage
And damn with faint praise
His hard-pounding ways
In preference to driver and carriage.

Bill Higgins[5] was one such a suitor,
No tearaway, screaming freebooter,
But esteemed local resident
And Oakley Club president:
Of society, a decorative voluter.

Mrs. Harvey thought William remiss
Of her Mary's domiciliary bliss
In not giving up
The chase and the cup
Forthwith, for benign synthesis.

Widow & Heiress

So William was put in his place,
Rejected, in matronly disgrace;
For his sport he was trounced:
Mrs. Harvey announced
The marriage would not now take place.

A LIFE-STYLE UNIQUE

No Wimpole Street town house like Barrett,
No poetry nor passing the claret:
Two nags in the cellar
And, under roof stellar,
Six couple of hounds in the garret . . .

And 'tween decks a family of eight
In a happy but humble estate,
Six children to feed
And nurture in need,
But nothing chalked up on the slate.

Thus young Osbaldiston[6] existed,
With starkest economy subsisted,
But hunted in season
Despite fatherly treason
Anent servant-girl ardently trysted.

On twenty-three shillings a week,
Lawyer's clerk with a life-style unique,
In decent black dressed,
He failed to attest
To poverty, paucity or pique . . .

Moonlighting in Holborn to earn
Butchers' offal, a meagre return
For keeping their books;
Grain from corn-chandlers' nooks
For his horses and spoiled brewhouse kern.

For hunting wayleave he would share
With the farmers his bag of prime hare,
Keeping one for the pot
Of ménage polyglot,
And one for the cupboard near bare.

A DEVON COURTSHIP

'Mid Dartmoor's stern country gleamed bright
Two beacons of neighbourly light:
Joint Masters, twin brothers
Ever mindful of others'
Well-being and sporting delight.

The Leamons were courteous, well-dressed;
Old gentlemen *sans* blazon or crest;
White-haired and refined,
Well-disciplined but kind,
Not wealthy but two of the best.

Past sixty, the bachelors one night
Considered the sorrowful plight
Of one left alone,
In old age to atone
For connubial neglect, oversight.

They decided that one ought to wed:
Each had the same name in his head . . .
An Okehampton *hoteliere*,
A buxom *vivandiere*,
Good provider and very well bred.

They tossed a deft coin to decide
Which should favour the designate bride,
And the brother who won,
The honours had done
Ere the sun reached its zenith noontide.

The lady accepted with grace,
Keeping house for the brotherly brace;
Nursing each to the end
As his wife or his friend,
Double dowry at last to embrace.

WINNING HIS SPURS

The hunting field quaintly afforded
Opportunities not otherwise accorded
To gentlemen o'er-gracious
And ladies flirtatious
For dalliance and sport unrecorded.*

A cast shoe, a lame horse, a kind deed
Recapturing a riderless steed,
Acquaintance betokened
By an awkward gate opened,
Or help to remount could oft lead . . .

To an empathy increasingly glamorous,
'Mid the pageantry colourful and clamorous,
And bridle and halter,
To bridal and altar,
Double-harness for th'achingly amorous.

When a handsome young subaltern espied
A young lady cut short in her stride,
Without introduction
Or thought of seduction
He gallantly flew to her side.

And for both it was love at first sight,
A meeting of rapturous delight:
Betrothal soon broached,
Noble father approached
But, sadly, affiancement to blight.

Troth plighted, then blighted, no hope
Of fatherly blessing or trope:
Swift horses persuasive
Of action evasive:
They must part or spur onwards: elope.

___
* Based on an anecdote by F. Palliser de Costobadie.

They sped to a borderside inn,
Determined on marriage or sin:
To witnesses declared
A destiny shared,
And repaired to their welcoming whin.

No sooner was bedroom door bolted,
The lovers, in riding kit, holted,
Then the laird came a-thund'ring.
Intent on a-sund'ring
The tryst and his prize filly colted.

As befitting a passionate nation,
Scots law required prompt consummation
Of the union, an act
To legitimise the pact:
A congress of firm predication.

"Quick, Bob!" urged the putative bride,
Casting habit and modesty aside;
"Into bed! Boots and all!"
Then with leap to enthrall
The Lancer lay close by her side.

Young Robert complied with all speed,
Ere door was down, doing the deed
In top boot and spur,
A willing *chasseur*,
Naught left for laird but to accede.

A LATE REPRIEVE

In the Bedfordshire county outback,
A notable harrier pack
And the owner's fair daughter,
Braving hell and high water,
Attracted a questing young Jack.

The young lady's dam disapproved
Of his footsteps becoming deep-grooved,
And nagged at the squire
To sell hounds and retire
From the chase, which he did, as behooved.

Within hours of this terrible wrench,
He was told that his waywardly wench
Had eloped with the bounder,
And was like to grow rounder
In a manner to make his wife blench.

Single-minded he sprang into action
To remedy disgrace and abstraction:
Sending messenger swift
To rectify the rift,
And recover the four-footed faction.

A NOCTURNAL CAPTURE

Renowned for his rousing reveille
In dawn-dewy Cumbrian valley,
John Peel could be reticent
When holding a lady's scent,
Engaged in romantical sally.

JOHN PEEL

Stout of heart, strong of limb, sporting yeoman,
Bred from stalwart, freeholding long bowmen,
Independent of race,
Ever bold for the chase,
A foxhunting, horn-blowing showman . . .

Past scree, ghyll and tarn to the fell
He would scramble, whoo-whooping, pell-mell,
Despite savins or sheep,
Or snow inches deep,
From the drag to the chase and the knell.

With the zeal of a reiver or cateran
And the patience and skill of a veteran,
Wielding gavelock and mell
He would rudely expel
The fox from his bield in the borran.

Young Peel set his heart on the daughter
Of a neighbouring farmer but sought her
Parents' consent
For the nuptial event
In vain; they gave him no quarter.

Not rejecting romantical condiment,
Her parents declared an impediment:
She was *far ower young*
From her hearth to be wrung;
But Peel swore he meant what he said he meant.

No second or third time of asking,
No lovers in self-esteem basking;
Four parents opposed
To the marriage proposed,
But *Pierrot* and *Pierrette* a-masking . . .

One night, with the parents a-bed,
John Peel took a hunter and sped
From Caldbeck to Uldale,
To song of the nightgale
And the girl he'd determined to wed.

Unwontedly tight in his tongue,
The joy of the chase mutely sung,
Young Peel held his whist
Till the rapt lovers' tryst
And his quarry from covert was sprung.

Then swiftly to Gretna they flew,
Ere the sun rose to sparkle the dew,
For their runaway marriage:
One horse but no carriage,
Nor best man nor bridesmaid in view.

Peel senior had scarce kenned the pith
Of the absence of heir, kin and kith,
When his son's **TA-A-LE-O!**
Struck his ears like a blow
On the anvil by some mighty smith.

Dismounting from saddle and pillion,
Like a radiant, revolving triskelion,
The groom swept his bride
And his parents, wide-eyed,
Into joyful, impromptu cotillion.

Recognising a neat *fait-accompli*,
And a ridingdress soiled and *ower-crumply*;
That by hammer and hand
No marriage could stand,
Mrs. Peel called the bans very promptly.

John Peel sired a brood of thirteen,
The eldest son, John, just as keen
For the thrills of the chase
At a hard-seeking pace,
And a whipper-in, skilled and serene.

'BY HAMMER AND HAND'

NOTES ON CHAPTER TEN

1. The Earl of Stamford and Warrington.

2. Freely adapted from Baring Gould's *Old Country Life,* 1890.
   The author had probably heard rumours about Le Comte de
   Jametel, a handsome but impecunious visiting Frenchman who

was in the habit of casually inquiring among hunt members whether they knew of an *héritière* to whom he might propose marriage. He visited Melton in the season along with Prince Louis of Bourbon, the Comtesse de Clermont Tonnere and an Austro-Hungarian contingent including Counts Charles and Rudolphe Kinsky, Heinrich Larische and Szencheny. Count Charles Kinsky distinguished himself by winning both the Pardubitz and the Grand National (1891).

3. Col. H. Fane rode with the Belvoir.

4. In the Mallow Field Club Journal (No.6, 1988) Mr Seamus Crowley relates that Hayes St. Leger, 4th Viscount Doneraile (1818-87), who was a great lover of animals, was bitten by his tame fox in January, 1887, and showed symptoms of hydrophobia in August that year. Local tradition had it that he declined treatment by Louis Pasteur and was smothered in his bed by the local gentry to end his misery when the rabies became acute. The coachman, one Barrer, was also bitten but took the treatment and survived.

4a On the subject of ambivalence of the hunter towards the hunted, *Scrutator* recalled (c.1860) the case of a medical man who rode to hounds. A fox was caught in a trap set for vermin of other species in his garden and had its leg broken. The doctor took infinite pains to set the bone and nurse the animal to recovery. He then set it free and hunted and killed it "in the legitimate manner".

5. William Higgins, suitor for the hand of Mary Harvey, was prepared to make the supreme sacrifice and give up hunting in the interests of connubial harmony. He promised Mary's mother, Mrs. Susan Harvey of Ickwell, near Biggleswade, Beds., he would do so but not until the close of the season, having earlier acceded to an earnest request by the Marquess of Tavistock to occupy the chair of the Oakley Club in the February. This would have been some time before the marriage. Mrs. Harvey was advised that William was too young to settle down. There were also private doubts within the family as to his means.

6. Osbaldiston, possibly an ancestor of the Leicestershire squire, was thrown out by his father, a gentleman in the north of England, for marrying one of the household servants. He worked at Gray's Inn and got his offal for the hounds in Clare Market.

CHAPTER ELEVEN

BREWS AND STEWS

A NORTHERN STEW

The fame of the old Wallsend Harriers
Wide-straddled the Hadrian barriers
On account of one, Potts,
And his hare-rousing trots,
And affinity with tinkers and farriers.

As befits complemental artisans,
And neat appellational scans,
The hunt's whipper-in,
To cacophonous din,
Was an iron-clad fellow called Pans.

Three times a week in the morning,
In dark green and black velvet mourning,
White cords and top boots,
And clamorous bruits,
They chased hare from his lair, rudely scorning.

Here the plot and the broth fairly thicken;
Hark to beat of the horses' hooves quicken!
Their greatest accord
Was with rich festive board:
Whisky-punch and hogs' tongue and boiled chicken.

CALCULATED CONDOLENCE

Mr. Hamilton, a relative of Dufferin,
A good-natured man and long-sufferin',
Was subtly cajoled
By a calculating scold
Into selling his horse without offerin'.

One day after Kilkenny hunt,
In which he was well to the front,
He stabled his horse
At the clubhouse, perforce,
When frost made the going too blunt.

Returning to hunt some days later,
To good scent in the Freshford theatre,
He ran his horse hard
With too little regard
For the out-of-condition young plater.

The animal sank lifeless beneath him
And Hamilton was forced to bequeath him
To elemental care,
Meanwhile to repair
To clubhouse, and later bewreath him.

LORD DUFFERIN

'Midst festive board banter and toddy,
Mr. Flood, his condolence to embody,
And sympathy to proffer
Made a fine, sporting offer:
Fifteen pounds for the hard-lying body.

Mr. H. said, "There's naught but the skin!"
But Flood, flush with charity and gin,
Was generously insistent
And, persuasively persistent,
Clinched the bargain with gratified grin.

After searching and failing to find
The body next day, he inclined
To endorse his intuition
Which swift found fruition,
With horse's hooves trotting behind.

He had guessed that the horse was hard-pumped,
Prematurely ridden fast and then jumped,
And that cooling night air
Would vitality repair:
Mr. Hamilton was sadly gazumped.

THE REEK OF THE WREAKE

Otho Paget showed an intrepid streak
In gathering the news week by week;
Amid postprandial blether
Or inclement weather,
He chronicled the brave and the meek.

Expert critic of foxhunting form,
Less concerned with society norm,
He weathered the weald
On behalf of *The Field*,
In sunshine, rain, hail, sleet or storm.

Once, swimming the Leicestershire Wreake,
He emerged at effluvious creek,
Recovered his horse,
Resuming his course,
Personal freshness not quite at its peak.

Run finished at Barrow-on-Sour
In a snowstorm; wet through, saddle-sore,
Many miles from his bed
But, Leicestershire bred,
He stole clothes from an absent friend's store.[1]

A CIVIC HUMILIATION

To the layman it may seem absurd
But, to single a stag from a herd
The hunt, in slow motion,
Must avoid a commotion
Or getting the animals bestirred.

Two horsemen and two or three walking,
Nonchalant, unobtrusively stalking,
Keeping herd gently moving,
Ever silent, soft behooving,
The victim-intended scarce balking.

The ungulate, by nature o'er-topped,
Much-walked and leg-weary, will opt
To lie down and submit
To the harbourer's remit,
Without being ostensibly stopped.

Assembled in parkland one day,
Mr. Berkeley's gay band spied a trey
Of besetting attraction
Inviting satisfaction
And determined to get him away.

But an ignorant and over-eager guest,
Misconstruing the Master's behest,
Spurred for'ard at speed,
Starting up a stampede,
To the huntsman's alarm manifest.

The first citizen,[2] for such was his calling,
Then described a manoeuvre appalling:
Tried to blanch the stampede,
Rode across without heed
But with magisterial presence enthralling.

THE MAYOR AND CORPORATION

Down the hill at a thundering pace
Came the deer, the mayor to abase;
They jumped, fore and aft,
Struck His Worship abaft,
Bowled him over in civic disgrace.

He rolled to the foot of the hill,
Rotundity aiding the spill,
But got up unharmed,
If somewhat uncharmed
At the rigours of staghunting thrill.

FATE'S FICKLE BECK

A hunt servant's life in the sport,
Rarely brutish but often quite short,
Promised liberal prize
Or a violent demise,
E'er in call of the Great Hunter's mort.

A Scotton Bar Boxing Day meet
Saw a trio[3] each destined to greet
The foxhunter's Odin,
Though two only rode in
A field fated life to escheat.

Huntsman Squires, jumping stile into road,
And applying too much of the goad
Was crushed by his jade,
Breaking one shoulder blade
And three ribs, in fraught episode.

Truman Tuff fell downstairs, broke his neck;
Jim Trivick, his head, hitting deck
When his horse's hoof stuck
In a tramline: ill luck
For three stalwarts at Fate's fickle beck.

HOLDING THE PASS

Man of Kent with his foxhounds in spate,
Arrived at a Sydenham gate,
But a *knight of the cleaver*,
An arrogant reiver,
Proved sentinel staunch, obstinate.[4]

He brandished the tool of his trade,
Indulged in a threatening tirade;
No Horatio he
But a knave, *cap-a-pie*,
A blockhead intent on blockade.

The sportsman, averse to game lost,
Resorted to gentle riposte,
But the Bloodied, Unbowed,
Refused to be cowed,
Belling barbarism with mayhem embossed.

By way of an action for *trover*,
The gentleman sought leave to **jump over**
The six-foot-six gate
To the butcher's estate,
Disarming the lamb-slaying drover . . .

Who swore that no Englishman could
Surmount it but should if he would;
So the sportsman drew back,
Steadied hackle and hack,
Cleared the five-barred stockade whence he stood.

The butcher was truly amazed,
Astonished, admonished, *bumbazed*:
He promptly surrendered,
Imperiously tendered
Right of way, in honour ukased.

A DUAL ROLE IN DRAG

Stout follower of Mr. Trelawny
And Dartmoor hounds, valiant and brawny,
Mr Newcombe up-staged
But never enraged
In brews and stews Mulligatawny.

His primary professional role
Was as actor, dramatic or droll,
And manager-lessee,
A strutting Grandee,
'Neath Plymouth's proscenium scroll.

Thirty years in the wake of the Squire,
Over granite, through treacherous mire,
In vulpecular jaunts
To the farthest-flung haunts
Of the quarry, in weatherscape dire . . .

One day after cross-country ride
To Reynard's remote knotted hide,
He rode sixty miles
To put on the guiles
Of the Dame, in burlesque eventide.

The curtain rung up long before,
He leaped from his horse at stage door
Into vast widow's weeds,
Thus concealing the deeds
And the duds of his day on the moor . . .

As a seventy-year-old Widow Twankey,
But nimble and hoydenly pranky:
No prompting or priming,
Professional timing,
An artiste in stage hanky-panky.

A CORNISH WRESTLER

A stag oddly named *Robin Hood*
On Morwenstow vicarage lawn stood,
Disdainful, impressive,
No *gallant* but aggressive,
No friend of the poor and the good.

Though owned by the reverend incumbent,
To clergy he ne'er was succumbent;
Hierophants his *bêtes noires*,
His bossy devoir
To render divinely decumbent.

Mr. Knight, a visiting minister,
A wearisome priest but not sinister,
Approached *Robin Hood*
As a deer-lover would,
A patronising pat to administer.

Rude *Robin* attacked *gentil Knight*,
Put him down for a weird Puseyite;
Made to gore the man ruddy,
A shrieking red study,
But rescued from desperate plight . . .

THE REVD. R.S. HAWKE

By the vicar whose Polkinhorne hold,
Restraining the ungulate bold,
Allowed Knight to escape
From undignified scrape,
Not confessing to sins manifold.

When the bishop came down from his perch,
Scolded vicar for live stag a-lurch:
"Mr. Knight *might have died!*"
The vicar replied:
"No great loss; he is *very Low Church.*"

Next day in approach sly and tricky,
Robin Hood grabbed episcopal dickey;
Tried to eat the mauve vest,
A rare feast to digest
In psalterium unhallowed and sticky.

The vicar heard Exon's loud cries,
Feared a painful, if high-flown demise,
Ran swift to the scene,
Rescued object obscene
From the beast he must de-demonize.[5]

AN ELEGANT BRUSH-UP

With the Grafton, a chimneysweep rode
In a chimneypot hat, *à-la-mode*,
And an ancient green smock,
A sartorial shock,
And a touch of professional woad.

Adam Sherwood,[6] adept at the science,
And keen on stylistic compliance,
Would analyse each chase
For the Hunt and his Grace,
To the huntsman's dismay and annoyance.

Whether riding or raking the ember,
He would talk to all classes of member
About chimneys Byzantine
And coverts labyrinthine,
With elegance and wit to remember.

Come evening, done huffin' and puffin',
He would sparkle at bluffin' and ruffin':
An ace card at whist,
As the ladies well wist,
And clever at luffin' and sloughin'.

A BREWING DEEP-BARMED

The Honourable George Grantley Berkeley,
Ex-Guards and a journalist clerkly,
A gentleman-huntsman
But never a stuntsman,
Led the Oakley as through a glass darkly.

Or so grand originals averred,
Keeping pot and plot steadily stirred;
They tried to unseat him,
Resolved to delete him
From the Mastership lately conferred.[7]

On a meagre one thousand a year
He tried to engender good cheer;
For four days a week
Endured pique of the clique
Over common and coppices drear.

Youngest son of the Gloucestershire Earl,
Mr. Berkeley was no plodding churl;
A well-seated rider
But mannered outsider,
Unordained: a *Bunyonesque knurl.*

Protagonist of local dissenter,
Sam Whitbread[7a] brewed up the fomenter
To a white-foaming froth,
An intoxicant broth:
A challenge to staid non-repenter.

The farmers were favourably inclined
But Lords Tavistock[7b] and Ludlow resigned,
So Berkeley urged Whitbread
To mind what he said
For fear of an injured behind.

Subtle Sam pleaded justification,
Fair comment above litigation,
A personal opinion
In the public dominion
On a gentleman's alleged malversation.

So Berkeley accused him of lying
And hypocrisy: forever denying
Malicious subversion,
Under solemn assertion
Of friendship and succour undying.

Through his lawyer Sam Whitbread declined
To reply to complaints ill-defined,
Wanting specified dates
Of libellous rates,
And depositions properly signed.

Berkeley's spring of long-suff'rance saw drought
But, eschewing litigious rout,
Undignified laundering
And longwinded maundering,
He determined to **call the man out.**

Lord Clanricarde advanced to be recognised
As a friend and a second: not minutiaezed
By wordy evasions
About private occasions
And damns and distempers swift sanitised.

As the sun o'er horizon upclimbed,
Town clock close the Swan solemn chimed,
George Berkeley *à outrance*
To Clanricarde, askance,
Handed over Joe Mantons due primed.

His friend was now greatly alarmed
At a brewing and stewing deep-barmed,
Urging Berkeley to name
His witness to blame
So the twain could retire, both unharmed.

But his witness to calumny and slander
Continued with facts to philander,
Pleading memory blanks,
Refused to break ranks,
Declining to aid the outlander.

So Clanricarde and Whitbread agreed
A third party might soft intercede;
Berkeley's letter withdrawn,
They stifled a yawn,
And vanquished the thought and the deed.

A LATE REAPING

Jem Morgan, dynastic progenitor
Of three generations in hunting corps,
Served many a master
Without personal disaster,
Earning fame, pride of place, a fine score.

LORD CLANRICARDE
a diplomatic skater

After fifty hard years in the field
And of foxes a bountiful yield,
He gave up the horn
To son, Goddard, third-born,
His contract most honourably sealed.

Then out with Old Berkeley for pleasure,
A grand septuagenarian's leisure,
Relaxed and replete
At a January meet,
His horse fell, long life to admeasure.

He remounted and jumped second fence,
Ere the switch of the scythe seared his sense,
Then to farmhouse repaired,
His soul swiftly prayer'd
And gathered to posthumous eminence.

ELEVATED POSTURE

In January, Eighteen-fifty-one,
A Meltonian fox on the run
Led the Belvoir a chase,
At a smart, clipping pace,
Ending up where they had begun.[8]

First he crossed Grantham Road to Thorpe Pasture,
Thence to Stonesby, in insolent posture,
Into Croxton Park Grove,
Where the pack vainly strove
To dislodge him from oak tree purpresture.

On the Belvoir side of the park,
Hounds bayed at the base of the bark
But, sixty feet up,
Like a mischievous pup,
The fox stayed secure in his ark.

A whipper-in ascended the oak,
Administ'ring a dexterous poke,
Whereupon he descended,
No surrender portended,
As to Stonesby via Saltby he broke.

Past Sproxton Thorns hard on the left
To Saxby, the hounds, fleet and deft,
Raced to Stapleford Park
And around in an arc
To the Melton gorse, whence he was reft.

There the hounds went away with fresh prey,
Leaving horses in sad disarray,
And riders perplexed,
And hunt servants vexed
At the masterly vulpine display.

Neither huntsman nor foxhounds were rated,
But the fox up a tree commemorated
In silver sculpturesque
Of that sporting burlesque,
Damning Belvoir ebullience o'er-stated.

HIGH DRAMA

In the February of Eighteen-eighty-six
A Blackmoor Vale fox in a fix
Left the scrub and the scree
To climb high up a tree,
In a hunting field drama prolix.

A whipper-in ascended the elm,
Up the steep-slanting trunk to o'erwhelm
The game creature, but he,
In a gesture of glee,
Adroitly manoeuvred his helm.

The animal then jumped forty feet
To land in the midst of the meet,
But instead of death throes,
He was up on his toes
And for'ard away, free and fleet.

For two miles he ran, straight and true,
Defying the Hunt's *view halloo*;
A *divertissement* proud,
Acclaimed by the crowd,
Till he kept his last rendezvous.

A SUMMONS TO DINNER

The Tedworth terrain far transcended
The merits of runs less extended,
But the going was marred
By a daunting hazard
When dense, swirling vapour descended.

The fog would appear without warning
At any hour of the morning,
Or late in the day
When, with view of the prey,
The Hunt pressed pursuit till the horning.

Local riders, aware of the danger,
Took a compass, but the visiting stranger
Could be caught unawares,
Cast adrift with his prayers,
A lonely, lamenting, lost ranger.

A novice sudden-halted one day[9]
On *Mortimer*, the Master's old bay,
In fog-bound disorder
On the Hampshire-Wilts border
Found his only recourse was to pray.

In that devilish, dispiriting cloud,
A sinister, enveloping shroud,
He drained his last dram,
Downed his last crumb of ham,
Then his soul towards Heav'n humbly prow'd.

Nigh on Eight 'cross the wolds came an answer,
As if from benign necromancer;
A summons by bell,
A Netheravon spell
Casting *Mortimer* as aural geomancer.

PRIDE GOING BEFORE

Riding high with the cream of the nation,
Sitting tall in a proud elevation,
Lord of all he surveys
In imperious gaze:
A scarlet-clad King of Creation . . .

Then th'horizon seems oddly to tremble,
Equestrian joy to dissemble:
A touch of unease
At seignorial knees;
A vague call for the wits to assemble.

But alas! He seems to be shrinking,
Diminished, inexorably sinking;
Exuberance laid low,
A descent sure but slow
Into underworld mouldy and stinking.

But wait! He spies lichen-lined wall:
Paved entry to Valhallan hall?
Or *descensus Averno*
To fire-bricked inferno
And hideous, ignominious thrall?

Then, deep in the dank, darkling dell,
Dishevelled, deflated, our Swell
Sees a rusty, iron pump
Wedged behind horse's rump:
Like Pussy, he's gone down a well!

Mr. Croome, in the gloom, proffers whip
To amend the unfortunate slip;
Mr. Pole, in the hole,
An unlikely troll,
Latches hold in a brotherly grip.[10]

NOTES ON CHAPTER ELEVEN

Paget's friend, Mr. William Martin, was away from home when his wardrobe was plundered but as one Leicestershire man to another he would not have objected.

The Mayor of Newbury was enjoying a novice's run at Hampstead Park, Berks.

Tom Squires succeeded Collinson as huntsman to the York and Ainsty in 1871. As Scarth Dixon put it, "An awful fatality seemed to hang over the York country at that time." Before Squires had completed his second season, he met with a fatal accident. The hounds met at Ouseburn Workhouse on March 13, 1873, and found in Grafton Whin. They ran their fox close to Marston Village . . On leaping an awkward stile into the road, Squires' horse fell and rolled over him, causing injuries from which he died in three days. Truman Tuff, whipper-in, took over and showed good sport. By the end of the season on April 10 the hunt had killed ninety-two foxes in one hundred and ten days' sport. Jim Trivick, late of the York and Ainsty, was whipper-in to Sherwood at the Cleveland and later carried the horn. Later he went to the Hurworth and then to the Ledbury at Malvern and was killed at the moment his hounds were killing their fox.

c1800

Based on an anecdote by S. Baring Gould. He says that R.S. Hawker, the eccentric vicar and poet, had two stags, the second called *Maid Marian*. The stags were a present from Sir Thomas Acland of Killerton Park, East Devon, whose one-hundred-and-fifty-acre deer park within a fifteen-thousand-acre estate held two to three hundred fallow deer.

Adam Sherwood of Stony Stratford, Bucks., c1842.

A meeting of hunt subscribers and members of the Oakley Club called by Samuel Charles Whitbread at the request of seven others on January 16, 1830, resolved that the Oakley country had not been efficiently hunted that season and called on the Master to engage a professional huntsman.

7a   Samuel Charles Whitbread (1796-1879) was the younger son o
      Samuel Whitbread M.P. for Cardington, Beds. He was educate
      at Eton and Cambridge and was a political ally of the Duke o
      Bedford. He was M.P. for Middlesex, 1820-30. He became
      partner in the Chiswell Street brewery in 1819.   He was
      founder of the Oakley Hunt but never Master.

7b   The Marquis of Tavistock was Master of the Oakley, 1809-1
      1822-29 and 1836-41 by which date he was the seventh Du
      of Bedford, having succeeded in 1839.

8.   The incident occurred at Croxton Park in 1851.

9.   Mr. Godfrey Webb, a London businessman, was a guest of S
      Reginald Graham, Bart. at his winter quarters, Netheravo
      House, Wilts.

10.   Based on an incident on December 24, 1851, when Mr. Hen
      Pole, out with the Vale of White Horse under the Mastership
      Mr. Henry Villebois, disappeared slowly from sight in a re
      from Lea Wood towards Fairford Park. Mr. Croome offer
      his whip to Mr. Pole and, with the help of Mr. Ernest Bowle
      pulled him out. After much plunging, the exhausted horse w
      brought out unhurt on a rope.

Charles at home.

CHAPTER TWELVE

FOREIGN FIELDS

A HORSE BEYOND PRICE

> Dump Parsons, twice London Lord Mayor,
> For hunting had penchant and flair;
> Prime civic pilaster,
> Ex-officio Master
> And City Hunt's titular heir.
>
> With royals and nobles he rode,
> Obeying the staghunting code;
> A shining exemplar,
> Equestrian Templar,
> A knight of the field and the road.
>
> But when fields of St. George and St. Giles
> Became cluttered with buildings for miles
> And the stag and the hare
> Had departed elsewhere,
> He quitted the Wells and Seven Dials . . .
>
> To ride with the Sovereign of France,
> In courtly demeanour to dance
> A quadruped quadrille,
> A close-order drill
> In stately and ordered advance.

Now it seems that citizenry Gallic
Attributed an uprightness phallic
To the First Citizen,
And offices akin
To Lord Chancellor's and likewise cephalic.

So when Parsons nosed pale palfrey for'ard,
The field thought his conduct was froward:
Astonishment reigned
And nobles disdained
Royal etiquette breached, stance unto'ard.

The spirited horse shot ahead,
Left the field far behind as it sped
To be first at the kill
To milor's acclaim shrill,
And the field-master's near-dropping-dead.

When the King of a courtier inquired
Who the gentleman was, the man, ired,
Said *Chevalier de Malte*,
A punning insult
To that isle and to brewer admired.

But the King, with Lord Mayor, in discourse,
Inquired for the price of the horse,
And his Worship replied
What could not be denied,
Beyond price, save as gift to the source . . .

Of all wisdom, nobility and light
In that realm of transcending delight;
So the King, much appeased,
Was graciously pleased
To grant Parsons stout import sole right.[1]

A PIGSTICKER UNSTUCK

After grief and agrom at Agra,
General Lake longed for Leamington Spa
But endured Indian heat
For Sindhian defeat
And rout of confederate Mahratta.

Lord Lake was a lover of sport,
With hunting, in total comport;
An officer off duty
Might chase porcine booty,
Subject only to cavalry escort.

Brigade-Major John Prester, devout
For nilgai[2] or pigsticking rout,
At dawn or abaft
The day's *wappenshaft*,
One day sought a post-tiffin bout . . .

Reared a hog in the scrub of the plain,
Chased him hard o'er unbroken terrain,
A wide circle describing,
Thick dust-storm imbibing,
Escort trailed like a caravan train.

THE WART-HOG, AN
AFRICAN COUSIN

Prester noticed, too late, the direction;
Straight for infantry lines: disaffection,
Then the tents of HQ,
A mad hullabaloo,
A hurricane-borne insurrection!

So, fearing the wrath of the corps,
He redoubled his bid for the boar,
Spurred Arab horse hard,
Both ball and bombard,
Tripping guy-rope, somersaulting to floor . . .

In a heap near the C-in-C's tent,
Pride and breeches indecently rent,
While the hog, charging on
Like a wild Amazon,
On murder and mayhem hell-bent . . .

Tore into the new quarter-guard,
Ripping two men to ribbon and shard;
Tossing sentinel high
Into arms stack nearby,
Then careering down neat boulevard.

Serried tents in disarray, scattered,
PBI and bombardiers battered
In frontal attack
Of ruin and wrack;
The peace of the camp rudely shattered.

The major got up, mounted horse,
Dodging tent pegs, eschewing remorse,
Speared the galloping boar
In mutual roar
As it challenged in swift counter-course.

The general regarded the swine,
The carnage and chaotic line;
"Worse than Castlebar"[3] he said,
With a shake of the head;
Then asked the young major to dine.

BEHIND THE THRONE IN KILKENNY

The forebears of Captain John Power
Afforded him generous dower;
Not short of a penny
He founded Kilkenny
Hunt Club at Derrynahinch bower.

He built up a fifty-couple pack,
Well bred with good pace and attack;
Reared many good horses,
Extended the gorses,
And combed the Kilkenny outback.

In a good scenting country, unenclosed,
With landowners keen, unopposed,
He sought vulpine prey
For many a long day
With hounds fleet of foot and well-nosed.

A tall, heavy man and well-read,
He provided a bountiful spread
At Rice's hotel,
The Hunt citadel,
With Sneyd's claret and old port before bed.

A Whig staunch for emancipation,
Influential with cream of the nation,
He was made baronet
For his foxhunting sweat
And high Tory Hill[4] denigration.

For forty-seven seasons he rode
With the pack from his Kilfane abode,
None harder or faster,
Pre-eminent Master,
In Erin's *preux chevalier* code.

The rules of the Kilkenny Hunt
Were hard on the socialite bunt,
But on days except Ember
Gave full rein to member,
Not forbidding equestrian stunt.

Non-members were rigidly excluded
From club-room: no stranger intruded;
One black ball kept out
The predatory scout;
No faction disrupted or feuded.

Lord Waterford, in deft escapade,
Climbed the stairs in equine cavalcade;
Jumped the refectory table,
Under gaunt, club-house gable,
In the face of Bath-bun cannonade.

GLOUCESTERSHIRE RUNNERS

When a follower can truthfully say
He's run eighty-odd miles in a day,
We need no soothsayer
To know he's a stayer:
A man who works hard at his play.

LORD WATERFORD

Jem Hastings[5] ne'er went to a meet,
Unless on his own ample feet;
Pigskin he detested,
So never invested
In horse-flesh and leather-clad seat.

He once ran nigh ten leagues to covert,
Five more, a stout fox to recover;
Then thirty miles back,
On the Cheltenham tack,
A badger by moon to uncover.

Another swift runner of Gloucester,
Though on the American roster,
Only once sat a horse
When, to lasting remorse,
He got stuck like the famed Doctor Foster.

Jonas Cattell, chief whipper-in and guide
To the New Jersey Club and the pride
Of its fleetest equestrians,
Though king of pedestrians,
Was a runner no fox e'er defied.

Athletic in form, six feet tall,
He was frequently backed to beat all
In twenty-mile races
'Gainst fleet Indian aces;
A performance the best to enthrall.

JONAS CATTELL

One day for a very small purse
He ran four-score, in going adverse,
From Woodbury to Cape Isle,
In brilliant and winning style,
And next day, eighty miles in reverse.

With the hounds at a loss for the scent,
He would help them recover their bent
By finding the track,
With an instinctive knack
And a vigilance vehement.

A GENTLEMAN'S GENTLEMAN

The son of a baronet's butler,
Tom Crane was as sharp as a cutler;
And as huntsman at war,
Complementing the Corps,
A sort of non-mercenary sutler.

Smartly-dressed, sharp of ear, keen of sight,
The top-boots much polished and bright;
In the left hand his whip
Planted firmly on hip,
And a loose-shaking rein in his right . . .

Though sinistral, an excellent horseman,
With the dash of a Viking or Norseman;
No dread hesitation
But swift levitation,
And a weather-tanned visage Olympian . . .

Brought up in the kennels of Fife,
He took leave of the hounds and his wife
And a fine saddleroom
To escort, as padgroom,
Colonel Puleston[6] to Emerald-Isle strife.

When the Colonel's black mare was shot dead,
And Sir Richard in sanguinary dread,
Tom Crane braved the fire,
Dashed up to the Squire
With a spare horse, unerringly led.

Serving later as batman in Spain,
And as Guards' Colonel's ostler and thane,
He was rescued from servitude
In a gesture of gratitude
To hunt fox on Peninsular plain.

Thus favoured by gentry and Duke,
Amid arid expanses to snook
After scent of the fox
In dry ravine and rocks:
A freebooting hunt mameluke . . .

His ardour in following the hounds
Oft led him to straits out of bounds,
But he did not retire
Till vedettes opened fire
In alarm at bizarre sights and sounds.

And once, 'mid the desolate plain,
In a lone, Torres Vedras[7] campaign,
He chased a stout fox
Beyond boundary rocks
Into dangerous, enemy terrain.

"Where my fox goes, then there must I go!"
He told the Field-Master, a-glow
With the thrill of the chase,
Brobdingnagian race
After Lilliputian foe.

The hounds killed their fox on French soil,
The French caught their man without moil;
By NCOs dined,
Then loosely confined,
Sent home at dawn, hunt to unroil.

In the field with the Sovereign of France,
Rebuked for o'er-reaching advance,
He alone cleared a hurdle,
Causing blue blood to curdle
And the British to look on askance.

Back home with the foxhounds of Fife,
He devoted the rest of his life
To improving the pack
And restoring the lack
Of foxes where riot ran rife.

His memory lives on to posterity,
Preserving equestrian verity:
A *native companion*,
A gentleman's gentleman,
Embodiment of skill and sincerity.

THE MIGHTY FALLEN

Nobly-visaged and handsomely hootered,
Commanding, assured, though self-tutored;
An iron demi-god
To Peninsular plod
But in hunting field louche, ill-accoutred . . .

He wore a red coat, cutaway,
Lilac waistcoat from ancient Cathay,
And kerseymere breeches
To roll in the ditches,
And Wellington boots to dismay . . .

Haute école and the *Beau Brummel manqué*,
Sartorial cloud over the day;
An inelegant seat,[8]
In advance or retreat,
Though undoubtedly *fortiter in re* . . .

And mighty in meadows of Mars,
A meteor marked out by the stars,
But cutting no dash
With equestrian flash,
Nor as one with his hunting Hussars.

He hunted from *noblesse oblige*,
Hoi polloi and the gentry to please;
To mix with his neighbours
And share in their labours,
And ducal pretensions to ease.

Three or four times a day the Duke tumbled,
A proud man ostensibly humbled;
Full exposure to risk
Being seen to be brisk,
A rough riding seat rudely rumbled.

A FANFARE FOR FOLLY

The character of James Thomas Brudenell,
Until that dramatic event befell
In the Valley of Thunder,
Of blockhead and blunder,
Was that of a military ne'er-do-well.

Promoted from Cornet to Colonel
In eight years of influence paternal,
He was martinet insular
Over officers Peninsular,
Autocratic and less than fraternal . . .

Of countenance highbred and patrician,
Of aquiline cast and volition
As matching his rank:
His eyes blue and frank,
Of seemingly kind disposition . . .

His figure was tall, long of limb,
His bearing, magisterial and prim;
A good riding seat,
Somewhat rigid but neat;
A cavalryman's paradigm.

A quarrel was not far to seek
In a man of his choleric streak;
His Lordship was partial
To frequent courts-martial:
An average of one every week.

LORD CARDIGAN

He ordered seven hundred arrests
In two years, when results of his tests
For conduct and discipline
Fell short of his paladin
Principles and stern manifests.

Instituting a system of spying
And petty, tyrannical prying,
He earned reprimand,
And lost his command
Of the 15th, 'mid censure undying.

His father endeavoured to wring
Another command from the King,
And procured for his son
A post second to none,
By pulling monarchical string.

In command of Prince Albert's Hussars,
Lately back from oriental bazaars,
Lord Cardigan pursued
Every quarrel and feud
He could find in the messes and bars.

His critics got very excited
When, for duelling, the Earl was indicted,
But a court of his peers,
The first for long years,
In collusive acquittal united.

He lavished vast sums on his regiment,
Among cavalry to make it pre-eminent,
But failed to win friends
Or offer amends
For a temper perverse and belligerent.

Though his notions of discipline were rigid,
And relationships with subalterns frigid,
Lord Cardigan was jocular
And generally popular
With ladies and men invalided.

A man of considerable wealth,
He gave away money by stealth,
Seeking no recognition
Or pressing petition
To cushion bad luck or ill health.

At home, in the galloping shires,
With sportsmen and hunting high-fliers,
He enjoyed much esteem,
Strange though it may seem,
As host to the gentry and squires.

In the field of Diana he rode
To daring, disciplinary code,
Every hazard to face
For fear of disgrace,
Courting danger where prudence soft strode.

Charging timber and water at speed,
He was cavalryman without heed,
And twice was near-drowned
In stunts to astound,
And non-swimmer's valorous creed.

His boldness implied immense pluck
Rewarded by suitable luck,
Independent of age
Or brave heritage
And a whiter-than-white dashing buck.

But of cowardice was there a dread?
Or conceit that swift-surged to the head?
An unbending tige,
Self-regarding prestige,
Or disdain of dying in bed?

The war saw his schizoid propensities
Expand to flamboyant immensities;
Adorned like a toucan
He quarrelled with Lucan,
Aggravating their sclerotic densities.

A man with opinions emphatic,
His character was odd, enigmatic;
Cross-grained, unpredictable,
Imperious, intractable,
Irrational and crassly schismatic.

While his men fried or froze in the field,
His own resolution was steeled
In the ease of his yacht:
Haute cuisine and silk cot,
And ladies who'd swooningly yield.

When the High Command order arrived
And Nolan and Lucan contrived
To garble the message,
Was Cardigan's dressage
The only dictate which survived?

Was he totally absorbed in caressing
His pride in immaculate dressing,
Ensuring subordinates
Maintained their co-ordinates,
Refrained from inordinately pressing?

Was it courage or insouciance sublime   CAPT. NOLAN
Which prompted that grim pantomime?
A frontal attack
In the teeth of the pack:
A tactically suicidal crime!

Was there spirited animadversion?
A plea for a flanking diversion?
Was it *noblesse oblige*,
Respect for his Liege
Which prompted that desperate excursion?

Or stoical, unthinking stolidity,
An arrogant, self-vaunting rigidity?
An obsession with form
In the eye of the storm:
An unbending, robotic torpidity?

The horse that he rode in that charge
Posed a nagging conundrum writ large:
Two white legs, two chestnut,
In mutual rebut:
A markedly mixed entourage!

First to reach the Russian redoubt,
Lord Cardigan at once laid about,
And then, in one bound,
Was seen to expound
A new maxim: first in, then first out!

His men he gave leadership none
'Midst the shock and the shell of the gun:
No pausing to rally,
No stirring reveille,
But instinct to keep on the run.

'Neath battlefield grime was there pallor?
Suspicion of imminent *malheur*?
Or a mere *riding huntsman*,
An elegant stuntsman,
Punctilio preferred to mere valour?

Four hundred and fifty men dead,
Five hundred mounts mortally bled;
A vainglorious victory,
A joust valedictory,
A fanfare for folly inbred.

Soon after that memorable charge
Lord Cardigan secured his discharge,
Coming home to acclaim,
To banquets and fame,
A hero's renown to enlarge.

Appointed Inspector of Cavalry
In apparent recognition of chivalry
And prowess in the field,
He proceeded to wield
A braggart's conceit without rivalry.

After fifty years' hunting the fox,
Innumerable injuries and knocks,
Twenty minutes of hell
'Mid a torrent of shell,
He died 'neath his own horse's hocks.

F/M LORD RAGLAN
C-in-C, British Army
in the Crimea

RARE RACING RIOT

The rarest of riot e'er run,
Under grey skies or tropical sun,
Must surely have been
In the hills, blue and green,
Of Neilgherry, by Scottish laird's son.[9]

Early entered to foxhounds in Fife,
Where riot, mostly roe-deer, ran rife,
Mr. Dalyell of Lingo
Knew a cat from a dingo,
Long before the great thrill of his life.

Civil servant in steamy Madras,
With the best of the mandarin class
He abandoned the plain
For the cooler terrain,
Of the hills, in the summer *impasse.*

There he hunted for three days a week
With an ex-Pytchley draft at its peak,
Substituting the jackal
Where the land seemed to lack all
Sign of the alopex clique.

On that plateau some twenty miles square,
In the cool of the high mountain air,
The hounds made their name,
Earning undying fame
In a contest defying compare.

The pack, which had had a good run,
Killing jackal, contrived to outrun
The whole of the field
Save two, in that weald
Of lush upland and bright summer sun.

Of a sudden from coppice came dashing,
Ferocious, blood-thirsting, teeth gnashing,
A fully-grown leopard,
Buff coat blackly peppered,
Razor claws, crushing jaws, whip-tail lashing.

The foxhounds at once gave pursuit,
Ire raised by the strength of the brute,
Without hesitation
Maintaining their station
At the heels of the shaven hirsuit.

The leopard, unused to attack,
Pursued an irresolute track,
Lacking victim ahead,
Being quarry instead,
With foe at his flank and his back.

Eventually the hounds rolled him over,
White side up in the grass and the clover,
But, excitedly yapping
And darting and snapping,
They failed to dispatch the tough rover.

The animal's impenetrable hide
The foxhounds' incisors defied,
But the cat, lashing out,
Fetched them many a clout
And a deep laceration beside.

Thirteen couple all strove to attack
But the pard drove them steadily back,
Not accepting defeat
But, regaining his feet,
Defying the impudent pack.

Once more the hounds took up the chase,
Their galloping foe to outpace,
And to corner their prey
'Neath a rock, in a bay
By a stream, the cat there to abase.

Then seven stone of sinew and muscle
Resumed the sanguinary tussle,
Inflicting more wounds
On the tenacious hounds,
In that marathon melée and justle.

The hounds, in full voice, braved the thrashing,
Gamely suffered the scoring and gashing,
Their number preventing
Any fatal tormenting,
Their courage undimmed, bravely dashing.

The huntsman and field joined the two
Who had witnessed the bloody *ragout*:
Tried to whip off the pack
And conclude the attack
But the hounds just ignored their *halloo*.

Then a rider rode up with a rifle:
No sportsman with niceties to trifle;
With bullet to head
He shot the cat dead,
Succeeding the *fracas* to stifle.

On the instant the foxhounds were still,
Of a sudden, the atmosphere chill:
No whisper disturbing
Nor gun-smoke acerbing
The air; nor ripple on rill.

Then the pack, as of single accord,
Turned and trotted from blood-speckled sward
In silent contempt
At a victory pre-empt,
The summary execution abhorred.

The leopard skin, richly rosetted,
Was stuffed and the incident gazetted;
The hounds were restored
By prolonged bed and board:
Celebrated, exhibited and fêted.

NOTES ON CHAPTER TWELVE

1. The incident occurred in September, 1725, at Fontainebleau with Louis XV.

2. The nilgai or nylghau is a large, short-horned Indian antelope the adult male being of a bluish or iron-grey colour. The head is long and pointed and the forelegs longer than the hinde pair. Height at shoulder averages 4' 6". Prester described the blue deer as being very fast and not unlike the wild, red deer of Exmoor which he had hunted with the Devon and Somerse Staghounds from Dulverton.

3. The Castlebar Races was the derisory description given to hasty cavalry retreat before the French under General Josep Humbert in County Mayo on August 29, 1798. Lord Lake recently appointed to the command, arrived to see the rout of troops under General Hely-Hutchinson. Ever afterwards he wa wont to compare any military setback as "worse tha Castlebar". Lake retrieved the situation by compelling the French to surrender at Ballinamuck on September 8. The following year Lord Lake became Commander-in-Chief, India While training the Bengal army from Cawnpore in the col weather of 1802-3, he joined in hunting tigers, wolves, jackal and game in the open country round the ruined city of Kanau He shot a large tiger about to spring on Major Naime who ha speared it. The general entertained his officers lavishly.

4. Tory Hill lies at the southern end of the county.

5. Jem Hastings ran with the Fitzhardinge Hunt for twenty-five years.

6. Lt.Col. Sir Richard Puleston, CO Ancient British Fencibles 1798.

7. Torres Vedras, 27m. NW of Lisbon, a much-fortified town i the Peninsula, was successfully defended by Wellington a yea before the incident.

8. Napoleon, too, had a slouching seat, made worse by short leg and a heavy paunch.

9. The incident occurred on June 22, 1869.

Brief Lives

APPERLEY, Charles James, pseud. *Nimrod* (1778-1843) was the second son of Thomas Apperley of Plasgronow, Denbighshire, scholar, author and friend of Dr. Johnson. The young *Nimrod* rode to hounds before he was twelve years of age, when his father was tutor to the then Sir Watkin Williams Wynn. His two sons were educated at Rugby in the beer-drinking days forty years before the advent of the reforming Dr. Thomas Arnold. In 1798 Charles Apperley went to Ireland with the local regiment of yeomanry and rose from cornet to first lieutenant in less than eighteen months, so heavy were the losses of his regiment in the bloody battles with the United Irishmen. Aged twenty-two, he married a second cousin of Sir Watkin. She brought with her a dowry sufficient to set him up as a country gentleman at Hinckley, Leicestershire. There he first rode with the Quorn under Hugo Meynell. He and his wife soon moved to Bilton Hall, near Rugby, within range of the Quorn, the Pytchley and the then Warwickshire Hunt. To supplement their income, Apperley sold horses he had trained as hunters. He was a presentable young man with a slender figure and handsome features. He had an attractive personality: intelligent, percipient, good-humoured and obliging. He was a bold and successful rider on the Turf and in the hunting field. His growing family soon proved to be a strain on his resources and, to reduce expenses, he moved to Bitterly Court, Salop. Not until 1822, from Brewood, Staffs., did he begin his career in sporting journalism with an article on foxhunting in the *Sporting Magazine*. The editor at once took him on the staff and provided three first-rate hunters and a groom to establish his credentials in the hunting field. His despatches tripled the circulation of the magazine and his earnings and expenses rose to exceed £3,000 p.a. at their peak. He was universally recognised as an authority and fine judge of horse, hound and hunt. Master and field were on their mettle when he was out. He was courteous in person and in print, generous with praise and temperate with criticism. He came to exercise much influence in the sport as well as providing entertaining reading. However, when his friend, the editor of the *Sporting Magazine*, died, in 1830, Apperley was pressed to repay several big loans. Unable to do so, he decamped to Calais, and later joined that other fugitive from creditors, his friend John Mytton. He did not return for twelve years, by which time most of his creditors were dead. When Ackerman's, the print sellers, started a rival paper, the *Sporting Review*, Apperley was taken on but failed to match his former brilliance. However, in 1838 he was asked to write for the *Quarterly Review* and his essays on the Turf, the chase and the road were considered outstanding. Once more, his earnings shot up. He died in his sixty-fifth year at his home in Belgrave Square, London, leaving sons and grandsons to carry on his distinguished equestrian tradition.

ARSCOTT, John (1718-88) of Tetcott, near Holsworthy, West Devon, was a rumbustious hunter before the Lord, in the wild, moorland country of the Holsworthy and Broadbury of the eighteenth century. According to the famous ballad, *The Hunting of Arscott of Tetcott* (1752), Arscott, in a furious chase from Pencarrow through Whitstone, Poundstock and St. Gennys to Penkenner, led the hunt over the cliff to the ocean five hundred feet below. In fact the fox and hounds went over the cliff, a sheer drop, flanked by a deep fissure on one side and Crackington Cove on the other, but the hunt drew up in time. The superstition that Arscott and his hunt still rode in ghostly riot on stormy nights persisted into the last century. Crossing, in his *One Hundred Years on Dartmoor*, states that Arscott kept no fewer than three packs of hounds: harriers, foxhounds and staghounds, in the untamed country, scarcely separate from Dartmoor. The local fox, a version of the Dartmoor greyhound fox, was known as the *Broadbury Tiger* and, uniquely, had the stoutness and stamina to survive in the hostile climate. An aged retainer claimed that Arscott also kept a pack of foumart hounds which he hunted by night. R.S. Hawker says Arscott was almost the last of the jovial, open-hearted squires of the remote West, and Black John, the last of the jesters, entertaining the company after dinner with droll stories and party tricks as the punchbowl freely circulated. Arscott was "Chinese" in his regard for amphibia, bats and birds and fed them with his own hand, "living like Adam in the Garden, surrounded by animals and pets." The Rev. Paul W. Molesworth, a rector of Tetcott in the last century, related that the last John Arscott of Tetcott was benevolent to children and a generous host, keeping open house. Though he followed the chase avidly, he was kind to dumb animals.

ATKINSON, the Rev. Charles (1833-1912), rector of Harswell, East Riding, was a keen rider to hounds, with good hands and a firm seat. At first he rode with the Holderness but on the death of his father, in 1880, he became rector of Kirby Sigston, North Riding and hunted the Hurworth country where he was equally popular for twenty years. When his cousin, Mrs. Slingsby of Scriven, died in 1901 he succeeded to the Slingsby estates, near Knaresborough, and assumed the name and the arms of Slingsby. From Scriven he rode with the York and Ainsty and sometimes with the Bedale or the Bramham Moor. Like his ill-fated kinsman, Sir Charles, he met his end in the field, though on dry land. Still enthusiastic but frail in his eightieth year, he died on November 15, 1912, when his horse made a peck and threw him forward and he broke his neck. Barely ten minutes before the accident he confided to Mr. Harry Preston of Moreby that he wished to meet his end in the hunting field when the call came. He was on his own estate near Red House when the accident happened. His funeral was attended by hunting folk from all Yorkshire and beyond, as well as by his own cloth. The Archbishop of York, Dr. Cosmo Gordon Lang, when dedicating a window to his memory at Nun Monkton church, said hunting was a sport which developed some of the finest qualities of human nature, namely courage, stamina, a readiness to take risks, comradeship and courtesy.

BARING GOULD, the Rev. Sabine (1834-1924) was educated at Clare College, Cambridge, and became rector of Lew Trenchard, West Devon, after assistant curacies in Yorkshire and elsewhere. He was a prolific novelist and a folklorist and antiquarian who corresponded widely to glean anecdotes and songs of country life. Over the hall fireplace at Lew Trenchard is carved a representation of an Elizabethan foxhunt. As to hunting parsons he opined: "Why not? . . A more fresh, invigorating pursuit is not to be found, not one in which he is brought more in contact with his fellow-men. There was a breezy goodness about many a hunting parson of the old times that was, in itself, a sermon and was one on the topic that healthy amusement and Christianity go excellently well together. Now the unfortunate thing is that the English clergy of the new epoch do seem to have been ordained because they are feeble and effeminate youths . . . thrust into the society of pious and feeble women and contract feeble and womanish ways . . . Ordination becomes a pledge of effeminacy . . . It would be a wholesome corrective if they could go after the hounds occasionally." Baring Gould had personal experience of the love "by the genuine Englishman" of all social classes for the hunt and for sport above all else . . "Let agitators come," he wrote, more than a century ago, "and storm and denounce in the midst of our people: they cannot rouse them to fury against the gentry because they and the gentry run after the hounds together, enjoy a hunt together and are the best of friends in the field. No, the great socialistic revolution will not take place till the hunt is abolished."

BASSET, Col. (d.1802) of Watermouth, a romantic creek on the North Devon coast near Ilfracombe, was Master of the Devon and Somerset Staghounds, 1775-84 and 1794-1801. Major, later Colonel Basset, was the first Master who was not a grantee of the Forest of Exmoor or a holder of the office of Ranger. He took over again on the death of Sir Thomas Dyke Acland in May, 1794. Col. Basset killed one hundred and twenty-four deer between then and 1801 when ill-health obliged him to relinquish office. The riotous mood of the pack in 1794 might have arisen from the lack of spring hind hunting because of the death of Sir Thomas. After the twelve couple were despatched, six couple of puppies were entered to restore the ranks. Sir Thomas had experienced sheep-killing in October, 1789, when drawing the Shillets with the pack. He told the huntsman to hang the lot and then himself but his anger was soon appeased by a fast run from Hawkcombe ending with a kill at Exford. Collyns commented more than once on the folly of drawing with the whole pack and blamed the Master of the day for permitting it. Col. Basset was again vexed by sheep-killing in the spring of 1795. He hanged three of the culprits and a buckhound from the New Forest believed to have been the ringleader. Among many vicissitudes the Master experienced was distemper in 1799 which reduced the pack to ten couples for the first stag meet at Porlock in August. The next year the pack was reinforced by several large foxhounds from different kennels.

BASTARD, Mr. Baldwin John Pollexfen of Kitley, South Devon: (d.1905), was descended from an illegitimate son of a Duke of Brittany, whose offspring came over with the Conqueror. As a young man he served in the 9th Regt. of Foot and fought in the Crimea. He succeeded to the family estates on the death of his brother. Kitley (7,557 acres with a gross estimated rental in 1871 of £11,221) was built of Devon granite at the head of one of the Yealm estuary's creeks, amid timbered parkland. It was acquired when the third William Bastard of Gerston married Anne Pollexfen, heiress to the estate, c1690.

BECKFORD, Peter (1740-1811) was the son of Julines Beckford of Stepleton, Dorset, and grandson of Peter Beckford, Governor and C-in-C of Jamaica. He was educated at Westminster School and New College, Oxford, where he was a contemporary of William Somervile, author of the celebrated poem *The Chace*. His education was thorough for it was said of him he could "bag a fox in Greek, find a hare in Latin, inspect his kennels in Italian and direct the economy of his stable in exquisite French." His famous book, *Thoughts Upon Hare and Foxhunting*, first published in 1781, has remained a sporting classic to this day, being the first treatise on hunting to combine science and literary talent. He was elected a Member of Parliament for Morpeth in 1768 but when he gave up politics and retired to Dorset his wife, Louisa (daughter of Lord Rivers) whom he married in 1773, sadly missed the gaiety of the London scene with its opportunities for flirtatious romances. She pined away while her husband threw himself into the joys of field sport. He believed in the conservation of foxes and held that no good country should be hunted after February.

He recommended rearing foxes in captivity and releasing them like pheasant poults. He maintained that foxhunting had become the recreation of gentlemen and no gentleman should be ashamed of it. Hunting was the soul of country life: it gave health to the body and contentment to the mind. Unfortunately, his wife thought otherwise. She was bored by country life and found her husband's visitors to be stupid, insensitive bumpkins and their wives, domestic and virtuous. Her paramour, William Beckford, was a cousin of her husband and a son of Alderman Beckford, a Lord Mayor of London famous for defying the King. Jorrocks thought he should have been displaced from his monumental perch in Guildhall in favour of Peter. The alderman left his son a million pounds at age twenty-one. After a Continental tour and publication of a novel, *Vathek,* written in French in three days and two nights, William set about designing Fonthill Abbey, a folly on a grand scale, with the help of Wyatt, the architect credited with despoiling much of Salisbury Cathedral. Work started in 1796 and went on for some years. In the form of a cross, the abbey had a huge Gothic tower at the centre. In 1823 William sold the abbey to John Farquharson for a third of a million pounds and moved to Bath. His affair with Louisa drove him to a state of delirium. The scandal and his wife's state of health obliged her husband, Peter, to take her abroad where Louisa died, in Florence, aged thirty-five, after a long illness. Beckford spent nearly twenty years in Italy and was acquainted with Sterne, Rousseau, Voltaire and Cardinal de Bernis. Peter Beckford published a book on Italy, *Familiar Letters . . to a Friend in England.*

BERKELEY, the Hon. George Charles Grantley Fitzhardinge (1800-81) was the sixth son of the Fifth Earl of Berkeley, and a godson of the Prince of Wales, later King George the Fourth. He was educated at Sandhurst and gained a commission in the Coldstream Guards, aged sixteen, resigning in his twenties for a life of sport, journalism and authorship. He was six feet, two inches tall, and weighed thirteen stone. He was also a pugilist with a somewhat sensitive sense of personal honour. He was MFH of the Oakley, 1829-34, stepping into the breach when the Marquis of Tavistock gave up from ill-health. Berkeley provided his own kennels at Harrold and built up a pack of hounds on a subscription of only £1,000 a year. He felt he owed little to the hunt subscribers and they, with the exception of the farmers, resented him as an outsider, though he took over as a result of their inaction. Berkeley was an M.P. for Gloucestershire (1832-52) under his brother's uncertain patronage, and an all-round sportsman. He was in advance of his times in the humane treatment of animals but opposed a Parliamentary Bill prohibiting the use of dogs as draught animals. Berkeley left Harrold Hall with a heavy heart. Despite unfair treatment it was the happiest time of his huntsman's life.

BISSET, Mordaunt Fenwick (1824-84) was the leading figure among those stalwart stag hunters who rescued the Devon and Somerset Hunt from its semi-moribund condition in the mid-Eighties and built it up by diligence and industry to rank almost as a national institution. He was Master from 1855-81. He married the heiress of the Pophams of Bagborough and took up residence near the Devon and Somerset border. His Mastership opened a new era. By tact, good management and ample means he won over the local farmers and residents, rooted out poaching and sheep-killing and restored the reputation and the fortunes of the hunt. Though a heavy man who frequently had to pay three hundred guineas for a horse able to carry him over the hilly country, he was always in front with the hounds and had the presence and authority to command the field, whatever the situation. When he resigned in 1881 to take his seat in the House of Commons, he presented his hounds to Lord Ebrington, who succeeded him as Master, and also handed over the kennels, stables and dwellings which he had built in the centre of the country at Exford. He made generous provision in his will for leasing the land on favourable terms. Mr. Bisset had been persuaded, rather against his will, to contest the West Somerset seat in the Conservative interest and found House of Commons life not to his taste, after a quarter of a century in the bracing air of the open moor. He died aged sixty.

BOOTHBY, Mr. Thomas (1677-1752) of Tooley Park, Leicestershire, was a Master of Foxhounds for fifty-five years between 1696 and 1751. He hunted over a part of the Quorn country with what was claimed to be the first regular pack in England. Little is known about his hunting establishment but the *Gentleman's Magazine* for August, 1752, recording his death, described him as one of the greatest sportsmen in England. Boothby was a son of lady Corbett by her first husband. They lived at Tooley Park from about 1648. Mr. Boothby married a Miss Scrimshire, an heiress. His son, who predeceased him, had a daughter, Anne, who married, as his second wife, Mr. Hugo Meynell who succeeded Thomas Boothby as Master.

BOWER, the Rev. John (1800-59) rector of Barmston, East Riding, was a rider of great determination, which he needed to be to succeed in a country like the Holderness on a poor horse. The Hon. F. Lawley described him as "lion-hearted" and said the cleric was seen at his best when he drove his horse at a drain which, in the Holderness country, appeared suicidal to any visitor. His face seemed always to bear the grim reality of a soldier's facing certain death. Captain Frank Reynard recalled that one of Mr. Bower's finest performances took place when he was chasing a poacher and his lurcher. His horse was exhausted and stuck fast in a drain at Barmston. He borrowed a four-year-old plough-horse, in working gear, with collar and chains, and rode her, after loosing the lurcher to find his master, bare-backed, neatly jumping the mare over her fences and running the offender down in a very short distance.

BRUMMELL, Captain George Bryan (1778-1840), English dandy and man-about-town was the recognised arbiter of male elegance. His father was private secretary to Lord North. George, known as *Beau* for his fastidious dress sense, after education at Eton and Oxford, became a crony of the Prince of Wales on the strength of his repartee. He was commissioned into the Prince's Own Regiment in 1794, leaving as a captain four years later. In the hunting field he was disinclined to risk soiling his clothes. Fellow riders joked privately that his heavy perfume obliterated the scent of the fox. Dick Christian, the rough-rider who always spoke his mind, said Brummell "couldn't ride for toffee". When Brummell, beautifully turned out, tried to keep up with the flying Quorn one day he finished in Sysonby brook. Brummell squandered a fortune of £30,000 and fled to France to escape his creditors. He died there in a charitable asylum.

CARDIGAN, James Thomas Brudenell, 7th Earl of (1797-1868), son of the 6th Earl, was descended from Thomas Brudenell, a strong supporter of the Royalist cause in the civil war. When Charles I was in captivity at Carisbrooke Castle on the Isle of Wight, Thomas Brudenell made him a loan of a thousand pounds which the King promised to repay as soon as he could by conferring an earldom. However, Charles I lost his head before he could make good his promise and his son, Charles II, after his proclamation, conferred the title of Earl of Cardigan, at the same time extracting another thousand. The Brudenells had resided at Deene in Northamptonshire since the sixteenth century when Sir Robert Brudenell, chief justice of the common pleas and a privy councillor under Henry VIII acquired the property. The 7th Earl, of Crimean fame, was born at Hampledon, Hants., and educated at Harrow and Christ Church, Oxford. He entered Parliament in 1818 and joined the army as an elderly cornet in 1824 in the 8th Hussars, rising by purchase within eight years to be lieutenant-colonel in the 15th Hussars. His harsh discipline and overbearing manner led to seven hundred arrests and a hundred courts-marshal within two years in a regiment of only three hundred and fifty men. Like Charles I and his belief in the divine right of kings, Cardigan believed that aristocratic rank and wealth gave him unfettered rights over his tenant farmers and absolute rule over the officers and men under his command. On the other hand he affected a rigid obedience to orders from his military superiors (with the notable exception of his brother-in-law,

Lord Lucan, whom he regarded with contempt), and spent hugely on horses and equipage for his regiment from his own pocket. Cardigan was the embodiment of despotic feudalism and arrogant *droit de seigneur*. The senior army appointments which placed Lucan one notch above Cardigan, in charge of both heavy and light cavalry, demonstrated the preference of the times for social rank before ability and experience. Neither Lucan nor Cardigan had combat experience. The benign incompetence of Lord Raglan, the C-in-C, and his HQ staff in the field, contrasted sharply with the unquestioning loyalty and bravery of the rank and file soldier under appalling conditions of service. Cardigan's running feud with Lucan was a prime factor in precipitating the ill-fated charge. Each man was irascible to the point of explosive fury and each was tactically inept in the deployment of cavalry in war, although Cardigan immediately grasped the suicidal nature of the garbled order conveyed by the impatient and excitable Captain Nolan and given by Lucan. Cardigan's stiff-necked conception of duty, honour, rank and caste, coupled with overweening vanity, drove him "into the jaws of death" though, miraculously, he himself survived. If Cardigan was afraid of anything, it was of being thought a coward. It drove him to recklessness, even in the hunting fields of the Shires where all but the fanatic, faced with a hazardous jump, preferred discretion to valour and went round by the gate. Cardigan was so jealous of his honour and so afraid of disgrace that he took quite unnecessary risks in leaping dangerous obstacles and plunging into fast-flowing water, although he could not swim. At the age of seventy he insisted on mounting a dangerously fractious horse he would not have allowed a friend to ride. As Whyte-Melville said, "The foundation of his whole character was valour: he loved it, he prized it, he admired it in others; he was conscious and proud of it in himself."

CAREW, Sir Walter Palk, Bart. (1807-74) of Haccombe House on the south bank of the river Teign, three miles from Newton Abbot, and of Marley, near Brent, had kennels at both seats. He was the third Master of the South Devon (1829-43) and a landowner and sportsman of the highest repute, renowned for taking the best line across a country. His motto was *Animo non Astutia*. After giving up the South Devon he became a notable rider in the Shires. He was also a good shot, a yachtsman and a respected team driver.

CATTELL, Jonas, took charge of the Gloucester Club pack in 1796. His knowledge of the country and of the fox's habitat enabled him to take short cuts and keep up with the hunt. He was always on hand to help hounds recover a line. He once stuck to the line of a stout red fox long after the hunt had given up and was present for the kill by two leading hounds under a full moon at midnight. He sold the pelt for a handsome three dollars. On the North American continent the red fox usually ran farther than the grey, often leading a pack all day until dusk fell, affording escape. Some old red foxes became renowned characters whose stratagems were much discussed where men gathered in court houses, clubs and churchyards. The grey fox tended to stick to home ground in a wide circuit. Cattell's hunting gear contrasted totally with that of the typical English hunt servant of the day. He wore a flannel shirt, a coarse, home-spun suit under a linen hunting smock, a woollen hat and fishermen's boots with canvas overalls as protection from bushes and thorns. Sometimes he ran, gun in hand and tomahawk in belt, like a frontiersman of former days.

CHAFIN, the Rev. William (1733-1818) of Chettle, North East Dorset, described as "a man mad upon sport", was the eleventh and last child of George Chafin and Elizabeth, a daughter of Sir Anthony Sturt of Horton. He was a classics scholar at Emmanuel College, Cambridge, and after taking holy orders became Rector of Lydlinch, of which his father was patron. Hunting was a family tradition and William's father and grandfather were Rangers before him. The Chafins acquired Chettle House, near Blandford Forum, about 1574. William inherited in 1776 and remained there until his death, caused by being struck by lightning a year before. He devoted his life to sport. For rabbits he kept a small pack of beagles, twelve to fourteen inches in height, which he carried to field in panniers on his own horse. The office of Ranger was held by a noble or gentleman. He supervised the keepers and foresters and within the bounds of the Chase had rights over all game, woodlands and pasture. Not even the landowners were allowed to kill game without his permission and he once demonstrated his authority by shooting the dog of a neighbour's servant who was out with a gun. The Chase was bordered by the rivers Nadder, Avon, Crane, Allen and Stour. It was partitioned into eight walks. Before 1600 it was held by the sovereign or one of his close relatives but James I severed the royal prerogative when he gave it to Robert Cecil whom he created Viscount Cranborne and later, Earl of Salisbury. Then the Lordship and franchise became a property to be bought and sold. Although the Ranger and his agents and keepers protected his rights, poaching was common and families were brought up in the tradition of deer-stealing. The standard fine was thirty pounds and many people were prepared to pay it, if caught, and repeat the adventure the following night. When Parliament decreed that a second offence be a felony, the penalty was much more severe. Hutchins, in his *History of Dorset,* wrote that the nocturnal amusement of deer "hunting" was not considered a disgrace among the local population. Many otherwise respectable persons were engaged in it and some ingenious hiding places were devised to conceal the carcasses. Fights between keepers and poachers with hanger and quarterstaff were not uncommon. William Chafin had considered views on the question of cruelty to animals. Cockfighting, deemed to be barbarous and cruel even in his day, he believed to be the least cruel of any diversion then in vogue (c.1816) and not on a par with horseracing in which animals were forced to perform beyond their strength by whips and spurs. Cockfighting was not against nature but the indulgence of natural propensities since cocks fully at liberty would seek each other out for battle. Similarly, a duellist met his opponent voluntarily and with artificial weapons but a pugilist was urged to fight for money or vainglory and was beaten to the point of death to amuse a crowd of insensitive spectators. Shooting, too, might be deemed cruel unless practised by unerring marksmen or "dead shots". If not killed outright, a wounded animal might suffer pain for a long time. Hunting and coursing might be cruel but it could not be known by human beings how far the cruelty extended. What an animal felt when being chased was unknown but the feeling was of short duration and decisively ended without afterfeelings. Chafin held that hounds and greyhounds were bred for the pursuit of their respective game and guided by natural instinct without restraint. There was no compulsion on their movements. The chase was an indulgence of their natural propensities whereas, on a race-course, young animals were obliged by whips and spurs to act against their natural propensities. Horseracing was "the most cruel and inhuman of all diversions."

CHALMERS, Dr. Thomas (1780-1847) of Anstruther, Fife, was a student of mathematics at St. Andrews at the age of eleven. In 1799 he was licensed as a preacher of the Gospel and in 1803 he was ordained minister of Kilmany but continued to lecture at University. His mathematical lectures were so popular that the authorities banned them for causing disruption of routine. He became famous for the enthusiasm of his ministry and for his writings on religion and economics. At Tron Church in Glasgow his preaching further enhanced his reputation. When he visited London, Wilberforce declared, "All the world is wild about Dr. Chalmers." In Glasgow his experiments in parochial organization and education made a great impact and he reduced municipal expenditure on the poor in one parish by eighty per cent in four years. In 1823 he accepted a chair in moral philosophy at St. Andrews but transferred to the chair of theology in Edinburgh in 1828. Chalmers held that good economic conditions were dependent on the right moral condition of the masses. As a political economist he pointed out the close connection between soil fertility and the prosperity of the community. Thus, he saw a clear economic advantage of the hunt to the locality, though he pictured the members as having "a certain dash of moral outlawry" and "an air of recklessness", all of which the Fife hunt chronicler denied as being out of date. In fact Dr. Chalmers was sixty years ahead of the Wee Free Kirk but in the 1840s stood at the apex of the movement for disestablishment and spiritual freedom, becoming first moderator of the Free Church of Scotland.

CHARLTON, Mr. Nicolas John (1847-92) of Chilwell, Notts., was never a Master of Hounds but a devoted adherent of the chase who showed fine qualities of horsemanship and fieldcraft and was a staunch supporter of the Belvoir. As a child he was a timid rider, describing his pony as an "evil beast", but later he became a bold rider and jumper who could ride well on a poor mount and brilliantly on a good one, when he appeared to *glide* over a country. At Eton and Cambridge he made friends with many young men destined to become distinguished Masters. An injured hand prevented service in the cavalry but he commanded a troop of the South Notts. Yeomanry for many years. Nicolas Charlton married, as his second wife, the Hon. Helen Scarlett, second daughter of General Lord Abinger.

CHEAPE, Mrs. Maude Mary (1853-1919) of Bentley Manor, Redditch, Worcestershire and of Grosvenor Place, London, was the daughter of Mr. Richard Hemming of Bentley, Worcs., Haselor, Warwickshire, and Glaschorrie, Perthshire. She was born amid a severe snowstorm in December, 1853, at Bentley. She was blooded by William Mawe, huntsman to the Worcestershire foxhounds about 1860, having begun her sporting career on a pony at an early age. She took an active part in hunting and breeding all her life and was widely known as a spirited but refined sporting rider. She married Col. G.C. Cheape, Master of the Western part of the Fife country when Col. Anstruther Thomson was hunting the remainder. The marriage took place in June, 1873, in Mull, for which place she held a life-long affection. Later Col. Cheape was Master of the Linlithgow Hounds (1887-89). He was obliged to go abroad in 1889 so Mrs. Cheape assumed command. Earlier she had formed her own pack of beagles. In 1891, on the death of her father, she inherited the Bentley estate and took up residence there and showed good sport with her pack for many years. She bred polo and Highland ponies and cattle on the Isle of Mull and had a famous herd of long-horned cattle. Mrs. Cheape was a cultured and generous woman who took pleasure in helping others. Her sons and daughters were brought up to be skilled and knowledgeable riders and to them she was mother, friend and riding master. By 1919 only two survived: Brigadier-General Ronald Cheape, CMG, DSO, MC., and "Maudie", Mrs. W.H.M. Ellis, who chronicled her mother's eventful life. Three offspring were drowned and one shot in the war.

CHUTE, William John, M.P. was Master of the Vine Hunt for more than thirty seasons. He was not considered to be a good horseman but was a good breeder of hounds. He took over the pack when his father died in 1790 and carried on until he himself died in 1824. He was a man of ready wit and was staunchly supported by members of the Vine, many of whom were rich and unbeneficed clergy, riding in black coats and white stocks.

COKE, William (1793-1874) was the son of Edward Coke of Longford, Derbyshire, a brother of the Norfolk agriculturist who became Earl of Leicester. Sometimes known as Derbyshire Coke, William designed the hard, felt hat which was, for a century, called a billycock. It was manufactured at Derby by a hatter called Bowler: hence its alternative name. Mr. Coke originated the expression used by jealous, hard-riding foxhunters: "The pace is too good to inquire!" When Mr. Greene of Rolleston had just cleared the infamous Whissendine brook and inquired, strictly *en passant*, "Who is that man under his horse in the water?", and Lord Forester replied, "Only Dick Christian, and it's nothing to him!", Lord Kinnaird exclaimed, "But he will be drowned!" Billy Coke chimed in: "I shouldn't wonder but the pace is too good to inquire!". *Nimrod* described Coke as one of the fastest England ever saw. Whyte-Melville recorded that Coke rode nothing but thoroughbreds in the hunting field. No animal less speedy than a race-horse could sustain the pace at which he liked to ride. His hunter, *Advance*, celebrated for being dangerous with his heels in a crowd, was of stainless pedigree. Another horse in his stables was called *December* from being foaled on the last day of the year, a premature arrival that lost him his year for racing purposes by twenty-four hours and transferred the colt to the hunting stables.

COLLYNS, Dr. Charles Palk (1793-1864) of Dulverton, surgeon and author of *Notes on the Chase of the Wild, Red Deer in the Counties of Devon and Somerset*, was a notable authority on wild deer and staghunting on Exmoor. His book, first published in 1862, had a tangential sequel in 1887 when the Hon. John Fortescue's *Records of Staghunting on Exmoor* brought the history of the hunt up to date. Fifteen years later Phillip Evered's *Staghunting with the Devon and Somerset* completed an unplanned and diverse trilogy to satisfy the keenest student of sport on the moor in the nineteenth century and earlier. Dr. Collyns was the youngest son of William Collyns, surgeon of Kenton (sometime home of the South Devon Foxhounds). He was born in September, 1793. His elder brother was destined to succeed to the practice so Charles had to follow his profession elsewhere, after training at St. Bartholomews and the Royal Devon and Exeter Hospital. He settled at Dulverton in 1814. While courting Miss Anne Moore of Spreydon House, Broad Clyst, he once covered ninety-six miles in the saddle in one day. He did a round of twenty miles, visiting country patients before breakfast, joined hounds at ten o'clock and ran a stag from Burridge Wood to the sea at Countisbury, rode twenty-four miles home, took refreshment and changed into evening clothes, mounted his third horse with pumps in his pocket and rode twenty-eight miles to Exeter for the Devon County Ball. He was in the ballroom soon after ten p.m., perhaps only too keen to ease his limbs on the dance floor. He married in 1816 and had eight children whom he supported and educated entirely on his earnings. He rode frequently to hounds and made a close study of the physiology and ecology of the red deer. His tombstone records that he succoured the poor, promoted welfare and upheld manly pursuits. In his fifty years at Dulverton he knew everyone and everyone knew him. He rode a stalwart bay horse which carried him over the moor on many severe runs but his sport always came second to his "arduous professional duties". However, the "noble and unique sport" was to him a source of gratification and recreation of the highest order. Had Dr. Collyns been alive today, he might well have taken up the study of bone loss in the human frame, pondering on the remarkable facility of the stag to replace horns mewed every year with totally new growth, that is, fourteen pounds of new bone grown in sixteen to eighteen weeks.

COOK, Col. John (1773-1829) was born at Christchurch, Hants., and took a commission in the 28th Light Dragoons. Although of slender means, he managed to spend most of his leisure time in the hunting field. The fruits of his wide experience are to be found in his slim volume, *Observations on Foxhunting*, published in 1822. It is one of the less well-known "classics" on the art and science of the chase but, as Lord Willoughby De Broke remarked a century later, "A modern MFH would do well to follow every word of advice it contains". He also concluded that the book demonstrated how little the essentials of the sport had changed since the battle of Waterloo. John Cook was entered first to hare and he and his pack had earned a reputation before he came of age. In 1800 he became Master of the Thurlow and stayed for four seasons. He married Elizabeth Surtees, a distant relative of Robert Smith Surtees, author of the sporting novels. Surtees quoted two sage remarks from Cook's *Observations* in his jolly burlesque, *Mr. Sponge's Sporting Tour (1853)*. A lack of foxes and of financial support took John Cook back to Hampshire and the Mastership of the Hambledon for three seasons. In 1808 he returned to East Anglia with his own pack as Master of the Essex and remained until 1813. It was here that he made his lasting reputation in the hunting field, not to say too much about the Dunmow dinner table. In

Jack Cole he had a whipper-in of parallel reputation and jocundity. Five years of popular success ended when his money ran out and he had to sell his pack and give up the country at the age of forty. He obtained a military post and again rode to hounds, in Staffordshire, for a while until the needs of a growing family obliged him again to retire from the field and live in France where he wrote his book. He died at Rouen in 1829, aged fifty-six. One can hardly imagine a greater contrast in approach and style between that of the robust Col. Cook and that of his near-contemporary, George Templer of Stover. Cook would have seen Templer, in hunting terms, as a foppish, eccentric aesthete, and Templer might have viewed Cook as a brash, headstrong Philistine. Neither would have been right.

CORBET, John of Sundorne Castle, Shropshire (1752-1817) succeeded John Warde as Master of the Warwickshire Hunt in 1792. Previously he hunted all country North of the Severn. He took his hounds to Stratford-on-Avon, established a hunt club, and had kennels also at Meriden, near Coventry. He lived at Clopton and shared the expenses of his seventy-couple pack with his kinsman, Sir Andrew Corbet. Every fortnight he dined with the club members at the White Lion, Stratford. There they sold horses by handicap at prices as high as seven-hundred and fifty guineas. *Trojan* hunted for eight seasons and his blood became famous at other kennels, so much so that a toast, "The blood of the Trojans", was drunk after the loyal toast at the Stratford hunt club dinners and farther afield. Corbet was a noted breeder and *Trojan* was his favourite. His country was forty miles in length and twenty miles across. His brother, Jack, whipped-in and his huntsman, Will Barrow, had a style all his own, riding with whip and reins in his right hand, and his left arm dangling. Under Corbet, the Warwickshire became a first-rate hunt. He was described as an ideal Master and a perfect gentleman. He was not a hard rider and rarely jumped a fence but he understood hounds and was one of the first Masters to separate his packs by sex. He paid "certain parties" forty pounds a year not to dig out foxes at Wolford Wood for sale as bagmen. In February, 1811, he was obliged to give up the country he had hunted successfully for nearly twenty years by ill health. In 1812 he sold his hounds, numbering seventy couples, to Lord Middleton for twelve hundred guineas. He died in May, 1817, aged sixty-five.

CRANE, Tom, became huntsman to the Fife in 1821 after being huntsman to the Duke of Wellington during the Peninsular campaign. He was a contemporary of *Nimrod* and was entered simultaneously to Sir Richard Puleston's hounds when Crane senior was butler and later steward to the baronet. Like *Nimrod*, Tom Crane accompanied Sir Richard to Ireland in 1798. He was lieutenant-colonel of the Ancient British

Fencibles, a light dragoon regiment raised by Sir Watkin Williams Wynn. Tom went in the humble capacity of a stable servant and later served as a private in Portugal where he became batman to Col. Freemantle of the Coldstream Guards. When a pack of foxhounds arrived, influence was exerted on Crane's behalf and he was made huntsman, enjoying a much elevated status on the Duke's domestic staff. When the Duke gave up the pack, Tom Crane went with them to the new owner, Lord Stewart, with the approbation of Sir Richard Puleston. He was in the field as an amateur, with Lord Stewart, when he so boldly ignored protocol to demonstrate his prowess over high hurdles before Charles X of France. Returning to Fife in 1821, he found the country bare of foxes and with dwindling support. In a country abounding with riot, Crane redoubled his efforts and succeeded in re-establishing the pack. After less than ten years in office, he went to earth in the long frost of 1830 at Cupar. Crane was described as a "super-excellent horseman", although left-handed, and a quick man over a country.

CRESPIGNY, Sir Claude Champion de, Fourth Baronet (1847-1935) of Champion Lodge, Maldon, Essex, exemplified the adventurous, intrepid, Victorian male, constantly testing his own manhood, daring and strength. He served in the Royal Navy (1860-65), on board HMS Warrior, the first ironclad, in 1862. Although very much the *beau sabreur*, he then transferred to the 60th Rifles where he was a soldier-jockey (1866-70) and from then on until his mid-sixties, a gentleman-jockey and steeplechaser, athlete, equestrian, pugilist, swimmer, yachtsman, balloonist and big-game hunter. He won his first steeplechase, aged twenty, beating the redoubtable Bay Middleton by a length, in Ireland during the Fenian troubles. He never won the Grand National. In India (1867-70) he won another race on an unpromising horse at 100-1 and saw for himself "the unrivalled smartness and efficiency of those three superb regiments, Probyn's, Robartes' and Hodgson's Horse" whose disbandment he deplored. Crespigny was blooded with the Essex and Suffolk Hounds at the age of seven. After his marriage in 1872 he lived in the West of Ireland and went hunting in County Clare and punt-shooting on the Shannon. He marvelled at the cleverness of a good horse when his blood was up. Out with the Cheshire hounds in 1870, his mare cleared a five-foot fence with a bound of thirty-one feet, then the second longest jump on record. In 1876 he was presented with the medal of the Royal Humane Society for rescuing a drowning man from the sea at Limerick where he was serving with the Artillery Militia. At various times he was out with the Tedworth, Luttrell, South and West Wilts., Essex, Chiddingfold, Lord Leaconfield's, Lord Radnor's, New Forest, Lord Portman's and the Vine and with the Devon and Somerset and the New Forest Staghounds. He once rode more than a hundred miles in a day and claimed to have walked two thousand miles of London pavement in a year. He was the first man, with a professional, to cross the North Sea in a balloon in 1882, being awarded the gold medal of the Balloon Society the following year. He was a war correspondent up the Nile in 1889 and a volunteer in South Africa in 1900 and in British East Africa in 1905, which service he combined with big-game hunting. He was "a glutton for hard exercise" and kept fit by walking, jogging, the regular use of clubs and dumb-bells, and cold tubs before breakfast. He never believed in shunning danger and thereby soiling the escutcheon of bravery, "the most precious possession of every good Englishman". He admired indifference to danger where a man's honour was at stake. Where there was a daring deed to be done in any part of the world, an Englishman should leap to the front to accomplish it. Crespigny had four sons who carried on his sporting tradition.

CROSS, George, gained a diploma as a veterinary surgeon and was assistant to Professor Dick at the Veterinary College, Edinburgh, before setting up at Monifieth, near Broughty Ferry. The practice failed and he joined John Walker as whipper-in. Later Mr. Whyte-Melville recommended him as huntsman to the Bedale in 1844 and he was there till 1850 when he moved to Atherstone as kennel huntsman and first whip to Col. Anstruther Thomson. When asked by the Master about wages, Cross replied: "I dinna care muckle about wages; gi'e me a bellyfull of hunting!" He was enthusiastic about hounds and made many good crosses and lost few puppies from distemper. In 1855 he went with Col. Thomson from the Atherstone to the Bicester country then, sadly, lost his reason and died in Warwick Asylum.

DALE, T.F., lived at Brush End, Burley, Hants. He wrote for the sporting press under the pseudonym, *Stoneclink*, and was author of several books on foxhunting, including histories of the Belvoir and the Badminton. He was educated at Queen's College, Oxford, and was a retired senior chaplain in Bengal and a steward for the National Pony Society. He died in 1925.

DALYELL, R.A., was the eldest son of Mr. Dalyell of Lingo, a Fife laird who married a sister of Sir Ralph Anstruther and, though a senior member of the Fife, was Master of a neighbouring pack, the Forfarshire hounds, from 1831. Young Dalyell first saw hounds at Burnside in Forfarshire at the age of three and was blooded in Hertfordshire with his father's hounds two years later. George Whyte-Melville had given him a clever Shetland pony in 1836. He was later one of a group of Fife boys who appeared at the East Neuk meets between 1844 and 1850. In 1851 he

joined the civil service at Madras and hunted a scratch pack at Ootacamund
on the Neilgherry Hills in 1853, and at Dopoor, near Bangalore, in 1854.
In 1862 he revived the Madras hunt which had always been the leading
pack in India until it failed in 1856 from want of finance. During his ten
years as Master the annual subscription list sometimes totalled £1,500.
He established the pack on a three-day basis and maintained it during the
close season. The Neilgherry Hills, 5,000 feet above sea level, offered a
plateau of grass about twenty-five miles square which was described as
similar to the Brighton Downs but more dotted with woodlands which
formed excellent coverts. The hottest weather never exceeded the heat of an
Italian summer. The incident on June 22, 1869, was reported in sporting
circles world-wide. All thirteen couples escaped death although
three couples were severely injured. Their number and exceptional courage
and tenacity in the face of a powerful enemy saved their skins. The leopard
was fully-grown and weighed seven stone, four pounds and measured seven
feet. In recognition of the kindness of Col. Anstruther Thomson, then
Master of the Pytchley, in supplying the draft of hounds, he was presented
with the head of the leopard, handsomely mounted.

DAVIES, the Rev. Edward William Lewis, was born in County
Glamorgan and educated at Eton and Jesus College, Oxford, being ordained
priest in 1837. He was vicar of Adlingfleet, Yorkshire, 1852 to 1874, and
rural dean, 1855 to 1874. He resigned and retired to Bath in that year and
is believed to have died there in 1890. His best-known works in relation
to Devon, which he appears to have visited frequently to hunt over
Dartmoor, were *Dartmoor Days* (1863) and *Memoir of the Life of the Rev.
John Russell* (1878). He checked the draft of the latter book with Russell
before he died, adding only the final chapter to record the sad event. In
Dartmoor Days he shows an intimate knowledge of Dartmoor and the
principal riders to hounds. Under his pen-name *Gelert*, identifying his
Welsh origin, he wrote a *Guide to the Hounds of England*, published in
1848, and as *Fores's Guide* in 1850. Davies had a keen eye for local flora
and fauna, was a highly literate hunting parson, and was intimately
concerned with the Teigngrace Cricket Club along with the Rev. Henry
Taylor and George Templer.

DRAPER, Squire William (1671-1746) of Beswick Old Hall, near
Beverley, Yorkshire, first hunted his Holderness pack in 1726. He came
originally from Nether Wooton, Oxfordshire, and married Ann, the only
daughter and heiress of Ingleby Daniels of Beswick. The Squire had
fourteen children. He first hunted the Boroughbridge country and Vale of
York with Edward Thompson, M.P. for York. The Daniels family had
been settled at Beswick for more than two centuries and the Old Hall, a

red-brick country house with mullioned windows, was a typical residence of its time. *The Sporting Register* recorded that Draper "bred, fed and hunted the staunchest pack of foxhounds in Europe" and brought up his family on an income of only £700 a year, kept a stable of excellent hunters and a carriage with horses. He lived in "the old, honest style of his country, killing every month a good ox of his own feeding, and priding himself on maintaining a substantial table but with no foreign kickshaws." His reputation as a Master of Foxhounds attracted guests of high social standing to his house, leading to a good start in life for his children. He was a lively and witty conversationalist and his company was cultivated by neighbouring gentry. In the field he rode with judgement, avoiding what was unnecessary. He helped his hounds only when they needed help. His youngest daughter, Diana or "Miss Di" was whipper-in and the subject of many hearty toasts at hunt dinners. The company drank "October", a local ale brewed since the early 1700s. Squire Draper was said to have been goaded into foxhunting by the widespread destruction of his lambs in the then mostly unenclosed country where foxes were not preserved and were wild and stout, having to travel great distances for food. Hence Squire Draper, known in the field as *General*, and his fellow-riders had some marathon runs, but usually returned triumphant with a brace of brushes. The land in those days was worth two shillings and sixpence an acre. As King's Huntsman for the East Riding, Mr. Draper paid his respects at Court annually, possibly wearing something more suitable than his habitual drab hunting coat and belt, in which he looked so shabby that a visiting male milliner from Beverley once mistook him for an ostler and offered him two-pence to hold his horse, a fee which the Squire insisted on having even after the mistake was discovered. The Squire died of a seizure in August, 1746, at Market Weighton. He was interred at Market Weighton where tombstones at the east end of the church record his death on August 18; that of his youngest daughter, Diana, in April 1772, aged fifty-six; and that of his second daughter, Anne, in October, 1776, aged seventy-five.

DUNTZE, Sir John Lewis of Exeleigh, Starcross, South Devon, was Joint Master with Sir Lawrence Palk of the Haldon side of the South Devon (1878-82). A landowner with eight hundred and fifty acres, he was the son of a wealthy, Exeter wool merchant and banker, and popular with all classes. He hunted in the Badminton country for many seasons before his semi-retirement to Devon. The duties of field-master fell to Mr. A.E. Palk, second son of Sir Lawrence, later the first Baron Haldon, during his absence. Sir John Duntze built his house close to the entrance of Powderham Park and at the extreme end of the South Devon country. Sir John was distinguished in the field by his low, felt topper and black coat with the Beaufort button. He was somewhat ahead of hunting fashion in using a whistle in preference to a horn. In those days the hunt was supported strongly by local farmers, several of them heavyweights, as well as local residents from many walks of life. There was also a contingent of officers from the RHA at Topsham Barracks, Exeter. Sir John died in 1884.

ELIZABETH, Amélie Eugénie (1837-98), consort of Francis Joseph, Emperor of Austria and King of Hungary, was the second daughter of Duke Maximilian of Bavaria. Her early education included hunting and climbing with her eccentric father. At Possenhofen, the country estate on Lake Starnberg, her father taught her to ride on either side of a horse, without stirrups, to promote balance. Elizabeth, known in the family as "Sisi", was shy and sensitive with people but had instant empathy with a horse. She was beautiful, except for her teeth, and all her life took great pains to preserve her complexion and figure. In 1848 Ferdinand abdicated and Franz Joseph was proclaimed Emperor at the age of eighteen. He fell instantly in love with Elizabeth at first meeting, in Vienna, and married her in 1854 when she was sixteen. She preferred the outdoor life to court ceremonial and affairs of state and spent much time with her horses. She was taught to jump by Holmes, an Englishman, who became her riding companion. She started a hunt at her estate at Gödöllö, eighteen miles from Budapest, under the Mastership of Prince Esterhazy and built up a stable of twenty-six English-bred hunters. She rode well but foxes went to earth all too often in the sandy terrain and much-wooded country and the season lasted only two months. When the Prince of Wales visited the Vienna exhibition of 1873 he kindled her ambition to hunt in England. In 1874 the Empress visited England but declined invitations to dine with Queen Victoria for fear of being bored. She stayed with the Duke of Rutland at Belvoir Castle and met Earl Spencer. A year later she hunted with the Grafton and rode with the Pytchley with Bay Middleton as her pilot. They excelled in the fast, grass country, clearing oxers and bottoms with ease and style. Middleton preceded her through high bullfinches to protect her face from scratches. Hundreds of riders turned out, immaculate in scarlet, to watch the spectacular pair. In his zeal to lead the way, Middleton sometimes over-rode the hounds, earning rebuke from the Master. Elizabeth was popular with the lower orders, especially in Hungary and Ireland, and enjoyed the rustic life, but her absences from home caused resentment. On her silver jubilee, a wit remarked that it celebrated twenty-five years of manège, not ménage. The Empress was fatally stabbed by a publicity-seeking anarchist in Geneva on September 10, 1898. John Welcome, the racing writer, gives a vivid account of her life in his *Sporting Empress*.

ELWES, John (1710-89) son of Mr. Meggot, a prosperous brewer of Southwark, and grandson of Sir George Meggot, M.P. for the borough, was an M.P. for Berkshire in three successive Parliaments. He changed his name to inherit a fortune of some £250,000 from his bachelor uncle, Sir Hervey Elwes, Bart., of Stoke, Suffolk (d.1763). He was educated at Westminster School and in Geneva where the master of the riding academy said he was one of the best three riders in Europe. As heir-designate to his uncle, a miserly hermit, he affected to emulate Sir Hervey's penurious habits and gradually adopted them. He lived off his land and never spent a penny on repairs to his main residence at Marcham, Berks. On the death of his uncle he hunted from Stoke, Suffolk, for fourteen years and kept a stable renowned for fine hunters. He was offered three hundred guineas for one at a time when a good horse could be had for fifteen pounds. His horses were not broken until the age of six. He spent no more than three hundred a year on his foxhunting establishment and it was said that his hounds had to be death-dealing or they would have starved. He left his money equally to his two sons who were the natural off-spring of Elizabeth Moren, a housekeeper at Marcham, but spent nothing on their education, believing that filling their heads would empty their pockets. As regards his hard-worked servant he held that a master who kept one servant had his work done. If he kept two, it was half done and if he kept three, he did it himself. The moral of his whole life was the vanity of wealth.

FARQUHARSON, James John (1784-1871), Squire of Langton, Dorset, was a MFH for fifty-two years (1806-58). His sobriquets included *The Nestor of the Chase,* the *Meynell of the West*, the *Pride of Dorset* and the *First Commoner of Dorset*. His immense wealth made him also *Lord of all he Surveyed.* It enabled him to hunt virtually the whole of the country and to do so entirely at his own expense. Far from being autocratic, he was widely acknowledge to be kind, courteous and considerate to all. Farquharson was the only surviving son of a wealthy East India merchant from the City who bought the manor and adjoining estate on the banks of the Stour in 1775 and left him the bulk of his fortune. After Eton and Christ Church, Oxford, he spent the rest of his active life chasing the fox, managing his estate and playing a prominent role in the county administration. He was friend of the renowned Peter Beckford who lived a few miles away at Stepleton Iwerne. From Beckford he gained his early "thoughts upon hunting". Farquharson kept two hunting establishments, one near his mansion at Langton and the other at Eastbury. He also had a hunting box at Cattistock. At Langton he kept more than thirty hunters, which he bred himself. His seventy-five couples of hounds were "of a large, useful, loping sort", up to twenty-six inches and well adapted to the country with its frequent hills, dingles and boggy bottoms. He was not successful at breeding hounds but was a noted cattle-breeder and agriculturist. He was out every day in the season with his peripatetic pack. A club comprising members and friends of the hunt held regular dinners every month at Dorchester, Blandford, Maiden Newton and elsewhere which the Master often attended. There were sonorous speeches and much toasting. During the twenty-one seasons with James Treadwell, his huntsman from 1837, they killed 1,344 brace of fox. Although Farquharson was universally popular and respected, especially as a MFH, as well as for spending his money in his native county, there were criticisms from time to time that his country was too vast to be hunted effectively by one pack. Anonymous comments of the sort in the sporting papers were dismissed as "peevish, sneaking nonsense." When Surtees visited Dorset in 1835, expecting to find the country "crawling with foxes" and "hounds chopping one every half-hour" in "a mountainous country full of impassable ravines, immense woods and yawning drains" he was readily surprised and dismissed the criticisms. But in 1857 the Blackmoor Vale Hunt, in a requisition signed by only three Dorset men, the rest being from over the border in Somerset, forced the issue and Squire Farquharson resigned at the end of his fifty-second season. He sold his hounds at auction for high prices. Treadwell retired to a cottage and pension provided by his employer. At a farewell banquet in Dorchester he was presented with a silver tankard and a silver hunting horn, each inscribed and finely engraved, and a cheque for £300. His sons carried on the family tradition as huntsmen, John with the Old Berkshire and Charles with the Bramham Moor. Foxhunting in Dorset seems to have been unaffected by the industrial unrest of the 1830s. Langton House and the hunt carried on with their lavish life-style despite agricultural riots, rick-burning and the wrecking of the new, labour-saving threshing machines not far away. Farm workers at Bere Regis, Tolpuddle and elsewhere in the county were paid only seven shillings a week compared with the nationwide average of ten shillings. A clergyman, writing to *The Times* in 1846, complained that the poor in the agricultural counties were sheltered no better than farm animals, and paid wages that kept them in a condition of intermittent pauperism. Their village greens and common rights, including gleaning in the fields, were rapidly being taken from them. At Tolpuddle, an hour's trot from Langton, the six farm labourers instrumental in taking and administering "illegal oaths" were arrested and later transported to Australia. There was another unsuccessful attempt to start a trade union in 1860 but a further attempt in 1872 prospered and boasted nearly one hundred thousand members within a year. It is an idle speculation but if the sums raised for presentations to the Master of the hunt in 1827 and 1856 had been subscribed for improving the pay of the local farm workers, some four hundred labourers could have been advanced to a wage of ten shillings a week for a year.

FROUDE, the Rev. John (1777-1852), Vicar of Knowstone-cum-Molland, Devon (1804-52) was the only son of the Rev. John Froude (1743-1803) and was instituted on his father's death. He was educated at Blundell's and at Exeter College, Oxford. But for his mutual friendship with John Russell and his mutual antagonism with Bishop Phillpotts and, more extraordinarily, the posthumous confusion in the public mind of Froude with the fictitious and wicked Parson Chowne, R.D. Blackmore's character in *The Maid of Sker*, his memory might not have survived so vividly. Undoubtedly he was a hard-riding parson who spent much time and energy on open-air pursuits, as did many of the educated and leisured classes of his day, but there is little evidence that he neglected his clerical duties or was ever apprehended in lawlessness. Although he defied his bishop, he was too wary to offend against the canons of his calling. He seems to have exercised a powerful sense of independence of authority, especially towards the Tory, high church bishop, and to have ruled the men of his parish with a rough tongue. He also indulged in practical jokes and a good deal of horseplay at the expense of his neighbours, but his conduct stopped short of mayhem and arson. Very likely he indulged in sharp practice in the buying and selling of horses. It was not uncommon in his day, even among acquaintances, but it seems that Prebendary Boggis's stricture that, save for baptism, he could hardly be described as a Christian in any sense of the word, was altogether too harsh. He lived in a rugged country in robust times, when the people of North Devon, then remote from civilising influences, were often a law unto themselves. It is often pointed out that if Froude was as black as he was painted, Russell would not have been his friend. Russell hunted with Froude as often as he could and described him as a most original man whose hospitality knew no bounds. Possibly Russell chose his words carefully. Most stories about Froude circulated long after his death. Bishop Phillpotts's own diary confirms his visit to Froude at Knowstone in 1831. The Bishop rapidly retired when told by Froude's housekeeper that her master was in bed with a severe fever, hinting at typhus. Cholera was then raging in Exeter. But Phillpotts noted: "The church good; house fair; in dining-room six fox's brushes, two of them bell-pulls."

GILLARD, Frank was huntsman to the Belvoir for twenty-six years, retiring when the Duke of Rutland resigned the mastership in 1896. He followed the tradition of his notable predecessors, Goosey, Goodall and Cooper, drawing covert as long as daylight lasted, with no regard to the distance from kennels. He was a dapper man, "brisk as a bee in all his movements" and doing a great day's work "because his heart and soul were in it." He was born in Devon in 1838 where his father was a kennel huntsman. First he hunted hare at Monkleigh but in 1859 became second whipper-in to the Hon. Mark Rolle's Stevenstone foxhounds. After one season he joined the Belvoir as second whipper-in, in 1860, for the Sixth Duke who succeeded Lord Forester in 1859. After three seasons he became first whipper-in and continued for four more seasons. In 1867 he became kennel huntsman to John Chaworth Musters with the South Notts. There he spent two happy seasons before migrating with his Master and his pack to the Quorn country. In the spring of 1870 he was released from the Quorn, then under the mastership of Mr. John Coupland, to go to the Belvoir at the express wish of the Duke of Rutland. There he reached the peak of his calling, becoming the fourth in a succession of huntsmen in a little under a hundred years to follow the same system of breeding and the same tradition of fine sport in the field. As the Duke became older and his gout grew worse, he delegated more and more of the hunt administration to Gillard so that he became virtually his own Master with authority over all aspects of the hunt. He controlled the field, supervised the kennels, engaged servants, bought horses, dealt with the finances and correspondence, kept a daily diary and visited the Duke every evening to make a report. When the seventh Duke succeeded as Master in 1888, Gillard was left even further to his own devices because the new Master preferred shooting to hunting. Gillard spent more time in the kennels and, according to Ridley, the historian, neglected the actual hunting, resorting to bagfoxes and other ruses to simulate good sport. The hounds became slack and went home halfway through the day of their own accord. Ridley records that Greenall, who succeeded Gillard in 1896, "inherited an impossible position" and was obliged to resign soon after criticism in the Press. So Cuthbert Bradley's *Reminiscences of Frank Gillard* were, perhaps, a shade eulogistic.

GOODALL, Will (1817-59) was the greatest of a family of great huntsmen, according to *Thormanby*. During his twenty-two years with the Belvoir he rose to the first rank of huntsmen and stood high in the estimation of the best judges of his day. After a spell as second whipper-in to the Bicester, he joined the Belvoir in a similar capacity in 1837 under Lord Forester, becoming huntsman in 1842. Lord Henry Bentinck held Goodall in high esteem. He said Goodall treated his hounds like women, never to be bullied, deceived or neglected. He would not intervene in their casting unless they appealed to him for help. He continually made much of them and, if he had to call them off a promising scent at dusk, he would jump off his horse and spend ten minutes consoling them. His technique was to get to the hearts of his pack. On October 28, 1854, the Belvoir experienced an extraordinary twenty-five minute run without check. Hounds found a brace of foxes in the Becks in Leadenham Park. They went away in parallel towards Broughton but on reaching the Newark Road the brace split left and right, with the pack dividing equally behind them and describing two circles back to the Becks where each fox was killed simultaneously within ten yards of the other. Will Goodall never carried food with him nor did he carry a watch because "my Lord [Forester] always draws until dark." They often had long distances to ride home at night and the toll on Goodall's strength, hunting five days a week, probably shortened his life. In fact he died from the effects of a fall which drove the horn, always carried in the breast of his coat, deep into the chest. As the hearse moved off at his funeral, the hounds set up a deep wailing, "not singing and not chiming", which permeated the crowd attending the last rites. The sound carried over the park to Knipton churchyard where he was buried, just inside the gate. He left a widow and eleven children who were well provided for by the Duke of Rutland, Lord Forester and members of the hunt.

GOOSEY, Thomas, was the first of four successive huntsmen to place the Belvoir in the forefront of English foxhunting. He became a whipper-in in 1796. After twenty years he became huntsman and continued in that post for twenty-six years with distinction until retirement in 1842. He was described as a fine, powerful horseman and a capital huntsman. With hunt servants and hounds he was a stern disciplinarian and although he did not mince words in the field, he always "begged leave" before rebuking a hunt member.

GRAHAM, Sir Reginald Bellingham, Bart., of Netheravon House, Wilts., ruled the Quorn for two seasons (1821-23), punctuating Squire Osbaldeston's two Masterships. He rode with many hunts in his day and hunted the Badsworth, the Atherstone, the Pytchley and the Hambledon. As Master of the Quorn he received the largest subscription ever collected: over £4,000. He was a heavyweight but kept up with the best and had the finest collection of big horses ever seen. He showed good sport but resigned in 1823 after a serious fall, though he escaped with bruises only.

HALDON, Lord (1818-83) of Haldon House, Devon, was the first baron of that name and was elevated in 1880. He was previously Sir Lawrence Palk, the fourth baronet, a major landowner of more than ten thousand acres and an M.P. As Sir Lawrence Palk he was joint Master, with Sir John Duntze, of the Haldon division of the South Devon Hunt, from 1878 to 1882, though obliged by ill-health during his last two seasons to delegate responsibility in the field to his second son, Mr. E.A. Palk. In his early days, Sir Lawrence hunted from Melton, for seven seasons, like his father before him, who was described by *Nimrod* as one of the crack riders of England. The first Lord Haldon was also a keen shot, a skilled team-driver and an enthusiastic yachtsman, owning two boats. He built the outer harbour at Torquay, at a cost of £70,000, making the town one of the best yachting stations on the south coast. The family fortune derived from his great-grandfather, Sir Robert Palk, who was Governor of Madras and amassed a great fortune while in India. He was created first baronet in 1772. He bought the estate and manor on Haldon. He died in 1792. His only son, Sir Lawrence Palk, became M.P. for Devon. By his second wife he had six sons and two daughters. He died in 1813 and was succeeded by his eldest son, Sir Lawrence Vaughan Palk. He died in 1860 and was succeeded by the fourth baronet, later Lord Haldon, who was educated at Eton and joined the 1st Dragoons in 1835, retiring in 1840. He became a Deputy Lieutenant for Devon, Colonel of the 1st Devon Artillery and was M.P. for South and, later, East Devon, 1854 to 1868. Among his other commercial activities, he was chairman of the Teign Valley Railway Company.

HAMES, Colvile George Hayter of Chagford House, a landowner, was Joint Master of the Mid-Devon for two seasons (1892-94). He was descended from a long line of Rectors of Chagford, on the edge of Dartmoor. One of the family became Bishop of Norwich, tutor to the Prince of Wales (later King George III) and finally Bishop of London.

HARRIS, Christopher Arthur, of Hayne, Devon, was the author of *Letters on the Past and Present Foxhounds of Devon*, 1861, a leading rider to Devon hounds and a friend and close colleague of George Templer and John Russell. He was educated at Eton and kept kennels at Hayne where he constructed coverts on the estate. He was a highly skilled equestrian. He was distantly connected to John Harris, of Hayne, Serjeant-at-Law and Recorder of Exeter, 1544.

HEATHCOAT-AMORY, Sir John, 1st Baronet (1829-1914) of Knightshayes Court, Tiverton was the son of Samuel Amory (1784-1857) a London lawyer and banker, who married Anne, daughter and co-heiress of John Heathcoat (1783-1861). He made a fortune from lace and silk manufacture at Tiverton. The business at one time employed more than one thousand workers and was the largest lace factory in the world. John Heathcoat-Amory left his brother-in-law to manage the business and took to politics and sport, including tennis, shooting, fishing and hunting hare, fox and stag. As a young man he campaigned for his grandfather, who was M.P. for Tiverton and later himself held the seat (1868-85). He bought the 200 acre Knightshayes estate and employed William Burges, the Gothic architect, to build the mansion (1869-74). The grounds contained English and Turkey oak, beech, lime, chestnut, hawthorn and conifer. An exceptional tree was the Wellingtonia Gigantea in the willow garden which was seventy-five feet high by 1897 and reached one hundred and fifty feet before the top was damaged in a storm and removed. Sir John, in the nineteenth century, built waterfalls, ponds and rockeries to the north-west of the house. Sir John was described as a type of man whose value to country life could not be over-estimated. By about 1900 he had made over his foxhounds to his brother-in-law, the harriers to his son-in-law and the staghounds to his son, Ian (1864-1931) who was later killed in a hunting accident. He kept harriers from 1860 but staghunting on his own account did not begin until 1896 when local farmers asked him to cull the red deer. He was a keen angler in the Exe and the Culm, and further afield in Scotland and Norway. In 1897 he killed a stag on Exmoor weighing 333 lbs with 5+5 points, the antlers measuring 21½ ins. tip to tip.

HILLS, Tom (1796-1873) was huntsman to the Old Surrey Foxhounds from 1816 to 1840 and from 1843 to 1861. During the three-year break he kept a public-house at Bletchingley but having decided he would rather draw coverts than ale, he overcame a "slight misunderstanding" with the hunt and returned to the saddle. He worked in the quarries at Godstone as a boy and began his hunting career as second horseman and assistant whip to Mr. Maberley, who was Master, 1812-20, with kennels at Shirley, Croydon. Tom was succeeded by Sam, one of his fourteen children. He carried on for thirty-two seasons until 1892. Tom was universally popular and a legend in his own long lifetime. He was described as a fine horseman and a born huntsman who showed good sport year after year in difficult country of big banks and ditches with lots of stiff jumping: not galloping grass but cramped, hilly and provincial. He was cheerful, wise, patient; a good kennelman with a great knowledge of the fox. He was also a good shot at partridge, a competent pugilist when necessary, with a fund of entertaining anecdote and an inexhaustible sense of humour. He used to carry a bugle and play tunes of popular songs to stimulate the pack but later gave it up for the straight horn. He was a heavyweight rider and when teased about his weight always said that his horse dared not fall for fear of being crushed under his rider. After the confrontation with the highwayman, Tom told his audience: "I could have downed him with my old hunting whip but I wanted to see a bit of sport." He was not lacking in courage, quite apart from facing the constant hazards of his chosen country. He had a long-standing difference with one, Deakins, gamekeeper of Titsey Park who was in the habit of snipping the brushes off foxcubs. After several quarrels, they decided to settle the matter with a fist fight. Like duellists, they met at the crack of dawn, on Botley Hill. It was a lengthy battle of many rounds. Deakins was taller, heavier and some ten years younger than Hills but Tom stood up to him with science and tenacity. A bystander likened the match to a pair of stallions, kicking each other to death. Eventually, Deakins was carried away, sadly battered. On a lighter occasion, after a long run from Long Coppice to Lord Stanhope's Park in November, 1860, the fox was killed under Lady Mary Stanhope's petticoats. Sam Hills, then a very senior first whipper-in, remarked: "I never knew a fox killed under such favourable circumstances." In retirement at Garston, Tom Hills enjoyed patriarchal status. His portrait was painted by Sir Francis Grant and his armchair was covered with the coat of his dark, chestnut hunter, *Paddy*. His chairs all had hound-skin cushions from nine of the best of seven couple killed in a one-hundred-foot fall down a Brighton line rail cutting in 1852. Tom died aged seventy-seven, a martyr to gout and broken bones. He had five sons in the profession, three of them huntsmen.

KINGSLEY, the Rev. Canon Charles (1819-75), priest, poet, novelist, naturalist, angler and rider to hounds, was born at Holne, on the South-east edge of Dartmoor, where his father was an impoverished curate. Later Kingsley senior moved to Clovelly, the picture-postcard seaside village on the North Devon coast, at a stipend of £350 a year. The striking scenery stirred the boy's imagination and coloured the graphic prose of his later books. After his father gained preferment to the fashionable St. Luke's, Chelsea, Charles completed his education at King's College, London, and Magdalene College, Cambridge. After ordination he became assistant curate and, soon afterwards, rector of Eversley on the North-east Hants. border. The rectory was his principal home until his death thirty-three years later. In 1844 he married Frances Eliza Grenfell, known as Fanny, youngest and prettiest of four well-to-do daughters of a recently deceased Cornish mine owner. They were religious but well-launched into fashionable society. At Eversley, Kingsley was an earnest parish priest, an ardent husband and father, and a prolific writer. He preached short, simple sermons for the unlettered peasants of the parish and at Windsor, where he was chaplain to the Queen, he gave short addresses with a Protestant flavour. From his canonical stall at Westminster he was prominent in religious controversies of the day, though his tenets were derivative rather than original. In later life he was prone to high-flown verbosity, as witness his address as president of the Devonshire Association for the Advancement of Science and Literature in 1871. He was forbidden to preach in Devon by Bishop Phillpotts on account of his Christian Socialist tendencies. During his not infrequent visits there to recover from bouts of nervous prostration, he occupied himself with nature studies on the coast, sometimes supplying specimens to Philip Gosse. Kingsley was deeply conservative beneath a veneer of radicalism. For instance, he enjoyed converse with the labouring poor and, indeed, sympathised with the poachers in his parish, but always maintained a distance befitting his social class. His heart bled for overworked beasts of burden but he did not share Mrs. Beecher Stowe's sympathy for "the poor fox" in what she called "a barbaric sport". The author of *Uncle Tom's Cabin* was not made aware of her *gaffe* during her brief stay in 1856 when the Bramshill hounds raced past the rectory windows one lunch-time. "Hunting a man would be far better sport", she declared, in apparent contravention of her principles. However, she failed to start a civil war in Hampshire. Kingsley's restless, mercurial temperament and his love of the open air made him a natural enthusiast for foxhunting. He knew "every fox covert on the moor and every pike hover and chub-hole" of the local streams.

LAKE, General Lord, 1st Viscount (1744-1808) entered the foot guards in 1758, becoming a lieutenant-colonel in the guards and a general in the army by 1792. He served in Germany (1760-62) and in the Yorktown campaign of 1781. He was later equerry to the Prince of Wales, later George IV. In 1793 he commanded the Guards Brigade in Flanders under the Duke of York. By 1794 he had sold his lieutenant-colonelcy in the guards and become colonel of the 53rd foot and governor of Limerick. In 1797 he was promoted lieutenant-general. When the Irish rebellion broke out in 1798, Lake took command of the troops. After an initial victory at Vinegar Hill he was sent by Cornwallis to oppose a French army which had landed at Killala Bay. Lake arrived at Castlebar to witness the retreat of British troops under General Heley-Hutchinson but compelled a French surrender at Ballinamuck on September 8. In 1799 he returned to England but soon left for India to take up duties as commander-in-chief at Calcutta in July, 1801. He instigated changes in all branches of arms to make the army more mobile. As a full general in 1803 he defeated Sindhia and the Mahrattas within a few months, being victorious at Laswari over a French-led army of thirty-one battalions with four hundred and twenty guns. Gen. Lake had further successes and Wellesley, later Duke of Wellington, attributed much of the success of the war in India to Lake's "matchless ability and valour". He was rewarded by a peerage in 1804 and was created viscount in 1807.

LEAMON BROTHERS, William and Thomas of Lamerton, West Devon, were twins, born about 1800, farming thirty-six acres valued at £90 p.a. William was Senior Master and Thomas whipped-in. They were assisted by Sam Lang, a foot-runner, six feet two inches tall, who telegraphed intelligence to the Master from high places. The brothers ran their establishment on a shoe-string, did their own kennel work and hunted in a systematic and business-like way with small, light hounds, "feathery on sterns and breeches", obstinate but obedient to the Master. Col. J.A. Thomson described the brothers as "thin, delicate-looking old men with white hair, red cut-away coats, white cords, black boots, caps and gloves: most respectable and riding low, well-bred bay horses." On the opening day of the 1871 season (October 12) Mr. William Leamon was presented with a silver hunting horn and an embroidered purse containing two hundred guineas by Col. Archer of Trelask in appreciation of their providing successful sport in the hunting field over many years. They were universally popular. Up to about 1840 the Lamerton country was hunted in two parts: North-West (Mr. Phillips) and South-East (Mr. Morgan). William Horndon subsequently hunted the two districts as one. The Leamon brothers ran the pack until the death of William in 1877.

LONG, William, succeeded Philip Payne as huntsman to the Sixth Duke of Beaufort in 1826. Long was a son of the stud groom at Badminton and was in service to three successive dukes for more than forty years. He was a whipper-in for eighteen years and rode the same horse, *Milkman*, for seventeen seasons. He was described by his contemporaries as a huntsman near perfection.

MARTIN, the Rev. W. Keble (1877-1970) was born at Radley while his father, Charles Martin, was warden (headmaster) of the College. His maternal grandfather, Dr. George Moberly, was headmaster of Winchester and later Bishop of Salisbury. Keble Martin was educated at Marlborough and Christ Church, Oxford, and spent his youthful holidays at Dartington, Devon, where his father was rector (1891-1910). There he had ample leisure to study the flora and fauna. Rabbits were a plague and he shot them and sold them for ten pence each in Totnes. His tutor at The House was later Bishop of Peterborough, and the Dean of Christ Church was later Bishop of Oxford. His bicycle was repaired by William Morris, later Lord Nuffield, the millionaire motor manufacturer. Despite his many distinguished connections, Keble Martin never secured high office in the church but was a devoted parish priest in Yorkshire and Devon, where he spent his last forty-eight years, pursuing his studies of wild flowers whenever possible. He was editor of the *Flora of Devon*, 1939, and his life-long work, *The Concise British Flora*, 1965, sold more than a hundred thousand copies in its first year of publication. He designed the special floral issue of British postage stamps issued in April, 1967.

MAYO, Richard Southwell Bourke, the Sixth Earl (1822-72) was a British statesman, born in Dublin. He was Master of the Kildare Hunt from 1857 to 1862. Lord Mayo was M.P. for Kildare, Coleraine and Cockermouth successively, and Chief Secretary for Ireland under three administrations. As Viceroy of India (1869-72) he consolidated frontiers, promoted public works, reorganised finances and put India on a paying basis. He was assassinated by a convict in 1872 at Port Blair, Adaman Isles.

MEYNELL, Hugo (1735-1808) of Quorndon Hall, Leicestershire, was the first Master of the Quorn (1753-1800). *Nimrod* called him the *Maecenas of hunting* and his friends dubbed him the *Jumping Jupiter* of his day. He claimed descent from the Norman Baron Hugo de Grente Mesnil, a friend of the Conqueror, and was a grandson of a Barbados planter. He was rich, cultivated, capable and an accomplished musician. He was High Sheriff for Derbyshire at twenty-three years of age and three times a Member of Parliament. His first wife died young and his second, Anne, a daughter of Thomas Boothby Scrimshire of Tooley Park, had two sons, Hugo in 1759, who died in 1780, and Charles, born in 1768, who became Master of the Royal Tennis Court. About 1754 he bought Quorndon Hall and transformed it into a hunting box. He sold it in 1800 to the Earl of Sefton on giving up the pack. Although Hugo Meynell was neither a big landowner nor an aristocrat, he was fully accepted by both for his ability and acumen in the hunting field and for his system of hound-breeding and kennel management which produced "the steadiest, wisest and handsomest pack of foxhounds in the Kingdom". He made Leicestershire and Northants. a Mecca for hard-riding foxhunters. He was courteous to yeomen, farmers, graziers and aristocrats alike and his occasional reprimand in the field was limited to banter or sarcasm. He had a sharp eye and a quick ear and could distinguish the tongue of every hound in his pack. Meynell rode a strong, black horse, fast and a perfect fencer. *Nimrod* recalled his grey locks beneath a black cap and a keen, piercing eye; a lop-sided seat and heels without spurs. He was regarded as the most intelligent and successful sportsman of his time and one who introduced a fresh era to the world of hunting. He was knowledgeable and a delightful companion. Dick Christian, the rough rider, recalled Meynell's shrill voice and good language. Meynell entered his hounds to hare, walked them among riot in the summer and, when the season commenced, hunted in woodlands for two months. In November they were divided into old and young, the old pack in the best country and the young in woodlands and in unpopular coverts. He seldom lifted hounds through sheep and rarely cast them once on a line of scent. He considered killing foxes a prodigality. Seasoned foxes were as necessary as experienced hounds. When hard riding came into fashion, horsemen of the older school, accustomed to hunting a slow fox with a full stomach, thought the sport less enjoyable, but what was lost in science was gained in gusto. The famous Billesdon Coplow run of twenty-eight miles in two and a quarter hours was commemorated in verse by the Rev. Robert Lowth, son of a Bishop of London. Meynell died at his house in Mayfair. He was buried in the family vault at Bradley, Derbyshire.

MEYSEY-THOMPSON, Col. Richard of Kirby Hall, near Knaresborough, Yorks. began his hunting career in 1859, on a pony with the York and Ainsty, and on foot with the Eton Beagles (Oppidan Pack). He was first whipper-in in 1865 when he was presented with the only whip he was to possess during the ensuing thirty-four years. He achieved the distinction of kicking a goal during one of the famous wall-games: a near impossibility. As a child he recalled the Crimea, where his grandfather served in the 4th Dragoons. He himself joined the Rifle Brigade and served in the Ashanti campaign in 1873 in the 2nd Battn. where he was nine years adjutant and five years commanding officer. Later he was an ADC in the Dublin District. Meysey-Thompson swam with his famous whip in several unsuccessful rescue attempts after the ferry capsize in the Ure. He and James Robinson were the first to arrive at the ferry station but the thirty-foot craft was on the far side. On its return the colonel gave way reluctantly to allow the Master and senior members to embark. Thus he was much closer to the bank when the ferry began to roll and, sensing danger, he leaped from the stern and swam ashore, returning to the water many times in attempts to save his comrades. His *Reminiscences of the Court, the Camp, and the Chase* published in 1898, contains a graphic account of the Newby Ferry disaster.

MICHELL, the Rev. Jack (d.1869) of Cotleigh, near Honiton, East Devon, was said to have preached as hard as he rode. He followed his father, grandfather and great-grandfather as rector and as Master of the Cotleigh and East Devon Harriers. The pack were dwarf foxhounds and hunted fox, hare and badger. Jack Michell was an all-round sportsman, shooting woodcock with a double-barrelled Manton muzzle-loader in the nearby woods and angling for trout with two favourite dry-flies, a Blue Upright and a Wrentail. Ill-health caused him to give up the living and the hunt in 1860.

MIDDLETON, Captain William George (1846-92) was born into a Scottish sporting family, his father being secretary to the Glasgow Hunt (Lanark and Renfrew) and his uncle, Master of the Fife. His family were landowners. In 1865 he joined the 12th Lancers at Cahir, Tipperary. His riding prowess was such that although still a cornet, he became Master of the Garrison Draghounds at Ballincollig near Cork City where his horn disturbed his commanding officer's afternoon siesta. He hunted the locality for three seasons with great dash, in a country of banks, ditches and stiff fences. He was known as "Bay" either from the colour of his hair or after the winner of the 1836 Derby. He was slightly deaf from a fall but had great charm and charisma and was popular with both sexes. He was a practical joker but also a shrewd Scot who needed to do well. In 1868 Gladstone made the Fifth Earl Spencer of Althorp Park, Northants., Lord Lieutenant of Ireland at the age of thirty-six. Under-employed and bored by administration, he frequently rode to hounds. He was a bold though not polished horseman, frequently far ahead of the body of the hunt, thus giving rise to anxiety for his safety at the hands of Irish rebels. Middleton was promoted Captain and appointed an extra ADC to Spencer's staff in 1870, in effect as a bodyguard, along with "Chicken" Hartopp, "darling of the Tenth", the pair being among the few who could keep up with the Lord Lieutenant in the hunting field. Spencer and Middleton became great friends and when Gladstone's government fell in 1874, Middleton resigned his commission and returned with Spencer to Althorp to ride with the Pytchley. In 1875 he became engaged to Charlotte Baird, member of a neighbouring mining family in Scotland and married her belatedly in 1882. Sir Claude Champion de Crespigny, Bart., a contemporary, said that Middleton rarely threw away a race from carelessness but had one serious fault as a rider: he spurred his horse in the shoulder, from sitting with his toes turned out. Some of his mounts were much bloodied in a hard run.

MOODY, Tom, whipper-in to Squire Forester of Willey Hall, Shropshire, was immortalised by Dibden to a degree more appropriate to his Master. Though a fearless, rumbustious, ale-quaffing swashbuckler, he never rose to be huntsman, but the Squire always said he was the best whipper-in in England. Tom Moody was apprenticed to a maltster and was making a delivery one day to Willey Hall when the Squire saw him putting his obstinate cob to a gate until he eventually leaped it. The Squire was impressed and took the boy into his stables. He had an agreeable disposition and was admired by the other servants for his dare-devil stunts on horse-back. Moody could bring up the tail end of a pack of hounds or sustain a long burst to the kill as well as any man. He allowed the hounds to cast without interference and had a wide range of hound language to suit any occasion, including one when he fell into an old pit shaft and had to *holler* from the echoing depths for a rescue. He was an honest, faithful fellow and a genuine sportsman, though some of his tavern stories to passing travellers strained credibility. He was buried

at Barrow in Wenlock in December, 1796, with horse and hunt in full
canonicals.

MORGAN, Jem (1785-1862) was the son of a tenant farmer in
Suffolk. He first rode with Mr. Lloyd's harriers at Hintlesham Hall,
Suffolk, as whipper-in, staying for eleven years. He moved to the
Tickham, Kent, as kennel huntsman and first whipper-in to Giles Morgan,
a sporting farmer, not related, then to Mr. Conyers to hunt the Essex from
1835 to 1850. He showed good sport and his reputation spread. He rode
well over the wide, deep drains in the Roothings. Next he went to the
Essex Union and stayed three seasons and resigned to retire but was
engaged by Lord Lonsdale, then Master of the Old Berkeley. He hunted
for six seasons, retiring in favour of his son, Goddard. In the first season
of his final retirement, at a Hyde Heath meet, his horse fell at "a little
trappy fence" and he broke his neck but survived long enough to jump a
second. Jem Morgan left four sons, all of whom were prominent in the
calling: Ben, Jack, Goddard and Tom.

MYTTON, John (1796-1834) of Halston, Shropshire, was descended
from a long line of Members of Parliament and burgesses of Shrewsbury.
Halston, three miles from Oswestry, had a sixty-acre lawn, a lake,
heronry, and extensive woodlands. During his seventeen-year minority the
trustees increased the annual value of the estate from £10,000 to £60,000.
As well as Halston, he inherited Habberly and three other properties in
Shropshire and one in North Wales. Mytton went to Christ Church,
Oxford, for one term on condition he never opened a book except the
Racing Calendar or the Stud Book, and then went on a Continental tour.
Aged nineteen, he joined the Seventh Hussars in France, as a cornet, and
at Calais lost a large sum of money at billiards. He married at the age of
twenty-three and had a daughter who died in infancy. Mytton was five
feet, nine inches in height and a young man of immense strength but
scarcely a day passed when he did not risk his life either falling from
horses when drunk or attempting wild feats of horsemanship, climbing or
swimming. He once chased and killed a bagfox soon after a fall and
fainting with pain from three broken ribs. He had a mercurial
temperament with a sudden and violent temper. At the same time he
could be kind and charitable. He was a good employer, a liberal landlord
and essentially a good sportsman but would never take advice and was
frequently deaf to reason. His pride excluded any sense of moderation or
prudence. He was extravagant in every way and his early addiction to
drink eventually ruined his health and his fortune. Mytton kept foxhounds
on a grand scale at his own expense, hunting two countries. He also had
twenty race horses in training at any one time. His game preserves were

lavish and he employed fifty keepers. His wardrobe included one hundred and fifty pairs of breeches and trousers and he often destroyed fine clothes and shoes at one wearing. He was dashing and popular, especially with the lower classes. He drank wine steadily throughout the day but it was good wine about eight years old and the effects were ameliorated by constant exercise in his earlier years. He was a good farmer and won prizes for clean crops of grain except one, a field of barley which contained wild oats. He hunted the Shropshire and Shiffnal (later the Albrighton) for five days a week over five seasons and later bought another pack which he hunted from Halston. His famous, one-eyed *Baronet* carried him for nine seasons, after service in the Hussars. He would inspect his stables before breakfast, in his dressing gown, regardless of the temperature. He rode excellent horses and asked a lot of them but never tired one to the extent that he had to walk home. He was said to have a magical influence over them. Mytton's success on the race course owed much to his trainer and jockey, William Dunn, and declined after Dunn was killed by a fall at Chester. He had thirteen gold cups on his sideboard at Halston but the expenses of his stud were enormous, partly from buying horses at top prices when in top form. Also, he ran virtual non-starters to afford sport to the race-goers. He rode himself, in green and white, before his weight went up, but was a jealous rider among friends. His first two horses were called *Hazard* and *Neck or Nothing*, which reflected his own character as a rider. He kept too many horses and too many not good enough, and rarely ran them fresh. Uncharacteristically, he rarely backed them and then not for much. Mytton was a good shot and marksman. He could split a ball on the edge of a razor at thirty yards. One winter's day, he and his brother-in-law, Mr. Walter Giffard, Master of the Albrighton in 1830, took the field at 11 a.m. and bagged six hundred head of game from their own guns before dinner. On another occasion, Mytton, *Nimrod* and a third gun, a cleric, secured a kill every three minutes for five hours in succession. On the first day of the season he shot fifty brace of partridge by his own gun and his daily average bag of grouse on his Merioneth moor was thirty brace. By 1831, Mytton's excesses had driven him to France. He told his long-suffering friend, *Nimrod*, there were three couple of bailiffs "hard at his brush." *Nimrod* found him a decrepit and tottering old man, bloated by drink, his mind and body in ruins. After a night out in Calais, he tried to cure an attack of hiccups by setting his shirt alight. Badly burned, he told *Nimrod* he wished to show him how he could withstand pain. His stout constitution and *Nimrod's* untiring efforts and constraints on his intake of brandy secured a good recovery. A few weeks later, anxious to see his estranged second wife, he evaded his friends and his mother and returned to England where "every bailiff in London" was after him. From Halston he was taken to Shrewsbury prison and thence to the King's Bench prison in London. In the former Mytton had refused an offer by his old county friends to take his affairs in hand. He died in prison. Thus ended a career of princely extravagance and notoriety in sporting circles. Three thousand people attended his funeral. As *Nimrod* wrote of his wayward friend, in a prophetic epitaph: "The pace was quick and therefore could not last / From end to end he went an arrant burst / Determined to be nowhere or be first." Or as Shakespeare might have put it:

> Oh, what a noble frame was thus o'erblown,
> And restless spirit wrested from its throne.

NEWCOMBE, John Riley, who died in 1888, was lessee and manager of the Theatre Royal, Plymouth, and known by the artistes and stage hands as "The Governor". He hunted with the Dartmoor during the whole of Trelawny's Mastership. He was described as a bold rider and genial companion who knew the moor intimately and never shirked its challenge.

NORTH, Dan, was huntsman to the South Devon when the controversial chase of the wild, forest stag took place on November 2, 1882. He came from Mr. Snow's in North Devon, where he was familiar with the Devon and Somerset Staghounds. He succeeded Will Nevard, first huntsman to the Haldon Hounds, who died prematurely after one season. As Tozer said, North was "rather on the noisy side" but appropriately so for the woods and hills of Devon where obstacles to the hounds' hearing could abound. North showed a good deal of sport and had a shrewd notion for the line of a fox. When the first Lord Haldon died in 1883, Mr. Studd readily resigned in favour of the second baron, though the change was not to the advantage of the sport. The new Master wished to hunt the hounds himself. He took no subscription and thus could not be gainsaid. Lord Haldon's hounds, after responding in the field for so long to Dan North, were confused when North was demoted to first whipper-in, though he remained kennel-huntsman. Any improvement in the smartness of the turn-out was matched by a deterioration in the quality of the chase. However, Lord Haldon had over-rated his finances as well as his ability as a huntsman and was obliged to give up the hounds after two years. He resigned in 1886. Mr. Studd took on the country again, though suffering an altercation with Lord Haldon over the return of his hounds, to which he was entitled. Dan North returned to Mr. Studd at Oxton when Lord Haldon gave up but when the enthusiastic members of the South Devon, East of the River Exe, decided, in 1890, to form their own hunt, the East Devon under the Mastership of Col. J.A.T. Garratt, who was to hold office for twenty-two years, Dan North left to join Mr. Bolitho's in the rugged Cornish country of the Western.

ORVYS, William, succeeded Will Danby as kennel huntsman and first whipper-in to Sir Charles Slingsby, Master of the York and Ainsty. Orveys was fifty-nine years of age when he met his death in the cause of duty. He was previously huntsman with Mr. Conyers in Essex and, before that, first whipper-in to Jem Morgan. At the Y and A he earned a good reputation in the kennel and the field. He was described as "the cheeriest of huntsmen and the most civil of servants." Within a month of the accident close on six hundred pounds was raised for his widow and family. *The Druid* wrote that Orveys was a mature, good servant and a right arm to his master; his hounds were always brought out in fine condition and he was a bold rider and "hard as pinwire". He combined a sense of humour with a squeaky voice. He married a housemaid at Scriven Park as his second wife about five years before his death. Orveys's son, Charles, was huntsman to the Warwickshire under Lord Willoughby de Broke, and his grandson, Algernon, succeeded Fred Hills as second whipper-in to the Eridge in Kent. William Powter, second whip to the Y and A was not on board the ferry but he was killed during the ensuing cubhunting season. He was found lying on the far side of a fence with his neck broken.

OSBALDESTON, "Squire" George (1787-1866), sixth Master of the Quorn and "the greatest all-round sportsman of the age", was the son of Mr. Humphrey Osbaldeston of Hunmanby Hall, Hutton Bushel, near Scarborough, Yorks. As a keen cricketer young George complained that he was robbed of his birthright by being born in Wimpole Street, London. His father died when he was six years old. George's mother moved to Bath on the death of her husband and her son soon became the star pupil of Mr. Dash's riding academy. At Eton he became the fastest athlete, the best oar, a noted cricketer and a doughty pugilist. In 1805 he matriculated as a gentleman-commoner at Brasenose College and again distinguished himself as a sportsman. Down from Oxford, he bought a pack of harriers from Lord Jersey and hunted the country round the family estate to the delight of local farmers. When he and his mother moved to Lincolnshire he bought Lord Monson's foxhounds and hunted the Burton for five seasons (1809-13) with great success, breeding "the finest pack of working hounds in the three kingdoms". After a spell in Northamptonshire he took the Atherstone, including with it Lord Vernon's Derbyshire country and most of his hounds. Having established kennels at Witherley, he hunted the country in great style but fell out with Sir Henry Every, a local magnate, and later challenged him to a duel. By then George Osbaldeston was reputedly the best shot in England so the baronet found it expedient to offer an apology. The Squire accepted but moved his establishment of ninety couples and thirty hunters to Derbyshire. In 1817 at thirty years of age, George succeeded the renowned Tom Assheton Smith as Master of the Quorn (1817-21 and 1823-27). He gave good sport in the wild days of hard-riding and hard-drinking young men, mostly visitors to Leicestershire, but broke his leg badly in 1826. In the days of relentlessly hard galloping, a man in the lead was in mortal danger both fore and aft. There were bullfinches to the front and jealous riders close behind. He was out of the saddle for a year and never so carefree a rider again. In 1827 he took the horn with the Pytchley and in one season had twenty-three fine runs in succession, killing more than sixty brace of fox. In 1822 the Squire had hunted the Thurlow country and he did so again during his Pytchley reign. It meant travelling overnight and was sure proof of his hardihood and stamina. Once he was active for two days and nights without sleep. He had three good runs with the Pytchley, rode to Northampton, hacked to Cambridge, danced all night, rode back some sixty miles to Sulby Hall, hunted and killed a brace of foxes and then rode fourteen miles home to dinner. His skill as a horseman was not confined to hunting. In an age of competitive riding, racing, coaching and shooting, he was well to the fore and frequently matched himself in feats of skill and endurance for large sums of money. A memorable event in the saddle took place in 1831 when he pledged himself to ride two hundred miles in ten hours for stakes of a thousand pounds. He was to have as many horses as he wished. He was then in his forty-sixth year and the veteran of numerous fist fights, falls and sporting accidents. He trained for the event by riding sixty miles every forenoon and shooting partridge for relaxation in the afternoon. The event was staged at Newmarket over four miles, starting and finishing at the Duke's stand. One betting man rightly guessed that the distance would be covered in nine hours; in fact Osbaldeston finished in eight hours and forty-eight minutes, riding twenty-eight different horses. The Squire made eighteen hundred pounds in bets on top of the stakes. (Peter Scudamore, retired national hunt jockey, rode two hundred miles at Newmarket Heath in eight hours and thirty-seven minutes on October 10, 1993, to break Osbaldeston's record. He used fifty mounts, including racehorses.) The Squire rode only the best horses. Osbaldeston retired from the mastership of the Pytchley in 1840 after some thirty-five years in the hunting saddle. In appreciation of thirteen seasons of fine sport the hunt gave him a handsome snuff box inscribed to "the best sportsman of any age or country". The Squire was also a noted steeplechase rider and was never beaten. Although a leading sportsman and a man with bottom who normally obeyed the conventions of a gentleman, he was no paragon; still less a purist. He aimed to get

there first. There were times when he bought bagfoxes to populate his
sparse coverts, though he insisted on "old, English foxes" and no "damned
French dunghills". His character was most open to question on the Turf,
though no more so than that of any of his fellow sporting socialites in the
matter of fixing races. He was accused at Doncaster of buying horses to
sell to the public. The volatile Squire was reported to have called out his
challenger and *parted his hair* at twelve paces, though in fact no shot was
fired. However, shots *were* fired when the Squire ran a horse at Heaton
Park which was favourably handicapped after a staged trial. He accepted a
bet of two hundred to one from Lord George Bentinck and the horse won
in a canter. On asking for his money when they next met, he was told the
affair was "a robbery". He got his money and made his challenge but Lord
George refused to respond. After further insults from the Squire they met
at Wormwood Scrubs early one morning. Each man shot wide and honour
was satisfied. At cricket, too, Osbaldeston could be petulant. He was a
great batsman and a fast, underhand bowler. When a match failed to go
his way at Lords, he scratched his name from the list of MCC members, a
reaction for which he was never forgiven. He was an unrivalled shot at
game, pigeon and snipe. He once killed ninety-eight pheasants out of a
hundred shots. Another time he was backed to shoot eighty brace of
partridge in one day. He killed ninety-seven brace and more were picked
up the next day, bringing the total bag to one hundred and three brace and
a half of partridges and nine hares and a rabbit: a slaughter claimed never
to have been equalled. The Squire did not neglect his social duties. As
well as being high sheriff he stood for Parliament, being returned for East
Retford. Later in life he fell on hard times. He was not profligate but his
gambling was not always successful and people took advantage of his
trust. When the youthful Willmott Dixon, who wrote as *Thormanby*,
first set eyes on Osbaldeston, then aged seventy-two, he was shocked at
his appearance and disillusioned that his hero was a man of such mean
stature and countenance. He saw a "short, square, dumpy little old man,
with a shrivelled, shrunken frame, round shoulders and limping gait, with
a hard, disagreeable face . . . almost as battered as that of an old-time prize
fighter, and dressed in loose-fitting, shabby garments as if from an old
clothes shop." He could hardly believe that "this ludicrously unheroic
figure" had been the idol of his boyhood and the Admirable Crichton of
sport. There was nothing to suggest the outstanding physical powers of
his halcyon days nor the triumphant sportsman who surpassed all others
in his heyday. *Sic transit gloria mundi!* *

PAGET, Otho, was born in 1860, the younger son of Arthur Paget of
Thorpe Satchville, five miles south of Melton Mowbray, and was related
to the Pagets of Loughborough. He first rode to hounds as a small boy

---

* Thomas Creevey, the whig MP and gossip, described Osbaldeston as a funny little chap with features
like a foxcub.

on a family pony and as a schoolboy hired a horse to follow the Quorn. After two years in the training ship "Conway", he went to sea as a deck officer where his only experience of hunting was catching rats when they emerged on deck for a breath of fresh air. He gave up the sea to farm and follow hounds. He started regular hunting in the 1880-81 season and rode with the Quorn and the Cottesmore, recalling that Morris, the local butcher, who often lent him a horse, rode to hounds in his blue butcher's smock. To augment his meagre income Paget contributed articles to *Bell's Life* and to *The County Gentleman*, with guidance from *Brooksby*, alias Captain Pennell-Elmhirst, whom he regarded as the pioneer of hunting journalists. He succeeded him as hunting correspondent of *The Field* in 1885 and continued as such until the outbreak of the first world war. As Leicestershire correspondent, he was obliged to report on the Belvoir, Cottesmore and Quorn and Sir Bache Cunard's, formerly Mr. Tailby's. Thus he was out six days a week and apparently having to maintain his own stable, though many hunt members loaned him horses from time to time. Like Trollope, he got his hunting from his job, in a sense, and greatly enjoyed it but concluded that the lot of a hunting journalist was not altogether a happy one. It was no light task to write a readable, fair and accurate account of a run. Like *Brooksby*, he complained of the heavy hand of the hunting editor. He worked hard for his living, burning the midnight oil regularly to write up the day's events, but remained a poor man, unlike the vast majority of his fellow-riders. After a fast burst with the Belvoir one day, he wrote that it was possible to compress a lifetime of mad excitement into a few seconds when on the back of a good horse with the hounds racing. Paget wrote as a practical observer and critic of hounds and hunting rather than as a mere society reporter. His experience in swimming the Wreake in the course of duty had a more unfortunate sequel on December 28, 1903, when his horse threw him into a deep ditch, full of thorns. It was also the village sewer and he went in, head down, through the thorns, legs in the air. He was in danger of drowning but his spurs were entangled in the reins and his horse's plunging pulled him out. He rode home but he was laid up for ten weeks and the ill-effects lasted ten years. Paget answered the call in 1914 at the age of fifty-four and served in the army until 1919, during which time he had one day's hunting.

PARKER, Admiral George, R.N. of Delamore (1,212 acres) near Ivybridge, Devon, was born in 1827 and was master of Dartmoor Foxhounds 1876-89. He was descended from a Nottinghamshire family but married the heiress to Delamore in 1857. His great-grandfather was Sir Thomas Parker, Chief Baron of the Exchequer (1742-72), and his father was Admiral of the Fleet, Sir William Parker, GCB, Bt. (1844) and

Senior Admiral when he died in 1866. George joined the Royal Navy in
1840 and served in the Mediterranean and the West Indies. In 1872 he was
appointed Rear Admiral on the Reserve List and promoted Admiral in
1884. He was seen as a born sportsman with horse, hound, rod and gun
and had the best woodcock coverts in Devon. William Boxall was
huntsman for the first six years of his mastership, succeeded by Robert
Yeo. The Admiral was a heavy man for the Dartmoor country but with
the benefit of local knowledge and sturdy mounts he usually contrived to
be near enough to his hounds and to be up at the finish. His grandson
also reached flag rank.

PARSONS, Alderman Humphrey (c1676-1741) of the Red Lion
Brewery at St. Katherines in Aldgate, East London, and of the Priory,
Reigate, Surrey, was Lord Mayor of London, 1730-31 and again, 1740-41.
He died in office on March 21, aged 65. He was also Member of
Parliament for Harwich (1722-27) and for London (1727-41). On the
death of his father, Sir John Parsons, M.P. and Lord Mayor (1703-04) he
succeeded to the family estates at Reigate and Dorking. He was one of
few aldermen to be elected Lord Mayor twice and in his October, 1740,
civic procession he was the first to ride in a coach-and-six. He was a
highly popular man and his Lord Mayor's show was a pageant of unusual
splendour. He was the subject of many adulatory broadsides and one of
1741 described him as a churchman and an incorruptible Tory "proof
against the bribery and wiles of the Whigs". Another sheet was entitled
"Whittington Revived and a City in Triumph". Parsons was a member of
the Wax Chandlers Company but translated to the Grocers, one of the
twelve major trade guilds, on election to the mayoralty. He was Sheriff in
1722-23 and president of the Bridewell and Bethlehem Hospitals (1725-
41). Humphrey Parsons owned "a brilliant stable" and was prominent on
the Turf as well as in the hunting field. He was portrayed in hunting dress
on the front page of the *Grub Street Journal* of December 3, 1730. His
contravention of royal hunting etiquette in the field at Versailles in 1729
led to a life-long friendship with King Louis XV of France who showed
him favour far beyond that extended to princes and ambassadors. In
February, 1731, the king gave him his portrait set in a diamond-studded
frame. The City Corporation held hunting privileges in Middlesex,
Surrey and the Chilterns for centuries, though they were poorly defined.
They were confirmed by Henry I (1100-35) in a charter but it failed to
mention the Forest of Essex which was a favourite country for red deer
and wild boar. The Corporation's huntsman was known as the Common
Hunt. He had ceremonial duties as well as those of maintaining a pack at
the dog house at Moorfields and later to the north of Finsbury fields when
the stench in the City became oppressive. People who obstructed the

City Hunt were brought before the Court of Aldermen to explain themselves. In the mid eighteenth century it was found that the Common Hunt had ceased to maintain a pack of hounds but was paying seven pounds a year to hire one from a huntsman as required. M.H. Oram in a paper read to the Guildhall Historical Association records that the City Lands Committee subsequently appropriated the rents then being charged for appurtenances by the Common Hunt and abolished the office in 1807 when the holder died.

PEEL, John (1776-1854) of Caldbeck was an informal MFH for fifty-six years in West Cumberland, under the Skiddaw Fells, where the greyhound fox plundered the poultry and lambs of the native Herdwick breed on which the economy depended. He was the eldest of thirteen children of William Peel, a horse-dealer, and Lettice Scott. In 1797 he married Mary White of Uldale, first at Gretna Green and again in Caldbeck Church under licence. Her dowry, including a farm, produced about £400 a year. Peel established his own pack of foxhounds about 1798 but at various times hunted other local packs. He kept twelve couples of all sorts, supplemented by dogs of every kind from the neighbourhood. They had good sport with hares but the fox was the real enemy and was hunted with great determination by Peel and the dalesmen, mostly on foot in the rocky terrain. Peel was a man of little formal education but knew every inch of the country and the line any fox would take. He stood over six feet tall, was broad-shouldered and hearty, and a skilled rider. His famous grey coat, made of the local blue-grey wool, was adopted, according to legend, after a Troutbeck soldier in regimental red, home on leave, headed a fox and spoiled the best run of the season. Peel said the man was enough to frighten a thousand foxes and abandoned his own bright green coat for the home-spun weave. He wore a battered box beaver hat, a choker necktie, dark corduroy knee breeches, long stockings and boots without tops, and rode a short stirrup. Cumberland farmers afterwards wore grey collars in his memory. The famous song, *D'ye ken John Peel* alluded to a run from Low Denton Holme, near Caldbeck, to Scratchmere Scar. It was written by John Woodcock Graves, born in Wigton in 1795, and sung to an old Irish tune, first at the Rising Sun, Caldbeck, where the pair drank freely at "the heel o' the hunt". The song took London by storm and there was a command performance before the Prince of Wales, and another at Drury Lane where a chorus of three-score young women in scarlet led the singing. The music became the March Past of the Border Regiment and was sung by soldiers in war and peace.

PHILLPOTTS, the Rt. Rev. Henry, Lord Bishop of Exeter (1778-1869) of Bishopstowe, Torquay, held the second longest episcopate known at Exeter, from 1831 to 1869. In 1833 there were more than six hundred benefices stretching over one hundred and forty miles from East Devon to Land's End. This was a formidable challenge in terms of travel alone, before the days of trains and telephones. Nevertheless he quickly acquired a good, working knowledge of the See and of most of the resident incumbents and their politics, ecclesiastical leanings and life-style. Phillpotts was a high Tory and a high churchman and for those reasons was disliked by most of his clergy. In addition, he had a reputation for nepotism, greed and belligerence, not altogether deserved. He was a born fighter who relished controversy but although pugnacious and litigious, he was usually well-informed and skilled in argument. He was a good administrator and far-sighted as to the needs of the church. He attacked Roman Catholics and radicals, condemned auricular confession and "apish imitation of Rome" but caused riots at St. Sidwells, Exeter, by ordering the wearing of surplices. News of the foxhunting proclivities of some of his incumbents soon reached him and he made efforts towards reform. He was not in any way concerned with the welfare of the fox. He considered foxhunting a clerical aberration and a distraction from the parochial duties of a country parson. Russell and Froude soon came to his notice and although he never got Froude to the palace for reprimand, nor found him apparently at home, he remonstrated more than once with Russell, but to no avail. His powers were limited and neither man gave cause for assault on his "parson's freehold" nor, indeed, as far as was known, neglected his Sunday duty or his parish. On one occasion, Bishop Phillpotts met Froude with a greyhound, known in Devon as a long dog, at his side. "And pray, Mr. Froude," asked the Bishop in carefully restrained tones, "What manner of dog may you call that?". "Oh!" said Froude, "that's what we call a *lang-dog*, my lord, and if yeu was on'y to shak' yeur appern to 'un, he'd go like a dart". There was no suitable episcopal reply to a racing certainty.

PRESTER, Major, later **Lt.Col. John** (1778-1856) came from the Cattistock country. After long and successful service in the army, he died at Millbrook, near Southampton. In India, he hunted every day, war permitting, either before or after his military duties.

PRICKMAN, John Dunning (1855-1913) of Riverside, Okehampton, was secretary of the Mid-Devon Hunt for many years and a regular contributor to sporting journals and local newspapers under the pseudonym *Pidgon*. A solicitor, he settled in Okehampton in 1880 and was active in public life. He was a coroner, clerk to Justices, Mayor of Okehampton in 1890 and the last Recorder of the Borough. He was an authority on Dartmoor and a noted raconteur in the Devon dialect.

RICHMOND, the Duke of, together with a group of aristocrats which included two other dukes, two earls, one viscount and three barons, formed the ancient Charlton Hunt into a regular hunting society on Sunday, January 29, 1737. Charlton was the Melton Mowbray of its day and the Charlton Hunt was the most famous in all England. It was a resort of the great and the wealthy and patronised by King William III and the Grand Duke of Tuscany among many high-born nobles. Charlton was a tything of the parish of Singleton in the valley of the Goodwood Hills and about a mile east of the highroad from Chichester to Midhurst, in West Sussex. The country included a wood of eight hundred acres, formerly the property of the Fitzalans, Earls of Arundel, who had a hunting seat at Downley. Charlton was the favourite resort of the Duke of Monmouth who declared that when he was king, he would hold his court there. At that time two packs of foxhounds were kept there, belonging to the Duke of Monmouth and Earl Grey. They were managed by a Mr. Roper, a Kentish gentleman. He was obliged to leave the country after the Monmouth rebellion but returned on the accession of William III and resumed management of the hounds, then the property of the Duke of Bolton. He was soon joined by the Marquis of Hartington (later Duke of Devonshire), who was a daring rider, and by Earl Halifax, the Dukes of Grafton and Montrose, various barons, and "half the aristocracy of England" for the hunting. The Charlton livery under the Duke of Richmond was blue, with gold cord and tassels to caps. One chase lasted nearly ten hours. (Twenty-three hounds ran a vixen on January 26, 1738, more than fifty-seven miles from 7.45 a.m. to 5.50 p.m.) The Charlton Hunt was regarded as one of the founding hunts of the sport in England. Some two hundred years before its formation on a formal basis, the country around Midhurst, including the Goodwood Hills and Forest, was hunted by the Earls of Arundel who owned most of the land. Edward Roper on returning from France went on until 1721 and died in the hunting field the following year at the age of eighty-four. Although the Duke of Bolton was devoted to the hounds, then at a peak of achievement, he was lured to London by an actress, Lavinia Fenton. He resigned the mastership in 1729 and gave the hounds to the second Duke of Richmond. The hunt was broken up in 1813.

RUSSELL, the Rev. John (1795-1883) was born at Iddesleigh, Devon, where his father, the rector, kept hounds and paying pupils. At Blundell's, Tiverton, he was nearly expelled for keeping four and a half couples, lodged with the local blacksmith. At Exeter College, Oxford, he hunted with the Heythrop, Bicester and Old Berkshire when opportunity allowed and represented his college and varsity in the boxing ring. He also took a keen interest in the then brutal sport of Cornish wrestling.

A fox-terrier bitch called *Trump* bought off a milkman was the progenitor of the famous breed he later kept in North Devon. At one time he hunted a country stretching more than seventy miles from Torrington to Bodmin. He learned much of the science from George Templer of Stover for whom he whipped in. Russell was six feet tall and muscular. He enjoyed great strength, vitality and stamina and rode vast distances to follow hounds. His large circle of friends included the Prince of Wales and the principal landowners in Devon: Fortescue, Poltimore, Portsmouth and Rolle. He rose and retired early, was abstemious at hunt suppers and never gambled, but he politely refused Bishop Phillpotts's admonitions to give up hunting. After several assistant curacies he became perpetual curate of Swymbridge with Landkey where he served two parishes and churches for forty-five years on a stipend of £180 a year with glebe worth £53, out of which he had to pay an assistant. He restored the church, built schools, held four Sunday services and raised much money for charity, especially the Barnstaple Infirmary which, by 1896, had nearly seven hundred patients maintained by voluntary subscription. He was prominent in Freemasonry, being invested provincial grand chaplain for Devon in 1835. In 1826 he married Penelope, a daughter of Admiral Bury of Barnstaple. Her income and encouragement tided him over some difficult times and enabled him to maintain his hounds and a couple of inexpensive horses. In 1879 he was presented to the living at Black Torrington (£500 p.a.) where he spent his few remaining years in relative comfort. When he left Swymbridge well-wishers gave him a cheque for £800. Perhaps the most famous and well-loved of all hunting parsons, Russell died a respected pillar of the church and society and a renowned sportsman.*

SEFTON, William Philip Molyneux, second Earl (1772-1838) of Croxteth Hall, Liverpool, traditional patron of the steeple-chase and coursing at Aintree, was Master of the Quorn (1800-1804). He bought Mr. Meynell's hounds in 1800 and added them to his own brought from Oxfordshire. He retained Jack Raven as huntsman to hunt the old pack two days a week in the best of the Quorn country, and Stephen Goodall who rode at twenty stone, to take the younger hounds through the woodlands on the other two days. Lord Sefton rode the best horses money could buy, often paying a thousand pounds for a good hunter. *The Druid* recorded that they all did him yeoman's service under "such a crushing hamper". Although a heavyweight he was adept at crossing a country. He disliked timber and contrived to push his way through blackthorn fences. Sefton, an unsuccessful Parliamentary candidate, was a good businessman and a fine coachman. One of his vehicles which caused a stir in St. James's Park comprised two large chaises joined in tandem with a rumble seat for the groom. The four-wheeled contraption carried eight

---

* HOSKINS (W.G) and FINBERG (H.P.R), *Devonshire Studies*, Jonathan Cape, 1952, took a different view, describing Russell as "the notorious hunting parson" who "ran through £50,000 of his wife's money, beggared and sold off the estates."

people in three compartments and was drawn by two horses. Lord Sefton was claimed to have started the fashion for reserve horses in the hunting field but the custom was not unknown three centuries earlier. William Blew recalled that Henry VIII, a man of similar proportions to the Quorn Master, once exhausted eight horses in one day. The Duke of Richmond and his aristocratic friends with the Charlton hounds at Goodwood in the 1730s were no less prodigal. Some ninety years later than Sefton, Earl Lonsdale ordered all second horsemen to keep to the roads and bridle paths. Lord Sefton changed mounts every fifteen minutes or so.

SLINGSBY, Sir Charles (1824-69) of Scriven Park, near Knaresborough, in the West Riding of Yorkshire, was not only a pillar of the county establishment but pre-eminent as a Master of foxhounds and a sportsman. That alone does not explain why his death, and that of his two leading riders, George Lloyd and James Robinson, in the Newby ferry disaster of February 4, 1869, led a leading hunt historian some thirty years later to write that "No social calamity of recent years has caused so great a shock as did this fearful accident." The poet, Egerton Warburton, had written of England's re-echoing Yorkshire's wail of grief. The day of the funeral was kept as a day of mourning "almost throughout hunting England." Maritime disasters, railway accidents and even the still vivid battles of the Crimean war seemed to fade into insignificance when "the thrill of horror ran through the whole country." If we are to believe the historian, Scarth Dixon, and his account of the event which "deprived Yorkshire of some of her best and bravest sons", the upsetting of the ferryboat and the drowning of the three riders, the huntsman and two ferrymen in a river of which most people had scarcely heard was the sole subject of conversation, among all classes of society "from one end of the land to the other." Clearly, even allowing for a measure of hyperbole, it was a dreadful accident, but its impact reflected the astonishing peak of perceived importance which sport, and foxhunting in particular, had then reached as an integral part of the social fabric of the country and especially that of the leisured classes. It was almost as though chasing and killing a fox, day after day, was the principal industry by which any male worthy of description as a gentleman could aspire to and achieve moral and social virtue. Oscar Wilde's jibe at the recreation of the English country gentleman would already have placed him further beyond the pale than his disgrace and prison sentence two years later, so closely interwoven was sport with the conception of manly and moral uprightness. Sir Charles Slingsby embodied all these virtues after some fifteen years as Master of the York and Ainsty, a leading and fashionable hunt after a mere fifty years of existence. He was appointed in 1853 and very soon headed a large field of hard-riding men who were "the best behaved in all England." He was a successful and enthusiastic breeder of hounds and was "perhaps the best gentleman huntsman that ever lived" and "one whose genial manners, and kind disposition endeared him to all." He never lost his temper or uttered a cross word. He was "a charming companion and a finished sportsman." He was quiet with his hounds, a patient drawer of coverts and understood the ways of a fox and conducted one of the best ordered fields in the Kingdom. He would return to the scene of a lost fox again and again to solve the problem of its disappearance, which characteristic goes far to explain the events of that fateful day.

SMITH, Thomas Assheton (1776-1857), Squire of Tedworth, Hants., and Master of the Quorn (1806-17) was born in Queen Anne Street, off Cavendish Square, London, in August, 1776. He was the second of eight children but his elder brother died in infancy, leaving him heir to his father's vast estates in Hampshire and extensive slate quarries in North Wales. He went to Eton at the age of seven and was there for eleven years, excelling in all sports including boxing, cricket and rowing. He had a famous fight with Musters who was later to be Byron's successful rival for the hand of Mary Chaworth. At Christ Church, Oxford, he acquired a deep knowledge of the English poets. He married Maria, second daughter of William Webber of Binfield Lodge, Berks., to whom he was a devoted husband. He succeeded Lord Foley as master of the Quorn and headed the hunt for eleven years before becoming Master of the Burton, Lincs., a country disliked by most Meltonians for its numerous drains and dykes. His remarkable jump from bridge to bridge was over a navigable canal called the Fosdyke where bridle and road bridges ran parallel at several yards distance. In 1824 he resigned and hunted with the Duke of Rutland for two years before returning to Hampshire and Penton Lodge, near Andover. When his father died in 1825 he moved to Tedworth and began to make extensive changes to the mansion, the estate and the pack. He converted several large woods including Colingbourne, Doles, Doyley, Faccombe and Wherwell into rideable coverts and for thirty years showed some of the best sport ever known from the finest hunting establishment in the Kingdom. Although his famous mount, *Screwdriver*, threw him more than once, he broke a bone on only two occasions. He built five yachts, including the famous *Menai*, which won many trophies at Cowes. Assheton Smith was a good farmer and a friend of the Duke of Wellington. W.C.A. Blew, the Quorn historian, reckoned that some of the "miraculous yarns" about Tom Smith's skill as a horseman should be taken with a big pinch of salt. He was undoubtedly a jealous and flamboyant rider but his courage and determination were unquestionable. His vast estates were left entirely to his widow but she survived him by a few months only.

STAMFORD, George Harry Grey, 7th Earl (1827-83) was the son of Lord Grey and succeeded to the barony at the age of ten and to the earldom and a great fortune on the death of his grandfather, the sixth Earl. He was Master of the Quorn (1856-63), after hunting the Albrighton country and, having moved to Bradgate Park and rented the Quorn stables, he hunted in magnificent style. At Eton and Cambridge he was a good athlete and later a noted cricketer at Lords. Lady Stamford was a fine, bold horsewoman. A writer in the 1860s recorded that Lord Stamford was so popular that farmers rejoiced to see him crossing their land and "villagers sent forth merry peals from the church bells when he honoured them with a meet." Leicestershire had never known a more popular Master. Lord Stamford resigned when he finally lost patience with the owners of coverts who had promised to preserve foxes for him but failed to do so. Some seven thousand people attended the sale of his horses at Tattersall's on May 9, 1863. They realised a total of 14,350 guineas. Special trains were run to the sale and the Emperor of France sent his superintendent of royal stables from the Louvre. The British aristocracy was well represented. Stamford died early in 1883, having caught a chill at his shooting box at Aviemore. His ancestor, Henry de Grey, was said to have carried the horn during the reign of Richard I.

STUDD, Edward Fairfax, M.A., B.C.L., barrister-at-law, of Oxton House, Kenton, S. Devon, was Master of the South Devon (Haldon Side) 1882-84 and 1886-91. He kept kennels at the Hang of Oxton. Though the impromptu staghunt of November 2, 1882 by Mr. Studd raised the ire of Sir John Duntze and Mr. Whidborne, ending the joint mastership with the latter, Tozer, the hunt historian, questioned whether Studd's action was so unquestionably a breach of any rule, usage or custom governing foxhunting. He held that hunting law arose only as between packs and usage or custom did not enter into the question because of the rarity of the wild, red deer in those parts. A Master of foxhounds would have been wrong to allow his hounds to hunt hare or fallow deer, which were common riot. He recalled that the Duke of Beaufort in 1863 took twenty-five couple to Poitou to hunt wolves. The difference was that the Duke sought out the animal whereas the wild stag sought out Mr. Studd. Moreover the red deer and the fallow deer were very different in scent and hunting attributes. When the fracas had died down, Mr. Studd provided some excellent sport and earned much popularity, discharging his duties with great energy and enthusiasm, despite Haldon's being a very hollow country. In the first season his total kill was only ten and a half brace but would have been much higher had he been inclined to digging. Besides drains and earths, the flints and gorse made the work of the hounds particularly trying. The circumstances of the staghunt of a year later involved no responsibility on the part of Studd or Dan North, who were both out as visitors with Mr. Tremlett's harriers. They found an exile from Exmoor at Newton St. Cyres and captured him near Ashcombe and lodged him with farmer White. After a week's rest and good feeding he was enlarged near the Lamb Inn, Longdown and eventually taken but not killed in an orchard behind Mr. Whidborne's stables.

TAVISTOCK, the Marquis of, was Master of the Oakley 1809-16. He took over from William Lee Antonie (1800-09) who was the first Master of the pack financed by subscription. It was a private pack until the Duke of Bedford withdrew before the turn of the century. However, he remained a subscriber. Antonie, of Colworth, was a Whig M.P. for Bedford Borough, 1802-07. Antonie was supported by Samuel Whitbread as a founder-subscriber. Tavistock resumed the Mastership in 1822 but gave up in 1829 from ill-health and sold the pack. The Hon. George Berkeley then took over on a subscription of £1,000 a year and built his own kennels at Harrold. He got on well with the farmers but felt he owed little to hunt subscribers. He found them insular. Tavistock took over again in 1836 and continued, after succeeding as Duke of Bedford, for two years.

TAYLOR, the Rev. Henry of West Ogwell, Newton Abbott, whipper-in along with Jack Russell to George Templer, founder of the South Devon, was described by *Nimrod* as "a very fine horseman" and "quite the clipper of the West." He was one of the "worthies of Devon" and a well-chosen member of the "Memorable triumvirate" riding from Stover. He was also a noted team member of the famous Teigngrace Cricket Club, founded in 1824 by a group of young men like himself, old Etonians. At Eton he was known as "Ninth Harry". His principal horse, *Nunky*, was given to him by his uncle, Mr. Edward Cooke, sometime Under-Secretary of State for Ireland under Lord Castlereagh. A contemporary writer described Taylor as "a clever sportsman and an unrivalled whip who could cast tail hounds to the head of a pack with great rapidity."

TEMPLER, George (1781-1843) of Stover House, near Chudleigh, South Devon, was the first Master of the South Devon Hunt (c1802-26). He was educated at Westminster School and was a poet, scholar and wit. George's grandfather, James (b.1722), who built Stover House in 1781, after making a fortune as a builder in London, was the grandson of Thomas, a *sope boyler* who died in Exeter in 1688. He was not descended, as a romantic legend has it, from a Col. Templer who served with the Prince of Orange. Another George Templer, M.P. for Honiton

(1790-96) was the fourth son of James Senior and an uncle of the MFH. C.A. Harris described Templer as "amiable, sincere, benevolent, gracefully erudite, a playful wit and charm of society." The Duke of Rutland took a draft from the Stover kennels in 1810, showing that Templer then had an established pack of a high standard. Harris said the hounds were handsome, symmetrical, with great roundness of loin and necks; heads and countenances that would have satisfied Osbaldeston himself. Russell said Templer was the best man over a country he knew and *Nimrod* thought him one of the cleverest sportsmen of the age. *Nimrod* hunted from Stover in September, 1824. He agreed there was "too much of the bag" about the hunting. Templer also coursed bag rabbits with terriers and tame foxes. William Scarth-Dixon recorded that as well as the dwarf hounds Templer kept up to twenty foxes in two fox yards, each with separate coop to which the fox was attached by a long chain and swivel but exercised regularly. Templer always tried for a wild fox first but had a bagman in reserve. A beaten fox was seldom killed. Templer's generosity and lavish hospitality coupled with his speculation in the granite tramway from Heytor to the Stover Canal, and the dishonesty of a lawyer depleted his inheritance so severely that he had to give up the pack, sell Stover and go abroad. A year later he returned and built Sandford Orleigh overlooking the Teign estuary. The canal, tramway and estates were sold to the Eleventh Duke of Somerset.

THOMSON, Col. John Anstruther, was born at Charleton, Fife, in 1818. He owed his rank to his sponsorship and command of the 1st Fifeshire Light Horse. As for many men of his time, service in the cavalry was synonymous with hunting and the latter soon took preference to soldiering. After education at Edinburgh Academy and Eton and a Continental tour much involved with military and equestrian affairs, he was commissioned into the 9th Lancers, a regiment renowned for hunting men, in 1836. He was stationed at Piershill in Edinburgh and began to "hunt in earnest" at a time when there were eight packs of hounds in Scotland. In 1840 he secured a captaincy at a cost of £5,000 but when the regiment was ordered to India in 1841 he transferred to the 13th Light Dragoons, preferring fox to jackal. He resigned his commission in 1847 when the Mastership of the Atherstone fell vacant. Thus he missed both the Crimean war and the Indian mutiny in his eleven years as a cavalry man but spent more than fifty years of his life chasing fox and stag and more than forty seasons as a Master. He was Master of the Atherstone, 1847-49, 1850-55 and 1870-71; the Bicester 1855-57, the Fife 1857-64 and 1872-90, and the Pytchley 1864-69. Thomson was six feet three inches tall and weighed sixteen stone. He had great charm and was a spontaneous leader of men of all rank and station. At Ipswich he had a colonel as whipper-in and at Cahir in Ireland he had two colonels whipping-in to him. Following Lord Spencer as Master of the Pytchley he provided great sport including the memorable Waterloo run of February 2, 1866. In the shires, his weight required him to crash through the hedges rather than leap over them. He tackled any obstacle with iron nerve and resolve and from the days of his first Mastership with the Atherstone the "long, Scotch gentleman" built up a reputation throughout England and Scotland. He rode with Farquharson in Dorset and Jack Russell in Devon and was as competent and collected over Dartmoor as in any country in the Kingdom. His housemaster at Eton had warned his guardian that young Thomson was in some danger of falling into "a reckless, coarse manner" and "an excessive abandonment to bodily rather than mental pursuits." His manners were never coarse and, while he was never an intellectual, his incessant physical activity was tempered by intelligence and a ready comradeship with his fellow men. One of the great pleasures of his life was to introduce, during Ascot week in 1881, the Rev. John Russell, then aged eighty-six, and Mr. J.H. Whyte-Melville, sometime Master of the Fife and father of the famous novelist. It was Major Whyte-Melville who induced Thomson to take the Pytchley in 1864.

TRELAWNY, Charles (1799-1883) was Master of the Dartmoor Foxhounds from 1843 to 1873. He held land in Devon and was Squire of Coldrenick, near Menheniot, East Cornwall. He was a patron of the Turf and bred light-weight hunters at Coldrenick. He claimed to have attended fifty-one consecutive Derby meetings. A retirement presentation portrait shows him seated on his favourite hunter, *Grimaldi*. Another favourite horse, for the 1842 Derby, called *Coldrenick*, proved unworthy of promise. Hawker's ballad, "The Song of the Western Men", with its rousing chorus,

> "And shall Trelawny die?
> Here's twenty-thousand Cornishmen
> Will know the reason why!"

was written in 1825 "under a stag-horned oak" in Stowe Wood. It alluded to the imprisonment in the Tower of London by the Roman Catholic King James the Second of seven Anglican bishops, including Sir Jonathan Trelawny, then Bishop of Bristol and later of Exeter (1689-1707), but no saint, according to Prebendary Boggis, for resisting two royal declarations of Indulgence. They were acquitted of a charge of seditious libel.

TROLLOPE, Anthony (1815-82) the novelist, had a roving commission in Ireland in the 1840s to inspect post offices. Later he had similar duties in the West of England and South Wales. He was paid a mileage allowance to maintain his horses and confessed to getting his hunting out of his job. In the '70s he hunted three times a week in season. Trollope thought hunting to be a peculiarly British pastime. He called it the national sport. He was a large, ungainly man, handicapped by short sight, but never lost his enthusiasm for the hunting field. He described the hunting scene in several of his novels and viewed foxhunting as a social leveller: a sport for all classes.

TUCKER, Sidney, huntsman to the Devon and Somerset Staghounds for seventeen seasons, was probably the best that hunt ever had. H.A. Bryden, who hunted with no fewer than sixty-seven packs during more than fifty years of sport, ranked him with Arthur Heal, a predecessor on Exmoor, and with Dale, Firr, Freeman, Gillard, Goodall, Thatcher and Sebright, which was high praise from a seasoned and percipient hunter. Sidney started with the Devon and Somerset in 1885 as second horseman, riding one and leading another horse over the wild, intricate paths; stretching his agility as a deft and clever rider to the full. After four seasons he became whipper-in to Anthony Huxtable when Heal retired, and in 1902 he took the horn and provided first-rate sport for seventeen seasons until he retired, at the peak of his powers. He was a man of middle height, compact and sturdy frame and great strength and endurance, as required by the severe climate of the moor. He had total empathy with horse and hound, getting the best out of his pack by an unspoken bond of mutual understanding of the task. As a rider he was bold and intrepid, with a keen eye, a quick ear and an intimate knowledge of the country and the run of a deer. Bryden admired Sidney for his dash, daring and resource and especially for his skill in rattling down the precipitous cliff face over narrow, zigzag paths to the sea from the summit at Glenthorne. His tactics, woodcraft and judgement were of the highest and he was a tonic to the pack. Sidney had some sixty couples. He preferred hounds of a medium size as being quicker up and down the steep hills and less subject to kennel-lameness. He put working capacity before looks, although the pack before the first world war was good-looking as well as hard-working. Sidney Tucker had all the attributes of the best of British huntsmen as depicted by Bryden; he was brave, hardy, resolute and enduring. He had strength, enterprise, high spirits, perseverance, firmness and decision and a spark of genius. Bryden held there was no other form of sport in the British Isles so completely wild, so unspoiled and uncontaminated as the chase of the red deer on Exmoor.

WALTERS, Miss Caroline, alias *Skittles*, was the daughter of a Liverpool Irishman, a master mariner who later kept an inn at Chester, where she learned to ride. She first appeared in the hunting field about 1860. Unlike the average lady of the *demi-monde, Skittles* had a quick wit and a social grace which placed her above her contemporaries. She was an outstanding rider with a good sense of fashion, and thus she was not highly popular with her own sex. She raised the ire of Lady Stamford, the daughter of a Norfolk gamekeeper who was rumoured to have gypsy blood in her veins. Lady Stamford asked her husband, MFH to the Quorn 1856-57 and 1862-63, to ban *Skittles* from the field, which he did, though with some reluctance. She then went to the Harborough country where Mr. Tailby, the bachelor-Master, refused to turn her off, having had no complaint of her conduct on the hunting field. On one occasion, when out with the Harborough, she lost her skirt entirely and was seen "stamping about in top boots and petticoat." The cry went up for a married man to go to her aid. An impudent young man asked a stuffy, clerical bachelor, "Are you a married man?" to his great annoyance. In 1884 the safety skirt was adopted. *Skittles* was reputed to have been the first of her sex to wear a shiny top hat for hunting. That style was superseded for most ladies by a low-crowned hat with a plume. By 1880 they wore top hats or bowlers. *Skittles*, who had been mistress to Lord Fitzwilliam, died in August, 1920, at her house in South Street, London, with her faithful friend, the Hon. Gerald Saumarez, at her side.

WARDE, John (c1752-1838) of Squerries, near Westerham, Kent, was a celebrated foxhunter for well over fifty years and a noted Master of the Pytchley, the Craven and the Bicester. He kept kennels in more than half a dozen countries in England from 1773 to 1826 when illness forced his final retirement from the field. Although preceded in time by Thomas Boothby of the Quorn and William Draper of East Yorkshire, he was pre-eminent with them in any claim to be the Father of English foxhunting. He was a heavyweight preferring large hounds, but extraordinarily active, always showing the best of sport. Even in the poor-scenting Craven (1814-26), he averaged forty brace of fox each season. His followers enjoyed some remarkable runs, including one in Oxfordshire in the early 1780s through thirty-two parishes. *Nimrod* described Warde as a great authority on the science and a real sample of old English foxhunting blood. Once, during penurious times with the Craven when he threatened to give up, his wife paid £1,000 anonymously into his bank account to allow him to carry on. The best horse he ever had he rescued from service as a carthorse at Newbury market place. John Warde died in his house at Charles Street, Berkeley Square, London.

WATERFORD, Marquis of (d.1859) gained notoriety at Melton and elsewhere by his high-spirited frolics and eccentricities which included painting a toll-house scarlet and amassing a huge collection of door-knockers without the consent of the owners. Lord Waterford was the subject of an extravaganza put on at Drury Lane theatre in April, 1838 and called "The Meltonians: An original, good-humoured and perfectly illegitimate drama"; an Easter novelty on a par with a Christmas pantomime. It illustrated the doings of a certain young nobleman. The tableaux included "Taking a five-barred gate in the drawing-room" and "Quick work by tip-top sawyers". A horse was made to jump the gate on stage. Waterford wore a black cap and a blue jacket and, mounted on *Yellow Dwarf,* he was a prominent figure at steeplechases in the Vale of Aylesbury. His riding was not stylish but he jumped as many fences as he could. He once aniseeded the heels of a clergyman's horse and then hunted him home with bloodhounds. It was in consequence of a joke he played on a Norwegian peasant girl that he was so beaten by a watchman that he was obliged to wear a wig. He won three four-mile steeplechases in one day at Eglinton Park. He lived the last seventeen years of his life at home in Ireland where he kept the Curraghmore hounds, a useful though unattractive pack. He was prominent on the Irish Turf. He died out hunting in 1859 when he fell at a fence and broke his neck. The manner of his death made the hunting cap unfashionable.

WELLINGTON, Arthur Wellesley, 1st Duke of (1769-1852), hero of the Peninsula and Waterloo, was born in Dublin, grandson of the 1st Baron Mornington. The Duke was a keen rider to hounds, at home and overseas, despite his poor seat. Like most military commanders of his day, he understood the superior skills which an experienced foxhunter could bring to the cavalry but deplored the unbridled enthusiasm of those who preferred a wild gallop at the enemy to a considered manoeuvre. Their fast horses made matters worse. In the Peninsula, he appointed foxhunters as *aides-de-camp* and kept a pack of hounds himself though he rarely killed a fox. Hunting from Paris after the peace, the Duke once annoyed the King (Charles X) by comparing open country at Compiègne with the delights of the Vale of Aylesbury. The Duke was a generous supporter of his local hunt and of the Vine and the Bramshill. He never complained about his many falls but lay still, counting the pairs of feet passing overhead. Surtees wrote that he never saw a man with less idea of riding. His seat was "unsightly in the extreme."

WHIDBORNE, John Sumner, solicitor and banker of Teignmouth, S. Devon, sometimes known as Squire Whidborne, was Master of the South Devon from 1851 to 1856. At the outset he defined the South Devon country as stretching from the Exe to the Dart and from Exeter to Totnes, extending north-westward over Dartmoor to the road from Two

Bridges through Moretonhampstead and Dunsford to Exeter (B3212), truly a vast tract of land. The country was also hunted by two harrier packs, the Dart Vale and the Haldon (amalgamated in 1947). Mr. Whidborne sometimes took his hounds, by invitation, into North Devon to hunt the indigenous greyhound fox, and even over the border into the stag country of Simonsbath and Exford Common. After the partition he was Master of the Newton side from 1882, when he was over sixty, to 1885. He died in 1890. After the split he built kennels at Lidwell on his farm which was about two miles north of Teignmouth and nearly four miles from Kingsteignton, where he took up residence, in the season, with his daughter at Brookside, his hunting box. Some of his own and his daughter's and the hunt horses were at Brookside and some at his Teignmouth home, so there was a great deal of hacking about before and after a meet. Tozer, one-time hunt secretary, recalled that the Master sometimes left Teignmouth an hour after midnight to start cubhunting at dawn. At Brookside he often provided mounts for visitors as well as breakfast and dinner. There was always excellent sherry and biscuits for callers at any hour. Whidborne preferred horses that were "long, low and lusty" as best suited to cross the varied South Devon country with its rough lanes, extensive woodlands, thick gorses, steep hillsides, open and knotted moorland and occasional plough. As well as being in private practice, he was clerk to the local magistrates and clerk to the urban district council. In the 1870s he held 542 acres of land.

WHITBREAD, Samuel Charles (1796-1879) was the younger son of Samuel Whitbread, M.P. for Cardington, Beds. He was educated at Eton and Cambridge and was a political ally of the Duke. He was M.P. for Middlesex, 1820-1830. He became a partner in the Chiswell Street brewery in 1819. He was a founder of the Oakley Hunt but never Master.

WHITE, Captain John (1790-1866) was born at Dalesford, Cheshire, and educated at Eton and Christ Church, Oxford, where, as a freshman, he kept three hunters and, during the three years he was up, never missed a meet within riding distance. On graduation in 1811 he took his horses to Lincolnshire where the famed Squire Osbaldeston was Master of the Burton (1809-13), having succeeded the Fourth Lord Monson. In 1815 he moved to Melton Mowbray and was soon a noted rider in the hunting field and a dashing young blade on the social scene. For seven seasons he and his friend, Captain Maxse, kept open house, in a spirit of roisterous fraternity, hunting hard by day and rollicking by night. *Nimrod* placed White, in his dual capacity as rider to hounds and amateur jockey, as among the hardest and best riders in England. He had an elegant seat, fine hands, a quick eye, good temper and undaunted nerve. White's physical stamina was once amply demonstrated when, after two runs in the field with Lord Lonsdale, he rode twenty miles back to Melton, changed his clothes, ate a light meal, and then rode seventy-five miles home to Park Hall, crossing the Peak of Derbyshire in a snowstorm and arriving at eleven p.m. after one hundred and fifty miles in the saddle since breakfast. White's zealous riding led to many falls and it was said there was hardly a bone in his body that had not been broken. His worst fall was in his early days in Lincolnshire when his horse fell on him in a drain. The saddle pommel struck his sternum and he broke three ribs, a collar-bone and an ankle. As a gentleman-jockey, he worked hard to keep his weight down. He had no time for steeplechasing but enjoyed shooting and preserved forty thousand acres but never laid a trap for a fox. He was also a patron of the cockpit and his famous black-reds sometimes won big stakes at Chester, epicentre of the then aristocratic sport. In 1842 he left Melton for the Mastership of the Cheshire hounds where he was always close to the pack and commanded a large field including many ambitious young riders from Liverpool and Manchester. They were impressed by his energy, coolness, courage and perseverance and always obedient to his deep, powerful voice. His commanding presence was demonstrated during the Reform Bill riots of 1831 when, in his capacity as captain of a troop of yeomanry, he dispersed a mob by threatening to order his men to charge and cut them down like so many Frenchmen. White also rode in the green collar of the Tarporley and with Sir Watkin Wynn's hounds when meeting on the Cheshire side of Denbigh. He gave up the Cheshire when Joe Maiden became huntsman, and retired to the Turf.

WHYTE-MELVILLE, Major George John (1821-78), the laureate of foxhunting, was the son of John Whyte-Melville of Strathkinness, Fifeshire, and a grandson on his mother's side of the 5th Duke of Leeds. He was educated at Eton and joined the Army in 1839, serving first with the 93rd Highlanders and later in the Coldstream Guards from which he retired in 1849 as a captain. When the Crimean War broke out he volunteered as a major of irregular Turkish Cavalry. That was the sole interruption to his literary career and his life-long devotion to the chase. He was entered to hounds by John Walker, huntsman to the Fife of which his father, a noted golfer, was Master for seventeen years. He first settled at Boughton, three miles from the Pytchley kennels, but moved to Wootton Hall, though still riding with the Pytchley, after inheriting a second large fortune. He finally moved to London. Apart from the Shires, his favourite hunting countries were Dorset, the Vale of Aylesbury, and Exmoor, for stag. His writing career began with a translation of Horace into flowing verse in 1850 but he soon embarked on a series of novels on the sporting scene which demonstrated an intimate understanding of sport and its characters. He became a respected analyst, moralist and a public influence of such note that his sudden death in the field in December, 1878, was whispered to Disraeli in the House of Lords within hours. Whyte-Melville gave all his considerable earnings from his pen to charity and endowed a working man's club and reading room in Northampton. His only serious fall before that which killed him was in January, 1867, when he broke an arm "riding a young horse like an old one".

WYNN, Sir Watkin, Bart. (1820-85) was a later baronet and he hunted on a princely scale from Wynnstay, the family seat in South-East Denbighshire. Sir Watkin Williams Wynn was educated at Westminster and Christ Church, Oxford, which he left prematurely because study interfered with his hunting. He spent four years in the Household Cavalry but in 1843 he shaved off his moustache, "the badge of slavery" then worn only by cavalry officers, and took over the family estate and the hunt, having already been elected Member of Parliament for his native county. He gave up his silk and membership of the Jockey Club and his race-horses to concentrate on hunting. He rode a dun brown mare and was followed for twenty years by Jonathan Phillips, his groom, with a second horse, for Sir Watkin was a heavyweight rider. He had a light hand, a quick eye, good nerve and a strong seat. He never pulled his horse's mouth about and seldom had a fall. His horses were always well-bred and over sixteen hands. Sir Watkin rarely flew at a fence but trained his mounts to jump the widest ditches and even the Grafton and Aldersey brooks at a stand and to creep through thick, high hedges, and jump the ensuing ditch when he dropped his hands, and gallop off. Thus he got over the ground quickly. He hunted large tracts of Shropshire and Cheshire. At Wynnstay he kept fifty-five couples of hounds and fifty to sixty horses. His servants' liveries, saddles, bridles and accoutrements were of the neatest. In 1858 a disastrous fire destroyed the mansion at Wynnstay and most of its contents, including many valuable works of art, though there was no loss of life. Sir Watkin and Lady Wynn decided to winter abroad and his hunters were sold at prices ranging from £40 to £650. After a break and rebuilding, hunting resumed under a new Master. Sir Watkin, in poor health in his later years, was last seen on a horse in the hunting field in April, 1883, by then ravaged by disease. For forty years he maintained his magnificent hunting establishment entirely at his own expense and hunted four days a week over four counties in each of which he was a deputy lieutenant and a substantial landowner. He was also a past provincial grand master, ADC to the Queen and a director of the Great Western Railway: a "Prince among Welshmen", loved by all. A few years before his death he was travelling on the Cambrian line when a fellow-passenger got into conversation and discovered that Sir Watkin knew the country well. Gazing at the passing countryside, he several times asked, "Whose property is this?". He always received the same brief reply: "Mine". At the terminus the stranger to Wales gave the train guard a friendly hint that his fellow-traveller was evidently a lunatic, suffering from *folie de grandeur*. Sir Watkin was succeeded by his nephew.

Lords of the Chase

INDEX

INDEX to HUNTS